Julian Klaczko, Mrs. Tait

The Two Chancellors

Prince Gortchakof and Prince Bismarck

Julian Klaczko, Mrs. Tait

The Two Chancellors
Prince Gortchakof and Prince Bismarck

ISBN/EAN: 9783337383732

Printed in Europe, USA, Canada, Australia, Japan

Cover: Foto ©ninafisch / pixelio.de

More available books at **www.hansebooks.com**

THE TWO CHANCELLORS:

PRINCE GORTCHAKOF AND PRINCE BISMARCK.

BY

M. JULIAN KLACZKO,

EX-DEPUTY OF THE PARLIAMENT OF VIENNA.

TRANSLATED FROM THE FRENCH BY
MRS. TAIT.

London:
CHAPMAN & HALL, 193, PICCADILLY.
1876.

PREFACE.

During the last few years various highly interesting publications have revealed to the world many of the most hidden secrets of diplomacy. The historian is forced to collect these testimonies, and to extract from them their teachings; although conscience, as well as State reasons, cannot but condemn these much-to-be regretted revelations, which compromise, in so striking a degree, every principle of authority, and every law of international relationship.

The Author is therefore anxious to make known that, although he has given up his political career since 1873, he still considers himself bound by the obligations laid upon him by professional secrecy, and by the elementary rules of State service.

None of the documents or despatches quoted in this work possess the doubtful merit of being unpublished; all are public property, and the minute information which is given as to their various origins and dates, renders it easy for them to be found in the works and Parliamentary papers indicated.

CONTENTS.

CHAPTER I.
PRINCE GORTCHAKOF'S MISSIONS 1

CHAPTER II.
FIRST APPEARANCES OF M. DE BISMARCK 37

CHAPTER III.
A NATIONAL MINISTER IN RUSSIA 79

CHAPTER IV.
A "FRONDEUR" DIPLOMATIST AT ST. PETERSBURG . . 104

CHAPTER V.
THE CAMPAIGNS OF THE VISTULA AND THE ELBE . . 133

CHAPTER VI.
THE WAR IN GERMANY 162

CHAPTER VII.

THE ECLIPSE OF EUROPE 205

CHAPTER VIII.

THE EAST AND THE WEST 247

CHAPTER IX.

THE FRENCH WAR 284

CHAPTER X.

A TEN YEARS' PARTNERSHIP 314

APPENDIX.

THE TWO CHANCELLORS.

CHAPTER I.

PRINCE GORTCHAKOF'S MISSIONS.

The Gortchakofs of History—Alexander Mikhaïlovitch—Lyceum of Tsarskoë-Selo—The Friendship of Pouchkine—Indiscreet good Wishes and brilliant Prognostications—Long Probation of Prince Gortchakof—The Leuchtenberg Marriage—A matrimonial Revenge—The Grand Duchess Olga and the Heir-apparent of Wurtemberg—Well-advised Patience—A Post of Observation at Stuttgart—The Revolution of February, and the Agitation of Unionists in Germany—The Frankfort Parliament—A Rising at Stuttgart: memorable Speech of the old King William of Wurtemberg—Restoration of the Diet of Frankfort—Prince Gortchakof Minister at Frankfort—Prestige of the Emperor Nicholas after the Revolution of February—The real Mission and benevolent Influence of the German Confederation—Friendship and Intercourse in Frankfort—A young Lieutenant of *Landwehr*—The *Salon* of the Joukofskis—Nicholas Gogol—Mystics and Signs of the Times—The Eastern Crisis—Prussia's Humane Politics—Fidelity and Devotion of the secondary States—Austria and its "Ingratitude"—The Russian Intervention in Hungary—Austria's Political Straits in Eastern Affairs—Its Conduct during the Crimean War—What it might have done against Russia—Prince Gortchakof at Vienna—Patriotic Sorrows and Anger—Conferences at Vienna—Diplomacy of bygone Times—Fall of Sebastopol—Austria's Ultimatum—Saying of Prince Gortchakof with regard to Austria—Congress of Paris—Napoleon III. suddenly changes his Policy—Prince Gortchakof as Minister of Foreign Affairs in Russia.

In common with the Odoïefskis, the Obolenskis, the Dolgoroukis, and many other noble families on the banks of the Moskva and the Neva, it is the boast of the Gortchakofs that they are the descendants of the Rouriks. More particularly, however, they trace their origin from one of the sons of Michael, grand-duke of Tchernigof, put to death towards the middle of the thirteenth century by the Mongolians of Batou-Khan, and since proclaimed a martyr to the faith, and even canonised as a saint of the orthodox Church.

The name of Gortchakof, however, is seldom met with in the sombre and stirring annals of old Russia. In the period which precedes the accession of the Romanofs we meet with a Peter Ivanovitch Gortchakof, an unfortunate commander of Smolensk, who, after an energetic and desperate resistance which lasted for two years, finally gave up this celebrated stronghold to the Poles. He was taken to Warsaw, where, in 1611, in company with the Czar Vassili, the two princes Schouyski, Sehine, and a number of powerful boyards, he was forced to take part in the celebrated "procession of captives" which the great constable Zolkiewski offered one day—*honorificentissime,* says the historian of the times—to the king, and also to the senate of the most serene republic. It is only in the second half of the last century, during the reign of Catherine II., that a Prince Ivan Gortchakof succeeded, chiefly owing to his marriage with a daughter of the wealthy and powerful Souvorof, in re-establishing the splendour of his ancient house, which since then has never ceased to distinguish itself in various branches of state service, and especially in the career of arms. The France of to-day retains the memory of two princes Gortchakof, two old soldiers of the Borodino, who added to the glory of their names during the war in the East. The one commanded the left wing of the Russian troops during the battles of Alma and Inkermann; the other, Prince Michael, was commander-in-chief of the Czar's forces in the Crimea, and joined his name for all time to the heroic defence of Sebastopol. He afterwards assumed the government of Poland, as the emperor's lieutenant, and became thus—striking example of the vicissitudes of history—the supreme representative of a severe foreign rule in that same town of Warsaw where, centuries before, one of his ancestors had figured in a procession of captives. However, if this coincidence ever presented itself to the mind of Prince Michael, he only drew from it a moral worthy of his mind, for he governed the conquered country with moderation and benevolence, leaving behind him the reputation of being as upright in civil administration as he was courageous in war.

The cousin of Prince Michael and present Chancellor of the Empire, Alexander Mikhaïlovitch Gortchakof, was born in 1798, and was educated at the Lyceum of Tsarskoë-Selo, which occupies a place of distinction in the scholastic history of Russia. Founded by the Government as a model house of education for the youthful aristocracy of Russia, the Lyceum shone with great brilliancy during the reign of Alexander I., although a Rollin or a Pestalozzi might have raised more than one objection to a college whose pupils were brought up only to adorn the higher circles, and which esteemed the weightier classical studies too heavy a burden with which to soar into the ethereal spheres of pleasure and elegance. Nearly all the professors of the establishment were foreigners, men bearing the stamp of the eighteenth century—freethinking, frivolous, and Voltairian. The most eminent among them, the professor of French literature—he who initiated the future chancellor into the language of Voltaire, of whose beauties and subtleties he is now so competent a master—was a Swiss of Neuchâtel, who, under the inoffensive name of De Boudry, concealed another of a far more terrible sound. M. de Boudry was no other than the brother of Marat, the infamous conventionalist.[*] It was the Empress Catherine who, in order "to put an end to scandal," compelled Professor Marat to change his name, without, however, being able to make him change his opinions, which remained "Jacobin" to the very end. He died impenitent, proclaiming with his last breath his deep admiration for the basely-maligned "friend of the people." From this doubtful style of education the young Gortchakof drew a generous and healthy sustenance. He left Tsarskoë-Selo rich in solid and varied acquirements, and, more extraordinary still, he left it a good Latin scholar, which last point has always been a source of astonishment to his fellow-students as well as to succeeding generations. It is nevertheless certain that the chancellor can quote Horace with all the *à propos* of the late King Louis XVIII. of sainted memory; one of his most celebrated despatches contains an

[*] Aus der Petersburger Gesellschaft, t. ii., p. 156.

eloquent passage, in which he quotes from Suetonius the distinction to be established between liberty and anarchy.

Next to his classical acquirements, the youthful memory dearest to the chancellor is the fact of his having been the co-disciple, and that he has remained the steadfast friend, of Pouchkine, the great national poet—memories that are all the more creditable to him, as, at times, this intimacy must have proved most embarrassing. When, in consequence of some obnoxious ode, the young author of "Rouslan et Loudmila" was exiled by the Emperor Alexander I. to an obscure village in the depths of Russia, two only, from among his former Lyceum comrades, had the courage to visit him and offer him their sympathy, and one of those intrepid youths was Prince Gortchakof. There are to be found among the works of Pouchkine a few couplets written in a style of gaiety and raillery, the interest of which is centred in the name of Alexander Mikhaïlovitch, to whom they are addressed. In one of these juvenile pieces, Pouchkine desires that " Love should accompany his friend to the shores of the Styx, and that he should fall asleep on the bosom of Helen even in the boat of Charon . . . ;" indiscreet good wishes of a kind to have offered ample food for scandal, had not the chancellor been wise enough to keep his old age free from all seductive deceptions and avoid even the appearance of a northern Ruy Gomez.

The poet's inspirations are more fortunate at a later period, when, in speaking of the difference in their vocations, he foretells the splendid destinies of Alexander Mikhaïlovitch, and calls him "Fortune's favoured son."

Fortune, however, was somewhat slow to recognise her child, and to award him the portion he merited. Entering, at an early age, the Office of Foreign Affairs, and becoming attached to the suite of M. de Nesselrode from the time of the Laybach and Verona congresses, Prince Gortchakof had already long passed that which Dante calls the "*mezzo del cammin di vita*," and at the age of fifty was only minister plenipotentiary at a small court in Germany. A fortunate event brought him at last under the benevolent notice of his master, and rescued him from that diplomatic limbo, those regions "free from tears but filled with sighs," which in diplomatic parlance are termed secondary appointments.

In a moment of paternal weakness the Emperor Nicholas had consented to the marriage of his daughter the Grand Duchess Maria with the Duke of Leuchtenberg—son of Beauharnais, and catholic officer in the service of the King of Bavaria—as it was mournfully whispered in the private circles of the Winter Palace.

Nicholas was not the man to retract his given word, but none the less did he feel the sting of what his surroundings termed a *mésalliance*, and the bitterness of his feelings increased when all the foreign members of the imperial family absented themselves from the brilliant *fêtes* which preceded and followed the nuptial ceremonies. As ill-luck would have it, soon afterwards a cousin of the newly-made imperial son-in-law, a daughter of the ex-King Jerome, espoused a Russian whose wealth sprang from commercial sources—a prince in the valley of the Arno, but scarcely a gentleman on the banks of the Neva— a disagreeable incident, which in the eyes of the horrified courtiers placed the Autocrat of all the Russias in the position *of relationship to one of his own subjects.* It now became a matter of necessity to wipe out all these painful impressions, and, by an alliance whose splendour should be incontestable, be revenged on so many mortifications. For awhile flattering hopes were held out that the Grand Duchess Alexandra might be accepted by an archduke of Austria, but finally a prince of Hesse had to suffice. For the Grand Duchess Olga, the most beautiful and best-beloved of the emperor's daughters, had been chosen the heir-presumptive to the throne of Wurtemberg, of the ancient and illustrious house of Swabia, he being at that time the only available royal prince.

This project was, however, not so easily carried out. The good Swabian people had no taste for it; a Russian alliance roused their fears for their constitutional liberties. What was still more serious, the old King William of Wurtemberg, an honest and liberal sovereign, but obstinate beyond belief, showed himself somewhat recalcitrant, and seemed to delight in proposing every dilatory objection he could think of. Other objections were raised on various sides; but the Russian plenipotentiary at Stuttgart, the former fellow-pupil of Pouchkine, set them aside with consummate ability; by dint of skill and dexterity he succeeded in establishing the Grand Duchess Olga in the royal family of Wurtemberg. The joy of the Emperor Nicholas was deep and wide-spreading, and the Winter Palace joined in the public eulogiums lavished on the triumphant diplomatist. After such a success, Prince Gortchakof might well expect to be advanced in his career, to be brought a few steps nearer to that ambassadorship at Vienna, which was the supreme object of his ambition. It was not to be, however, and the patience he displayed was admirable—like that of the Patriarch Jacob serving Laban, son of Nahor. To the term of four years which he had already served at Stuttgart, Alexander Mikhaïlovitch declared himself ready to add another term still more lengthy, if necessary; he promised the empress-mother to remain any length of time near the Grand Duchess Olga, to be her guide and counsellor in a strange country among strangers. However barren the prospect, he did not despair of improving his position while sunned by such rays of beauty and grace, coming, as they did, direct from the great northern sun, and, in fact, he retained his post at Stuttgart for another long term of eight years. *Tenues grandia conamur!*

But every post of observation is of use to him who knows how to fix his telescope and question the stars. The minister plenipotentiary at Stuttgart was the recipient of wide-spreading information, and found means to inform his government of many things which occurred far beyond the narrow limits of the little kingdom of Wurtemberg. Then came the year 1848, with its terrible catastrophes, with its revolutionary shocks, adding to the experience of the most experienced, lighting up with sudden brilliancy the hitherto unknown depths of human nature, and, to use Milton's language, making the nethermost darkness light.

Such a lesson in history did not pass without leaving its impressions on the former pupil of Tsarskoë-Selo, as can well be imagined. Saloons and cabinets had long ago confided all their secrets to him; now he became the recipient of those of the forums and the byways.

The close vicinity of Frankfort, seat of the celebrated parliament, permitted him to study from life, and in all its extent, the agitation prevailing in Germany at this memorable time. He noted, in advance, its various phases—at first simple, then burlesque and odious—and predicted, at an early hour, the inevitable miscarriage of a revolution whose vanquished floods were yet, however, to scatter their impotent foams over the usually tranquil streets of Stuttgart.

It was the month of April, 1849. Anticipating by twenty years the formidable work of 1870, the Parliament of Frankfort had just constituted a German empire, to the exclusion of Austria, offering the crown to the King of Prussia, Frederick William IV. The king hesitated and finally refused it, and the other German princes were still less anxious to accept a decree which implied their abdication. But this did not meet the views of the German demagogues. Seized with a sudden enthusiasm for a constitution which the day before they had denounced as reactionary and inimical to the liberties of the people, they tried by force to impose on the various sovereigns of Germany the vassalage of Prussia as decreed at Frankfort.

In Wurtemberg the Chamber of Deputies voted an address of a pressing and imperious nature, with the object of extorting from the king the recognition of the Emperor Frederick William IV. The monarch replied by a refusal. Rioting took place in the public square, and the court had to take refuge at Ludwigsburg from the frenzy of a delirious capital.

"I will not submit myself to the house of Hohenzollern," said the old King William of Wurtemberg to the deputation from the Chamber. "I owe it to my country not to submit; I owe it to myself and to my people. But it is not for myself that I speak thus; I have but a few more years to live; it is my country, my house, my family that impose this duty on me."

When an agitated witness of these stormy scenes, and of the pathetic appeals of the father-in-law of Olga for "the house, the family of Wurtemberg," Alexander Mikhaïlovitch little thought that one day, as chancellor of the Russian Empire, he would become the most useful auxiliary, the most faithful support of an audacious and enterprising policy that would realise in every respect that riotous programme of Stuttgart, and make Queen Olga a vassal of the Hohenzollerns. This was, however, but the stormy prologue of a drama still hidden in the future; and the year 1850 even hoped it had seen the last traces of an agitation which had only astonished Europe, instead of enlightening and warning it. Towards the end of the year 1850, the German Confederation was re-established on the terms of the old compact of Vienna; the Bundestag was about to resume its peaceful deliberations, and Prince Gortchakof naturally found himself appointed representative of the Russian Court at the Diet of Frankfort. From that time Alexander Mikhaïlovitch occupied a marked place in that great centre of political affairs, where the personal merits of the minister borrowed an additional brilliancy from the extraordinary prestige which late events had created for his august master.

Russian influence, at all times very considerable at the courts of Germany, had grown prodigiously; and, it will be recollected, had reached its height in consequence of the whirlwind of February. Standing alone as the only country untouched by the revolutionary storms which had devastated nearly all the other continental States, the empire of the Czars appeared then as the solid bulwark of every principle of order and conservatism.

"Humble yourselves, nations: God is with us!" the Emperor Nicholas had exclaimed in a celebrated proclamation; and without being too much dazzled by a language that in some sort made God the accomplice of a gigantic human vanity, monarchical Europe had but acclamations for a prince who, in truth, was working with a remarkable disinterestedness to re-establish legitimate authority and to maintain the world's equilibrium.

It is but just to recollect that during those turbulent years 1848-50, the Autocrat of the North made use of his influence as of his sword, but to consolidate tottering thrones, and enforce respect for treaties. He effectively protected Denmark, towards which the rapacious hand of Germany was already pointing, and was the most energetic in calling together a council of the Powers that ended by tearing from the Germans their much-coveted prey.

He interfered personally in Hungary, and sent his troops to crush a formidable insurrection which had shaken to its very foundations the ancient empire of the Hapsburgs, already mined by internal troubles and an aggressive war waged against it on two occasions by the kingdom of Piedmont. Already but little inclined by his principles and his interests to favour that united Germany,* "whose first wish was for an unjust extension of territory, and whose first cry was a cry of war," he employed all his influence to bring about the re-establishment, pure and simple, of the German Confederation on the basis it occupied before 1848.

The ties of family and of friendship which united him to the Court of Berlin, were never powerful enough to make him abandon for a single instant the cause of the minor sovereigns and of the independence of their states; and in spite of the sincere affection he felt for "his brother-in-law the poet," he spared King Frederick William IV. of Prussia neither the evacuation of the Duchies nor the irksome

---

* Expressions contained in the Russian circular of July 6th, 1848, from Count Nesselrode to his agents in Germany.

conditions of Olmütz. Defender of European rights on the Oder and the Main, of monarchical rights on the Theiss and the Danube, peacemaker in Germany, and, so to say, chief justice of Europe, Nicholas possessed at that period of history a grandeur and a prestige well merited on the whole, and that increased the influence of the agents who were charged to represent abroad a policy whose perfect uprightness and immovable firmness none dared contest.

In accrediting Prince Gortchakof to the German Confederation, the Emperor Nicholas, in an autograph letter dated the 11th November, 1850, recognised in the reunion of the Frankfort Diet "a pledge of the maintenance of general peace," and characterised thus, by a stroke at once profound and judicious, the honourable and liberal mission awaiting this Diet in the order of things created by the treaties of 1815. However legitimate may have been the objections of liberal Germans to the internal politics of the Bund and its antagonistic attitude with regard to the development of a constitutional *régime*, one cannot deny that from an European point of view, and with regard to the equilibrium and the universal peace of the world, it was a marvellous conception, well calculated to ensure the independence of States, and prevent all great perturbation in the Christian community.

Chimerical and mercantile spirits of the time, leaders of the Manchester school, and writers rich in at least "one idea a day," had just persuaded themselves that now the moment had arrived to declare "war against war," to insist on universal disarming, on the abolition of military slavery; and they assembled for this object noisy peace congresses at different points of the globe. They had even one day the simplicity to assemble one at Frankfort, not suspecting that at their side, and precisely in this Bundestag of modest appearance, had existed for some time past a genuine and permanent peace congress—a congress that strove to do good within the limits of possibility, and that had, moreover, the great advantage of not appearing ridiculous. Placed as it is in the very centre of Europe, separating by its massive and immobile bulk the great military forces which border, so to say, our old continent, its power forcibly neutralised and placed almost in the position of arbitrator on those vast plains where once the destinies of empires were decided, the German Confederation formed a body of States sufficiently coherent and compact to repulse all shocks from outside, but not sufficiently so to become aggressive itself, and menace the security of its neighbours.

Many years later, when a minister holding in his hands the reins of the empire, Prince Gortchakof was yet in a celebrated circular to render homage to the salutary combination of the Bund—"a combination purely and exclusively defensive," which permitted the *localisation* of an inevitable war, instead of *generalising* it, and giving a character and proportions to the contest which sometimes outrun all human foresight, and which in every case accumulate ruins and shed torrents of blood." *

In truth, if, during the long half-century which separates the congress of Vienna from the unfortunate battle of Sadowa, the frontiers of the different States have altered so little in spite of the great changes which have taken place in their interior politics; if the revolution of July, the campaign of Belgium, and even the wars of the Crimea and of Italy have been able to take place without notably disturbing the equilibrium of the nations, or injuring them in their independence, we have to thank this misjudged Bundestag, which, by its very existence, and by the wheels within wheels of its complicated machinery, prevented each conflict in its turn from becoming at once a general conflagration. It is much to be doubted whether the cause of humanity and civilisation, or the cause which the Russian chancellor represents more especially with such facility and splendour, have gained by seeing this ancient "combination" replaced in our days by another, much more simple, it is true, but perhaps much less reassuring. At the same time that he was performing the duties of his mission to the German Confederation, Alexander Mikhaïlovitch continued to occupy the post of minister plenipotentiary at Stuttgart. He made it a point of honour to fulfil to the end his mission of confidence and friendship to the Grand Duchess Olga, and divided his time between the free town on the Main, the seat of the Bund, and

* Russian circular of May 27th, 1859, à propos of the Italian war.

the little capital on the banks of the Neckar, where he always met with a warm and amiable reception.

At Frankfort, he was especially fond of the society of his Prussian colleague, a young lieutenant of *Landwehr*, and a perfect novice in the career of diplomacy, but for whom waited a prodigious future. There also had settled for many years a great Russian celebrity, a poet who was at the same time an influential courtier, and who could not fail to be sought after by a diplomatist fond of literature and a former co-disciple of Pouchkine.

The good and gentle Vassili Joukofski had certainly none of the genius of Pouchkine, nor had he his independence and vigour of character. A clever versifier and ingenious translator rather than a creator or an originator, of a nature somewhat soft and contemplative, the author of "Ondine," once so renowned, had at an early date made his peace with that official society which the despotic will of Nicholas had created, and had ever since basked in the rays of imperial favour. Dignities and honours did not fail to be awarded him during his long career as pleasing courtier and right-thinking poet. He received an important and honourable mission in being selected to direct the education of Alexander, the heir-apparent and present emperor, and also that of his brother, the Grand Duke Constantine. Joukofski devoted himself to this task with zeal and intelligence, and retained the affection of his young pupils to the end of his life—witness a correspondence which he maintained with them while he was at Frankfort, and which has recently been published. After completing their education, Joukofski took a pleasure trip through Germany; and, finding in Dusseldorf a companion of life, who, though much younger than himself, shared not only his tastes, but even his charming weaknesses, he decided to settle down on the banks of the Main at Frankfort. As has happened to many of his fellow-countrymen, although remaining abroad and showing the greatest repugnance to return to his native land, Joukofski devoutly considered the Western countries miserably fallen to ruin and corrupted, and centred all his hopes in " Holy Russia " as the deliverer of a world invaded and possessed by the demon of revolution.

The occurrences of February only served to strengthen these sombre visions, and to envelope Joukofski more and more in an unquiet state of mysticism, sometimes of an irritating nature, but more often inoffensive, and not without a certain feeble grace.

The campaign of Hungary caused a momentary diversion to these sad thoughts, and filled him with joy. It was not so much the glory which covered the Russian army that cheered his spirit, nor even the triumph of the Russian sword—that sword of St. Michael, "smiting the foul beast;" his prayers, his hopes, soared far higher. He hoped—thus he writes to his imperial pupil—that the great Czar would profit by the power God had placed in his hands, and "solve a problem before which the Crusaders had recoiled; that is to say, that he would drive the infidel from Byzantium, and deliver the Holy Land.

Madame Joukofski, though born a Protestant,

was in unison with her melancholy spouse; her soul required a "principle of authority" which failed her in the Reformed Church, and which she sought, to the great joy of the poet, in the arms of the orthodox faith, without, however, finding perfect peace.

The *salon* of the Joukofskis was the arena of the strangest and most varied of discussions on literature, politics, the glorious destinies of "Holy Russia," the inanity of modern civilisation, "the necessity for a fresh outburst of Christianity," and many other topics treating of the invisible and "ineffable." From time to time appeared in their midst, like a fantastic apparition or spirit from another world, a genius far superior in its originality and power, but also far more tormented and ravaged, than the good court poet and preceptor of grand dukes. After tearing with ruthless and implacable hands the veil from off the hideous sores of Russian society, after having presented to his nation, in the "Dead Souls" and the "Inspector," a frightful picture of its vices full of truth and life, Nicholas Gogol suddenly gave up all hope of civilisation, of progress, of liberty, and turned to adore that which he had formerly despised. He esteemed nothing but barbarian Muscovy, saw no salvation but in despotism, believed himself to be in a state of "unfathomable" sin, and set to work to find a divine mercy that ever fled before him. He journeyed from St. Petersburg, sometimes to Rome, sometimes to Jerusalem, sometimes to Paris, seeking everywhere rest for his tortured soul; then from time to time he would return to the Joukofskis, spending weeks together in their house, exhorting them to prayer, to contrition, and to the contemplation of divine mysteries. Then followed endless discussions concerning the heathens of the West, on a supposed approaching crusade, on the redemption of erring humanity by an untarnished race which had retained the faith. On several occasions the doctors had to interfere and break up an intimacy that was not free from peril. One day Gogol was found prostrate and insensible from inanition before the holy images in whose adoration he had lost himself! . . . We trust this short digression may be pardoned us; it gives an insight into the minds of a certain class of Russian society towards the close of Nicholas's reign, and adds a singular trait to the tableau of causes which led to the Eastern war.

It is interesting, too, to imagine Alexander Mikhaïlovitch in this *salon* of the Joukofskis, on such or such an evening, during some spiritual assault of arms with poor Gogol. The diplomatist, as deeply versed in literature as he was sceptical, was certainly well capable of recognising the lightning darts full of fire and life that pierced the clouds of a great but disordered mind, and to unravel more than one powerful and striking thought from among the strange vagaries that treated of an approaching crusade or of the deliverance of Zion.

Yet, who could have believed it? these mystics, these visionaries, were possessed with correct presentiments and read the true signs of the times! While Joukofski was composing his "Commentaries of Holy Russia," and Gogol was mortifying himself before his images, the Emperor Nicholas was revolving in his mind the great scheme of a crusade, and was preparing, under the profoundest mystery, the mission of Prince Menschikof. . . . That the monarch who had contributed so much towards the peace of Europe and the balance of power should suddenly have resolved to cast such a torch of war into the midst of the Continent, at that time scarcely settled, and yet that he should have waited for this period of comparative calm and for the re-establishment of general order to announce his designs, instead of boldly carrying them out some years before during the revolutionary shocks which were paralysing nearly every State, when his armies were already in the very heart of Hungary, and dominating the banks of the Danube—will be for the impartial historian a striking proof of the good faith in which the Czar undertook his fatal campaign, of the mystic blindness which possessed his spirit at this moment, and of his profound conviction that his cause was a just one.

Did Prince Gortchakof share his master's delusions to the same extent?

We are permitted to doubt it; we are permitted to suppose that, in common with Kisselef, Meyendorf, Brunnow, and all the most distinguished diplomatists of Russia at that time, including the chancellor of the empire—the old Count Nesselrode—he was aware of the enormous error into which a prince too proud to listen to objections, and who insisted on being his own minister of foreign affairs, was falling. This did not, however, prevent the Russian envoy to the German Confederation from fulfilling his duties with all the zeal that such a critical period demanded, nor from exerting, in the service of his country, all his varied mental resources in the sphere of action that was reserved for him. The events which took place in that sphere did not fail to prove of the first importance.

In the Bundestag were not only concentrated all the efforts of the secondary States of the German Confederation, but there also were conceived and ripened all the plans, preparations, projects, even to the slightest wishes, of the two principal powers of Germany, whose concurrence, Russia on the one side, and France and England on the other, were equally desirous of securing.

Prince Gortchakof had not much reason to complain of the attitude things were assuming in Germany. The fidelity of Frederick William IV. was proof against everything. The Czar might rely in any emergency on his brother-in-law the poet, and Alexander Mikhaïlovitch had an equally faithful supporter in his colleague of Prussia, the young officer of *landwehr*. The Cabinet of Berlin, though consenting from time to time to unite in the representations that the Allies were sending to St. Petersburg, and to sign, in concert with them, such or such an identical, similar, or concordant note, showed before long that it was acting thus only to slacken their progress, and turn them aside from any energetic resolutions. When the decisive moment came it stopped short, and stood aside, asserting that it wished to keep its "hand free" (*freie hand*). Even far more sympathetic and more openly expressed in their feelings were the other members of the Bund; they saw nothing exorbitant in the demands of the Czar on Turkey, and cared very little for the health of the "Sick Man."

They also maintained their right to keep their "hand free," closed up their ranks in the famous conferences of Bamberg, and now and again were ready to draw the sword. In truth, Alexander Mikhaïlovitch showed in later days, during the fatal year of 1866, a very short memory, very little feeling or distributive justice towards these poor secondary States, who had proved themselves so devoted, so serviceable, so unshaken in their attachment to Russia during the Eastern crisis.

While London and Paris were vehemently discussing the celebrated despatches of Sir Hamilton Seymour, and were denouncing the ambitious projects of Russia; Hanover, Dresden, Munich, Stuttgart, and Cassel were equally loud in their condemnation of the proceedings of the Allies and their "usurpations;" and Berlin groaned to see Christian kingdoms espousing so hotly the defence of the Crescent. One solitary German power—the greatest among them, it is true—assumed a different attitude, and was of one mind with the Allies, seeming even at times inclined to make common cause with them. And this power was Austria—Austria, that but lately had been succoured by Russian arms; rescued by the Czar's strong and generous hand at the very edge of the precipice, saved by him from sudden destruction! The astonishment, the stupefaction, the exasperation of the Emperor Nicholas knew no bounds; the whole Russian nation shared his sentiments, Alexander Mikhaïlovitch in common with every other Muscovite patriot.

"The immense ingratitude of Austria" thenceforward became the unanimous cry, the *siboleth* of every political creed in the vast empire of the north, and has remained so to our day. . . . . It is of importance to dwell upon this feeling which arose in Russia after the Eastern conflict, and to discuss its true basis, for this sentiment has had the most gigantic consequences. It has largely contributed towards recent events. It has dictated more than one extreme resolution in the Cabinet of St. Petersburg, has caused it to abandon secular traditions, principles consecrated by the experience of generations, which till then had seemed to be immovable, and which had become the very *arcana imperii* of the descendants of Peter the Great; and this same feeling has dominated, so to say, the politics of the successor of Nesselrode during the last twenty years.

It is incontestable that Russia had every right to reckon on the gratitude of Austria after the signal and important services she had rendered her in 1849. The armies which the Czar sent to help the tottering empire of the Hapsburgs contributed powerfully to stifle a dangerous and menacing insurrection; and if it is true that in order to obtain this help it was sufficient to remind the Czar Nicholas of a promise previously made, in a moment of friendly effusion, the action becomes still more meritorious, and does still more honour to the heart of the autocrat.*

It is undeniable that the intervention in Hungary bears the stamp of a generous and chivalrous nature, and was in itself an undertaking that astonished its contemporaries and confounded the wisest. The most skilful statesmen of Europe, who, during that troubled period, had sufficient leisure to glance occasionally towards the Danube, Lord Palmerston among others, remained for a long time quite incredulous, and tried to guess the reward that must have been stipulated upon in return for such assistance. Was not the Czar to retain Galicia? was he not to receive some positive assurance about the Principalities? were questions repeatedly asked in Downing Street. Yet no such thing happened. The Russians quitted Austria as unencumbered by

* A writer, whose position as a former Under-Secretary of State during the ministry of Prince Schwarzenberg gives his statements weight, offers the following account of the origin of the Russian intervention in Hungary, tracing it back as far as the year 1833, to the celebrated interview at Munchengratz, between the Emperor Francis I. of Austria and the Emperor Nicholas. During one of the confidential conversations which then took place, Francis spoke sadly and apprehensively of the sickly and nervous state of his son and presumptive heir, and begged the Czar to continue the same friendship for the son which he had always entertained for the father:—"Nicholas fell on his knees, and, raising his right hand to heaven, swore to give the successor of Francis all and every assistance he might ever stand in need of. The old Emperor of Austria was deeply touched, and laid his hands on the head of the kneeling Czar in sign of benediction." This strange scene had no witnesses, but a few moments later both emperors related it to an officer who then commanded the army division stationed at Munchengratz. This officer was no other than Prince Windischgraetz, who later on, in 1848, being appointed commander-in-chief of the Austrian armies at the time of the Hungarian insurrection, took upon himself to write to the Emperor Nicholas, reminding him of the promise given at Munchengratz. The Czar replied by placing his whole army at the service of his Imperial and Apostolic Majesty.—(Cf. Hefter, "Geschichte Œsterreichs." Prague, 1839, t. i., pp. 68, 69.)

any reward as they had entered it free of any after-thought, and the troops of Paskevitch evacuated the land of Carpathia with hands empty of any sign of booty.

A young and stormy orator in the Prussian Chambers bearing the then unknown name of Bismarck—he who fifteen years later was to meditate "the death-blow" of Austria, and arm the legions of Klapka—admired at that time the brilliant conduct of the Czar, and expressed his patriotic regret that this magnanimous task should not have devolved upon his own country of Prussia. It was for Prussia to render assistance to its elder Germanic brother—"its old companion-in-arms."* But we are at liberty to suppose that, even by a king as loyal and poetical as Frederick William IV., things would have been managed less romantically than by the barbarian of the North, and that a similar assistance lent by Prussia would have cost the House of Hapsburg either a portion of Silesia or a share of its influence on the banks of the Main.

But are we then to understand that in intervening in Hungary the Emperor of Russia was only acting from the purest feeling of chivalry and platonic friendship, regardless of his personal interests and the welfare of his empire? No, certainly not; and the Czar was too frank to conceal his ulterior motives.

He intervened in Hungary not only as the friend of the Hapsburgs, not only as the champion of the cause

* Uttered in the sitting of the Prussian Chamber of September 6th, 1849. This speech does not appear in the official collection of M. de Bismarck's speeches, published at Berlin.

of order against the cosmopolitan spirit of revolution, but because in the ranks of the Hungarian army were to be found Polish generals and officers, whose aim it was to carry the war even into countries subject to the dominion of Russia. In his manifesto of the 8th of May, 1849, Nicholas expressed himself as follows: " The insurrection maintained by the influence of *our Polish traitors* of 1831 has given to the revolt of the Magyars an *importance* which is becoming more and more *menacing*. . . . His Majesty the Emperor of Austria invites us to take arms against our *common foe*. . . . We have commanded our forces to advance, to stifle revolt and anarchy, and to destroy those audacious rebels who not only disturb the peace of Austria, *but who threaten that of our own provinces.*" This language was clear and open, such as beseemed a sovereign conscious of his power and dignity. In rendering this service to his ally, Nicholas did not neglect the interest of his own country. He extinguished a conflagration on his neighbour's domain because it menaced his own, and accomplished an act of intervention simultaneously with one of self-preservation.

Now it will be granted that every sense of justice dictates that gratitude should be measured by the service rendered, and that the law of self-preservation—supreme law of nature—should bear with equal force upon the recipient as upon the giver of favours. There has never been a policy in the world, not even in Scripture, which has counselled voluntary slavery, and there is no law, however sublime one may choose to deem it, which places suicide among the duties of gratitude. Well, it was nothing less than complete slavery—complete abnegation of its position as a great European state, that Russia demanded of Austria in proposing that it should subscribe to its pretensions in the East.

In geographical position, in spirit of race, in religious feeling, Russia, in its intended enterprises, would have struck a death-blow at the empire of Hapsburg, if that empire had allowed them to triumph.

A Danubian power herself, Austria had to take care that the Lower Danube remained neutral, lest it should fall into the hands of a powerful neighbour, who would thus become master of this great river.

A Slavonic power in her Eastern provinces, she had to guard against coming into immediate contact with an empire that was traditionally Pan-Slavonic, and could not wish to see it implanted in the Principalities, in Bosnia and Herzegovina.

Lastly, as a Catholic power, it was forbidden her to recognise the influence and the protectorate which the Czar claimed over the Christians of the Greek ritual, whom she counted by several millions among her subjects.

"My conduct with regard to the Eastern question is inscribed on the map," said, at Vienna, Count Buol, the Austrian minister, to his brother-in-law, M. de Meyendorf, the Russian ambassador; and he added that it was equally inscribed in history. "I have introduced no innovation, I have only continued the policy bequeathed to me by M. de Metternich." And in truth, in former years, during the Greek insurrection-

and the war of 1828, the great chancellor of the Court
and of the Empire had upheld the principle of
Ottoman independence with a steadfastness nothing
could shake; had upheld it during eight years, bearing the brunt of the storm, discouraged neither by
the unpopularity of the Turkish cause, nor by the
desertion of France.

How then could the Russians expect that Austria
would now desert a principle of such vital importance
to her, and at the very moment when she was about to
triumph over the indifference of the West, and reckon
England and France among her warmest champions?

Divided—whatever may have been said to the
contrary—between the keenest feelings of gratitude
and a great political necessity, the Austrian Government certainly gave to the cause of gratitude what it
owed. It overwhelmed the Emperor Nicholas with
warnings, with prayers, with offers of service, with
attempts at mediation. Austria forgave Russia more
than one want of respect, more than one burst of ill-humour; forgave it even the light tone in which her
Government was spoken of in the despatches to Sir
Hamilton Seymour; the manner in which a certain
autograph letter of the Emperor Francis Joseph was
received at St. Petersburg; the scornful, almost provoking attitude of Count Orlof during his mission at
Vienna. She was unceasing in her endeavours to calm
the irritation of the Allies, to modify and attenuate
their programme, to make the most of any conciliatory
disposition on the part of the Czar, and to the end
hoped against hope. All that Austria pleaded for

was a return to the *statu quo*, repudiating any idea of humiliating or circumscribing Russia; she only demanded the liberty of the Danube, the renunciation of the protectorate; and refused to join the Allies in their demands concerning the Black Sea. Unfortunately, but, as it happens only too often to those who wish to act justly and equitably by two antagonists, the Austrian Government succeeded in offending both France and England, and at the same time exasperated the Russians. In the summer of 1854, when Prince Gortchakof was exchanging his post of ambassador to France for that of Vienna, a celebrated political writer, Eugene Forcade, who was then, so to say, the mouthpiece of the generous impulses of the West, almost despaired of Austria, and exclaimed bitterly that over there, at the *Burg*, the Russian alliance was held in as sacred a light as a religion, as fixed as a law, as popular as a fashion! In the spring of the following year, the Cabinets of Paris and London rejected, as too favourable to Russia, a fresh project of arrangements presented by Count Buol, and the French Government took this opportunity to reproach Austria, in the *Moniteur*, for offering "an expedient rather than a solution."

The solution the Emperor Francis Joseph certainly held in his hand, and it only depended on him to make it as radical and as decisive as the direst enemies of Russia could have wished.

Why should we not confess it? When we consider the bitter fruit gathered by Austria as the harvest of her honest endeavours during the Eastern crisis, when we recognise the implacable hatred and the cruel disasters her attitude at the time has since drawn down upon her, we find ourselves regretting that the Cabinet of Vienna was so scrupulous during that memorable epoch; we find ourselves reproaching it for not having shown that selfishness of heart which now, alas! is becoming every day more necessary—more indispensable to the independence of states. Had Austria been a little less grateful and a little more politic during the war with Turkey, she would have entered the fray side by side with France and England, and instead of keeping the Allies prowling for years round the confines of Russia in the Baltic and Black Seas, would have opened for them the gates of Poland and gone in with them. Instead of "tickling the feet of the Colossus or cutting one of his nails," as was later remarked by Russian writers, a death-blow would have been dealt him such as the great hermit of Varzin knows so well how to devise and how to strike.

It was certainly not in the Cabinet of the Tuileries that any objections would have been encountered, for M. Drouyn de Lhuys, in his despatch of March 26th, 1855, boldly proposes the Polish question; nor, certes, would the Cabinet of St. James have raised any serious objections.

As to the probable result of such an enterprise, it suffices us to remember that Russia had come to an end of her resources; that Prussia had not yet reformed her military organisation—was not yet in possession of her "instrument;" and, lastly, that on the Hohenzollern throne sat Frederick the Romantic, and not William the Conqueror.

The human spirit quails as it contemplates the awful results that must have ensued upon such a decision on the part of Francis Joseph! The face of the globe would have been changed; Austria would have known no Sadowa in 1866, Europe would have never seen the dismemberment of Denmark, the destruction of the Bund, nor the conquest of Alsace and Lorraine.

It was, we have already said, in the summer of 1854 that Prince Gortchakof was made envoy to the Court of Vienna. He replaced, at first provisionally, but definitely in the following summer, the Baron de Meyendorf, to whom the post had become very painful on account of his near relationship to the Minister for Foreign Affairs in Austria. Alexander Mikhaïlovitch held at last the office to which he had so long aspired, and which, during the reign of Nicholas, was, in common with the same office in London, held to be the greatest prize—the marshal's *bâton*—in the diplomatic career of Russia; but his honours were now steeped in bitterness, for what patriotic sufferings were now joined to a distinction once ardently desired, but now accepted through love of king and country!

On the ground once so smiling and pleasant the envoy of the Czar would now see nothing but weeds and thorns; in a capital renowned for its wild and frivolous gaiety, he received nothing but the most disastrous, heartrending news; finally, "*that Austrian* *ingratitude"* which he had only heard of and combated from afar at Frankfort, he had now to see face to face and meet with a smile .... There is a greater sorrow than the *ricordarsi tempi felici nella miseria*, and it is to wake from dreams of happiness to a reality of misery; and one can easily imagine what a store of bitterness that sojourn at Vienna must have accumulated in the heart of the Russian patriot.*

It would be superfluous to mention the activity displayed by the Czar's new envoy during this painful mission, the infinite variety of resources which he employed in his country's service, notably during those conferences at Vienna which were held after the death of Nicholas, and on the accession of Alexander II.

Nothing could be more touching or more sublime than the aspect then presented by the two Gortchakofs, one behind the ramparts of Sebastopol, the other before the ministerial table at Vienna, each defending his country with equal tenacity, fighting with desperation

---

* May we be allowed, in reference to this subject, to relate a piquant scene, which has also its instructive side. At the Viennese Foreign Office there was, at that time, a most original being, an usher, whose singularities are still remembered at the *Ballplatz*. He bore the odd name of Kadernoschka, and, placed in the large hall outside the cabinet of the Minister, it was his duty to escort the different visitors to his chief. His style was of the grandest, and, having been appointed to the post by the old Prince Metternich, he loved to recall the fact of his having exercised his functions as far back as the time of the celebrated Congress of 1815 ! . . . One day, after a long interview with Prince Gortchakof, M. de Buol was surprised by the entrance of Kadernoschka, whose countenance was more than usually solemn, and by the news that he wished to lay before his Excellency information of great importance to the State, which turned out to be that the Russian envoy, after leaving the cabinet of his Excellency, had demanded a glass of water, had paced the great hall for nearly half an hour, gesticulating violently, muttering to himself, and from time to time exclaiming in French, "Oh ! they shall pay for this one day; they shall pay for it ! . . ."

for every inch of ground, driven to the last extremity, but honoured to the end by their loyal and chivalrous adversaries.

To-day, when an epoch of "blood and iron" has accustomed us to the summary proceedings—we had almost said to the executions—of Nikolsburg, Ferrières, Versailles, and Frankfort, and when martial law laid down by helmeted diplomatists has taken the place of that which old-fashioned and prejudiced Europe formerly called the rights of the people; we say that, witnessing the present order of things, we cannot refrain from a sentiment of astonishment, almost of incredulity, when we glance over the protocols of those Viennese conferences, where all was propriety, politeness, urbanity, and mutual respect—we fancy ourselves carried back to some far away and idyllic time, quite to a world of *bonshommes Jadis.*

M. Drouyn de Lhuys, Minister for Foreign Affairs in France, and Lord John Russell, then Prime Minister of England, did not consider it beneath their dignity to go in person to Vienna, in order to discuss with Prince Gortchakof the possible conditions of peace.

Russia had lost several great battles, the allied fleets were blockading all its seas, and menacing even its capital; this, however, did not prevent the English and French plenipotentiaries from treating it with the utmost respect, and with all those attentions which diplomatists made use of in the good old times. They displayed a perfect art in the invention of polite terms; striving to find the softest expressions, terms the most acceptable to the representative of a vanquished power.

The worthy Lord John Russell carried his good nature to such a pitch as to refer, and that in the presence of M. Drouyn de Lhuys, to the far harder and more humiliating conditions which England had imposed on Louis XIV.; this was, perhaps, the only want of tact that could be reported during those conferences at Vienna; and it was but a pleasantry from one ally to another.

As to Austria, she never wearied in watching over the susceptibilities of Russia, and ended by presenting a project of arrangement that was considered inadmissible by the Cabinets of London and Paris, and that drew down upon her that reproach of the *Moniteur Officiel*, of which we have already spoken.

The negotiations were broken off, and nothing remained to be done but to await the issue of the final encounter that was taking place under the walls of Sebastopol.

The Russian plenipotentiary awaited the result, enduring alike the combined anxiety of a patriot and a kinsman.

The bulwarks of the Crimea fell, and Russia found herself in a most critical situation. She was exhausted, far more so even than Europe supposed; and any prolongation of the war would undoubtedly have carried hostilities into Poland. At this juncture Austria again intervened.

She supported the demands insisted upon by the Allies at the conference at Vienna; even the clause which, until then, she had rejected as too injurious to Russia—namely, the neutralisation of the Black Sea; indeed, it was almost impossible to refuse this satisfaction to the Allies after the fall of Sebastopol. In truth, they were the mildest conditions ever imposed on any power after so long and sanguinary a war, and after such undoubted conquests. Austria went even farther, and sent these conditions under the form of an ultimatum, declaring that she would make common cause with the Allies if they were not accepted. And Russia accepted.

Here was, in truth, a service rendered to a young sovereign, who had inherited a disastrous war. It offered him, at the same time, the means of guarding the memory of his predecessor and the pride of his people; it allowed him to state that he only concluded peace in the face of this new enemy which had arisen by the side of the former ones, and whose existence his father had not suspected.

This was the report circulated in Russia, and which was believed all the more readily as there was such satisfaction in believing it. The Russian people were soon reconciled to the conquerors of the Alma and the Malakof; one power alone remained in their opinion responsible for every disaster—that power which, during the whole war, had never drawn its sword! To this very hour every Russian heart beats with indignation at the thought of Austria, at the thought of her colossal ingratitude, her profound treachery. Alexander Mikhaïlovitch shared these bitter feelings, these rancorous popular views, and became their most energetic and outspoken advocate, giving vent to his sentiments on these topics in a manner that at times bordered on ostentation. A saying of his was quoted, made at Vienna, while the Congress held still their sittings in Paris: "Austria is not a state, she is only a government." This saying preceded him to St. Petersburg, and made his fortune there. Public opinion pointed him out as the future avenger of Russia, as the man destined to offer his nation the means of a terrible retaliation; and the cunning diplomatist had no wish to give the lie to so favourable an opinion. Besides, at this Congress of Paris, certain tendencies, certain inclinations, were revealed, which opened out fresh vistas and inspired new hopes. The name of Italy was pronounced; even Roumania found unexpected favour.

During this singular Congress, in which the conditions of peace that France, England, and Austria imposed on Russia were finally decided upon, Austria appeared sombre and morose, England irritated and nervous; France and Russia alone exchanged the most polished amenities, the most gushing expressions of cordiality. The sword of Napoleon III. seemed transformed into the lance of Achilles, healing where it had wounded, wounding where it had healed. "There was balm in Gilead," and hope could still be placed in the sovereign presiding at the Tuileries .... The day after the Congress, in the month of April, 1856, the old Count Nesselrode, pleading his advanced age, retired, and Alexander Mikhaïlovitch became Minister of Foreign Affairs.

CHAPTER II.

FIRST APPEARANCES OF M. DE BISMARCK.

The Bismarcks of History—Their Ancestor, Rulo, Master Clothier—The Grandfather, the "Poet," and the Great-uncle, the "Adventurer"—Otto Edward Leopold de Bismarck-Schœnhausen—The "Grey Cloister" and the "Georgia Augusta"—Disputed Question of the "State Examination"—Cultivation and Mind of M. de Bismarck as compared to Prince Gortchakof—The Orator—An Effort of Oratory derived from the "Freischütz"—The Writer—Letters to Malvina—The Style of M. de Bismarck—Failures in the Administrative and Military Careers —"Years of Storms and Torment"—Life as Country Gentleman at Kneiphof and Schœnhausen—Bismarck "the Furious"—Aspirant to the Post of Superintendent of Dykes—Parliamentary *Début* of M. de Bismarck—His Share in the "Cross Party"—A Resolute Adversary of Modern Ideas and Constitutional Theories—The Christian State— Opinion on Schleswig-Holsteinism and German Unity—The Attempt of General de Radowitz—Prince Schwarzenberg and the Humiliation of Olmütz—M. de Bismarck as Champion of Austria—Minister at Frankfort—"His Excellency the Lieutenant"—Friendship with Prince Gortchakof—Letters to Malvina on the Diet of Frankfort and the Diplomatists of the Bund—Lassitude and Disgust—The Eastern Crisis —Growing Antipathy to Austria—Community of Antipathies with Prince Gortchakof—*Ferro et igne*—Contests with M. de Rechberg— Agitation and Travels—Minister Plenipotentiary at St. Petersburg.

DURING the four years which Prince Gortchakof spent in Frankfort, as the representative of his Government with the German Confederation, he had, as we have already seen, formed an acquaintanceship, and, indeed, was on the most intimate terms with a colleague, whose singular qualities, both of heart and mind, he peculiarly appreciated.

The two friends separated in the summer of 1854, when the Russian plenipotentiary left in order to fulfil his painful mission at Vienna; but they were to meet again before long, and to find in each other that complete community of ideas and sentiments which they experienced during the early days at Frankfort, and which lasted uninterruptedly during twenty-five years: *grande mortalis ævi spatium.*

This friend, won by Prince Gortchakof on the smiling banks of the Main, was no other than M. de Bismarck, the future Chancellor of Germany.

Otto Edward Leopold de Bismarck-Schœnhausen was born on the 1st of April, 1815, at Schœnhausen, the ancestral seat of his family, in the Old-Mark of Brandenburg, and cannot pride himself, as may his friend, Alexander Mikhaïlovitch, on having the blood of saints in his veins. His biographer mentions, with an evident complaisance, that at least two of his ancestors were excommunicated by the Church, and died impenitently under the ban. What is still more serious is, that some of the best historians of the Mark of Brandenburg, M. de Riedel among others, deny that his family springs from a noble origin; they show that the first of the line of whom mention is made in any authentic document of the fourteenth century was called Rulo Bismarck, and also that he was "Prevost of the Guild of Master Clothiers" at Stendal, a small borough in the Old-Mark.

The fact does not appear to admit of a doubt; but might not the burghers of Stendal, in common with those of certain towns of Tuscany, have obliged every country noble who wished to inhabit the city to inscribe his name on one of their guilds? Such is the opinion on the Tory side of this curious genealogical question; and to give it credence one must believe that the good burghers of Stendal occupied in the fourteenth century a social status similar to that of the great citizens of such towns as Florence and Pisa, and that Rulo Bismarck was a master tailor as much as Dante, his contemporary, was an apothecary. The Whigs, on the contrary—those biographers whose standard bears the "National-Liberal" colours—take a different view, and one of them concludes, ingeniously, that however it might have been, Rulo, the ancestor, "must look down from heaven with pride and satisfaction on the splendid imperial mantle that his descendant has cut for King William out of the cloth of Europe. . . . ."

In more modern times the house of Bismarck presents, in common with many other noble country families of Brandenburg, an uninterrupted succession of modest and faithful servants of the state, sometimes fulfilling military, sometimes civil duties.

The eighteenth century offers us two specimens of a rather more interesting type, the grandfather and the great-uncle of the Chancellor, the one surnamed "the Poet," the other "the Adventurer."

The poet, we are sorry to say, composed his verses in French, and the best known is an "elegy or epitaph to the memory of Christina de Bismarck, born at Schœnfeld, by Alexander de Bismarck, Berlin,

1774." It is to the memory of his defunct wife that the retired captain of cavalry has thought proper to raise this monument of words and bad rhymes, full of the sickly sentimentality of the age.

The adventurer, Ludolf-Augustus, does more justice to his name. In a fit of rage he killed his servant; was pardoned; entered the Russian service; and, becoming mixed up in some political intrigues in Courland, was exiled to Siberia.

Pardoned for the second time, he entered the Russian diplomatic service, fulfilled several missions, and, as a general officer, fell at Poltava.

It may here be mentioned that this Ludolf was not the only member of his family who served under the Russian flag, and that, in consequence, the name of Bismarck had for years been well known in St. Petersburg. His Whig biographers make a great point of the fact that the mother of the youthful Otto, "an intelligent, ambitious, but somewhat austere woman," was a burgher's daughter, a Miss Menken, a member of a well-known family of learned scholars in Leipsic.

In this manner they love to show that the restorer of the empire springs, on his mother's side, from the middle classes — from those studious and learned middle classes which constitute the great strength of Germany; though on his father's—who was a retired captain of cavalry, as was his grandfather the poet —from the nobility.

These abstruse Germans have, as we know, a weakness for symbolism, and give this name to what.

is often a mere insignificant trifle; and thus they attach a certain importance to the trivial coincidence of the young Otto having been confirmed at Berlin by Schleiermacher, the celebrated doctor of divinity, whose science was of a far more respectable nature than his life, and say "that thus, for one fleeting but solemn moment, the youth who was called to such an eminently active life was brought into contact with our learned theology and our romantic philosophy.

They also do not fail to remember the name of "Grey Cloister" (*Grauer-Kloster*) borne by the Lyceum at which the future destroyer of convents pursued his early studies; nor to note the French origin of one of its principal professors, Doctor Bonnell, a descendant of a Huguenot family which had sought refuge in Brandenburg after the edict of Nantes.

After having finished his studies at the Lyceum of the Grey Cloister, Otto de Bismarck went to the university of Göttingen, to the celebrated Georgia-Augusta, professedly to take his degree, but in reality to lead the life of those sons of the muses who have at the same time the good or bad fortune to be also sons of the nobility, *cavalieri*. Here, neglecting all else, he adopted as his chief pursuits hunting, riding, swimming, gymnastics, and fencing. Otto de Bismarck fought more than twenty duels, and fully justified the proud title of *bursche*,* which clung to him for many a year, even when replaced by the graver titles of ambassador and minister.

One can easily imagine that, devoting so much

---

* Fighting student.

time to bodily exercise, he could have little left in which to attend to any mental cultivation, or to pursue the study of law; and even the removal from the noisy Georgia-Augusta to the calmer and quieter academy at Berlin was found to be a remedy more heroic than efficacious.

Did M. de Bismarck ever pass that "government examination" (*Staats Examen*) which in Prussia forms an indispensable prelude to every public career? A serious question, which was freely and lengthily discussed in Germany, and used as a weapon for twenty years against M. de Bismarck when chief of his party, when deputy, when ambassador, and when prime minister. It is worthy of notice and thoroughly characteristic of the formal and pedantic spirit of the nation, that M. de Bismarck had defied all Europe and dismembered the Danish monarchy, and still the opposition papers in Germany were exploding from time to time, like tardy fireworks, over this much discussed and problematic question of his "government examination."

It is only since the period of Sadowa that this misplaced spite has ceased: Sadowa cast a veil over this and over many other irregularities assuredly of a far more serious nature.

This is perhaps the fittest time in which to ask what benefits M. de Bismarck derived from his university education, and to scan, if but cursorily, the cultivation and style of his mind. It certainly appears that M. de Bismarck is neither a studious nor a scientific man, and that his liberal education presents more than one gap.

What a curious contrast is presented by the two chancellors, Russian and German—the one educated in a Lyceum of more than doubtful worth, the other having frequented the most renowned *gymnasium* and *alma mater* of the learned Germans; and yet it is the pupil of Tsarskoë-Selo who, in point of classical learning and true *humaniora*, shines superior to the fortunate nursling of the Georgia-Augusta. Still, we must not omit to state that M. de Bismarck quite fulfils, and even exceeds, the rules laid down by the witty and lamented St. Marc Girardin, as being necessary for a well-educated man of the world. "I do not ask," says this writer, "that they should know Latin; I only ask that they should have forgotten it."

From his university career, however, the German Chancellor still retains certain fragments of cultivation, of which he well knows how to make use at times; and he possesses a very ample knowledge of his Bible, his Shakespeare, his Goethe, and his Schiller, four elements that are usually included in the most ordinary German education—precious and much-to-be-envied *quadrivium* of the children of Armenius! Prince Gortchakof possesses all the subtleties, joined to all the weaknesses, of the man of letters; the expressions he employs are highly finished, his sentences are modelled and remodelled; and, from the extreme beauty of his compositions, he has been surnamed the Narcissus of the desk. In his exquisite tastes and artistic instincts he shows a marked superiority over his former colleague of Frankfort; but this latter rises to his level when we consider the stamp of originality which he is capable of giving to his thoughts and words, when we note his individuality, his creative power, the *mens agitans molem*—that mysterious and powerful something which the antique sculptors depicted so ingeniously by placing a flame on the brow of certain of their statues. The Chancellor of Germany is not a man of letters in the strict and somewhat vulgar acceptation of the word ; nor is he, to speak correctly, either an orator or a writer. He cannot develop a theme, or graduate his arguments, or thoroughly weigh his speeches ; he cannot construct his periods, and does not endeavour to do so ; he is often troubled to find suitable expressions, in the rostrum as when holding the pen ; his style clashes, is often very incorrect, and as little academic as possible ; he is even confused, halting, and trivial at times. With many reservations we might compare his style of expression to that of Cromwell ; but even more than in Cromwell are we forced to admire the lightning-like thoughts, the powerful and unforeseen imagery, those words which strike and penetrate, and remain indelibly engraven.

Lately, during an argument of a somewhat incoherent and embarrassed nature, which treated of his conflict with Rome, he suddenly exclaimed : " Rest assured of one thing, gentlemen, *we shall not go to Canossa !*" expressing in that one sentence a kind of menacing *cæterum censeo*, and a whole world of memories and passions. In a very different spirit, in a time already long past, it is true—twenty years ago, perhaps—speaking one day of the principles of revolutions and counter-revolutions, he said, meaning to imply that no parliamentary debate would ever decide between these two principles: "The decision will only come from God; from the God of Battle, when He shall shake the iron dice of destiny from His hands."

We fancy, in hearing such phrases, that we are listening to M. de Maistre; and, similar to M. de Maistre, the German Chancellor has uttered a passage suitable for an executioner—we mean his invocation of iron and of blood; an invocation that must be placed side by side with the events that produced it in order to extract its value from its incontestable brutality. The invocation was made in the days when the National-Liberals, now so subservient, so obedient to him, would have opposed his army reforms, but demanded at the same time the union of Germany. The man, feeling in his soul the rising storms of Sadowa and Sedan, thundered back the defiance which he has since carried out but too truly. "It is not by speech-making that you will unite Germany; to cement this union, what is wanted is blood and iron!" . . . . The orator is not at his ease in the tight uniform which he never quits, and he generally confines himself to short sallies and freaks of speech.

It is with effort that he piles up the clouds of his rhetoric—though in the end the lightning glances from them, illuminating the entire situation. In order to be understood he will employ the loftiest or the most familiar imagery, and will cite as may be most apposite Shakespeare or Goethe in the same breath with "*les Guêpes*" of Alphonse Karr or some Vaudeville couplet.

One of these most happy, most memorable inspirations he suddenly wrested on one occasion from the libretto of the "Freischütz." May we be permitted to call to mind this episode, even at the risk of losing a little time in preliminary explanations which a German audience, well versed in all appertaining to the "Freischütz," did not, of course, require. In this opera of Weber's, Max, the good but unfortunate hunter, borrows a cartridge from Robin, the evil genius, and with it immediately brings down an eagle, one of whose plumes he proudly fixes in his cap.

He asks for a few more of these cartridges, but Robin tells him that they contain "magic bullets," and in order to possess them he must sell his soul to Satan. Max draws back, and Robin then informs him, amid infernal laughter, that it is too late now to draw back, that the compact is concluded, and that he is already compromised by the cartridge of which he has made use. "Dost thou think yonder eagle was a free gift?" . . .

Well! when, in 1849, the young Brandenburg orator implored the Prussian Chamber not to accept the Imperial crown offered to the king of Prussia by the Frankfort Parliament, he ended by exclaiming: "It is the hand of Radicalism that offers the king this gift! Sooner or later Radicalism will rise up before the king, will ask for its recompense, and, pointing to the emblematic eagle on the new imperial flag, will say: 'Dost thou think this eagle was a free gift?'"

An imagery as striking and profound as it was ingenious! One cannot make use with impunity of the "enchanted bullets of revolution, and one cannot conclude a compact with the demon of popularity without giving up some shreds of one's soul. Sooner or later the evil genius whose help you have invoked, the Robin of the woods and streets, will rise up, and, grasping your salvation, will tell you that he is not in the habit of working for nothing."

This splendid burst of oratory on the part of the youthful deputy of the Mark might well have been remembered with pride, and been the source of fruitful meditation to the Chancellor on more than one decisive occasion; on the day, for instance, on which he overthrew such or such a secular throne, or on the day when he gave the signal to begin *the war of civilisation.*

What he is as an orator he is also as a writer, and in mentioning this last acquirement we have most prominently before us the intimate and familiar letters which have been published in George Hesekiel's book, and which have met with such well-merited success in Germany.

We find in these letters the same obscurity, the same halting elocution, the same confusion, yet lit up from time to time by life-like and original expressions, by the most astounding figures of speech, by a bitter and derisive humour, which grinds and crushes with cruel voluptuousness.

The letters are mostly addressed to his sister, his "dear Malvina" (married to an Arnim), and we shall have to glance more than once at their pages during the course of these remarks.

In them have been pointed out to us certain descriptions of nature—of moonlight, of the North Sea, of the Danube from the heights of Buda-Pesth: pictures not without merit, and somewhat in the style of Heinrich Heine; as we might also say that there is a something of Hamlet (and what a Hamlet!) in the following sentence, the only one breathing the slightest sentiment of melancholy among so many robust and sanguinary outbursts:

"Thank God everything is in reality but a question of time—countries and individuals, wisdom and folly, peace and war! After all, everything in this world is but hypocrisy and jugglery, and, *once denuded of their fleshly mask*, the fool and the sage must be wonderfully alike; and, *their skeletons properly prepared*, it must be very difficult to distinguish between a Prussian and an Austrian. Surely this ought to cure us of any very special patriotism." And these are lines graven by the same hand that has since—guided, we must suppose, by a very *special* patriotism—handed over so many *subjects* to the skeleton makers!

One sees in these letters that M. de Bismarck began early to practise the style of irony in which he is now a past-master; irony of the coldest, most contemptuous kind, merging from time to time into bitter laughter. It appears in his speeches, in his conversations with ministers and ambassadors, and in his diplomatic negotiations, at moments of the utmost historical importance.

At such times his irony will take the form of the greatest openness or the most urbane politeness; but an openness that inclines one to fall down and worship the first tolerably decent lie, and an urbanity that makes one welcome an outspoken incivility as a positive relief.

Once, on the eve of the war of 1866, Count de Karolyi, Austrian ambassador, acting in the name of his Government, summoned M. de Bismarck to declare categorically whether his intentions were to annul the Treaty of Gastein. "No," was the answer; "I have no such intentions; *but, if I had, should I have given you a different answer?*" This is an example of a frankness that utterly puts one to rout, that dismays, and cries in one's ears with the devil in the "Inferno"—

"Tu non pensavi ch' io loico fossi!"

As to that cloak of murderous politeness in which M. de Bismarck's sarcasm at times veils itself, we may cite as an example the speech which he cast in the faces of the negotiators of Versailles, when they came to him to treat of the surrender of famished Paris, and offered two hundred millions. "Oh!" exclaimed he, "Paris is too important a town to be treated so meanly, let us do it the honour of a thousand millions;" and this is the peculiar form which the emulator of Heine gives to the *maxima reverentia* which we owe to misfortune! . . . When in riper years one is destined to exercise one's wit at the expense of princes and countries, it is not surprising that in youth one should have exercised the same wit over so trivial an object as a poor Pomeranian peasant who had drunk too much water.

In one of his letters to his dear Malvina, the youthful country gentleman speaks with the greatest hilarity of an inundation which had just covered one of his domains traversed by a little "affluent" of the meagre river Hampel. This inundation had cut him off from his neighbours, and had carried away several barrels of his *eau-de-vie*, "causing an interregnum of confusion from Schievelbein to Damm;" and he concludes his letter with this stroke—"I am proud to be able to say, that, in my little affluent of the Hampel, a waggoner, along with his horse and load of tar, has actually been able to drown himself!" . . .

With what an increase of pride this gentleman must have witnessed, later in life, when Europe had become his domain, a chief and his army, an empire and its ruler, vanish beneath another inundation, whose waves were blood: *currus Galliæ et auriga ejus!* . . .

Yet, in spite of this, at another time the youthful country gentleman threw himself bravely into the water to save his groom, and gained that medal for saving human life which for years was the sole decoration on the broad breast of the Minister of Prussia at Frankfort. On being questioned one day, by a colleague at the Bund, as to his decoration, of the nature of which the diplomatic corps was ignorant, he replied, in that tone of voice peculiarly his own, that once by accident he had saved a man; in a moment of idleness, of course; and it would have taken but little further questioning for him to have replied that it was but to take exercise in swimming that he had done it.

But now to resume. From the days of his apprenticeship at the Grey Cloister and the Georgia-Augusta, Otto de Bismarck carried away with him a load of literature neither weighty nor complete, but which has proved sufficient, and has enabled him to travel round the world of politics with care and honour. And even at that early period his mind revealed many precious qualities which still distinguish him—a lively and powerful imagination, a rare wealth of expression, at times full of grandeur, at times vulgar, but always striking; and, lastly, a humour which has not its equal, and which, to use the expression of Jean Paul, "is a sirocco to the mind." But in all this there is a complete want of grace, of charm, of distinction, of delicacy—no generous fibres, no soft or sympathetic chords, none of that "milk of human kindness" of which the poet speaks, an utter absence of the charity which, according to the great Christian moralist, is the celestial perfume of the soul. As to the art, or rather the trade, which consists in the laborious study of sentences, in the consideration of their affinity and their coherence, in the introduction of harmony and light into the different parts of a speech—in one word, as to his *style*, M. de Bismarck has either never learnt or always scorned it.

If we dared to apply to his style one of those trivial but expressive comparisons of which he himself offers us many examples, we would willingly compare it to a certain strange and almost incredible beverage which the Chancellor of Germany has always loved—namely, a mixture of champagne and porter. His language is like his beverage, containing the piquant, sparkling elements of the champagne at the same time as the heaviness, blackness, and especially the bitterness of the stout.

Finally, we must consider the strange anomaly that the man who was one day to impose the severe Prussian bureaucratic and military rules on all the German States; who was, to use his own expression, "to place Germany in the saddle," and to restrain it in the bonds of obligatory service—who indirectly, even, was to excite all Europe to military exercises, and make it leave the plough for the sword, quit liberal occupations for summer and autumn manœuvres;—we must consider the anomaly that this man himself could never bow his neck to scholarly tasks, nor endure the regular work of an office or of a soldier's life. We have it on his own confession that a space of two hours was the whole extent of time ever devoted to any course of lecture during his stay at the Georgia-Augusta. His university life being terminated, he made several attempts to pursue an administrative or judicial career; he tried it at Aix-la-Chapelle, at Potsdam, at Greifswalde, then again at Potsdam; but each time abandoned it, either in disgust at the monotonous office work, or from quarrels with his superiors. Touching on this last reason, there is on record a piquant answer from the young *referendarius* (barrister) to his chief, who had made him wait in the ante-room.

for upwards of an hour : " I had come to ask you for a short holiday ; but during this long hour I have had time to reflect, and I now beg to offer my resignation." He afterwards twice tried the army, without attaining a higher rank than that of lieutenant of *landwehr*, a rank which he, however, greatly prized, and the uniform of which he wore on every solemn occasion, even as minister at Frankfort ; we know that since then Sadowa has brought him the insignia of a general.

Those ten or twelve years which filled for M. de Bismarck the period between his much-discussed government examination and his entry into the Prussian Chamber, are honoured by his German biographers with the fine-sounding title of "years of storm and struggle," which calls to mind the name given to one of the most brilliant epochs of German literature.*

They were certainly years filled with miscarried schemes of every description, financial embarrassments, and, perhaps, with a disappointed love. We are inclined to believe this last fact from a passage taken from one of his letters to his sister Malvina : " It is in vain for one to rebel ; I know I shall marry * * * the world expects it ; and nothing, perhaps, is more natural as we are *restés tous les deux sur le carreau*. She does not inspire me with any warm affection, it is true ; but none of them do that ; and after all one is not so badly off but what one can change one's feelings as one does one's linen, however long the latter may have been worn."

* *Sturm und Drang Periode*—early period of Goethe and Schiller.

He seems to have felt a sincere affection for this sister, and lavishes on her the tenderest epithets; sometimes he calls her "his dear little one," or " dear little Malvina," " his good little Arnim," his " Creusa," and sometimes he calls her (forgive him, oh ye gods of Walhalla!) simply, and in *French,* " *ma sœur!* " In all his letters of this period, dating in a great measure from his estates of Kniephof or Schœnhausen (it was only in later years that M. de Bismarck purchased the famous estate of Varzin), we trace, mingled with his usual bitterness of mind, a certain disenchantment; also traces of pecuniary troubles, while his views for the future are of the most modest description, and rarely touch upon politics. In 1846 he attaches great importance to being nominated captain of the dykes for his district (*deichhauptmann*). "The place is not a remunerative one," he writes, "but is of importance with regard to Schœnhausen and other estates, for on its occupant depends, in great measure, whether we shall be under water, as during last year. . . . Bernard (a friend) insists on my going to Berlin; I should like to know what he means by it. He maintains that my inclinations and character adapt me to the service of the State, and that sooner or later I shall enter it."

Then suddenly, and on the very eve of the meeting of the first Prussian Parliament, one is taken aback by his planning an immediate journey to the Indies, with the probable intention of making his fortune and settling out there; and involuntarily the mind turns to Cromwell, who once intended to embark for America on the eve of the Long Parliament.

My readers must not, however, fancy that time passed sadly at Kniephof or Schœnhausen; on the contrary, the style of life was that of the German *junker* (country squire), and the officers from the neighbouring garrisons afforded company of a merry and substantial nature: "We empty great cups filled half with champagne half with porter; we waken our guests in the morning by firing off pistols close to their pillows; we terrify our lady-cousins by letting loose four foxes in the drawing-room; and we do justice to the name given to the proprietor of the domain by the whole neighbourhood—namely, that of 'the mad Bismarck (*der tolle Bismarck*).'"

We hear of his violence and of his duels with sword and pistol, and even to his condescending now and then to a pugilistic encounter. One day, being in a beer-saloon at Berlin, the former pupil of the Georgia-Augusta broke his mug of beer over the head of an unknown person, who had delivered himself of certain disrespectful speeches concerning a member of the royal family—not, however, without having previously addressed a charitable word of warning to the insolent speaker, nor, afterwards, without quietly and politely asking the waiter the cost of the breakage. This occurred in 1850. M. de Bismarck had already occupied the post of deputy for several years, and was on the point of becoming minister plenipotentiary to the German Confederation.

It was not only at Kniephof and Schœnhausen that

the future Chancellor of Germany bore the name of *" der tolle Bismarck;"* the Berlinese themselves had no other name for him for a long time, during the whole parliamentary career of the young deputy; from the time of his maiden speech and his first appearance in the tribune—when, after provoking an indescribable tumult by a violent attack upon the Liberals, he drew a newspaper from his pocket and sat down tranquilly to peruse its pages, awaiting the subsiding of the storm—till his last speech of the 3rd of December, 1850, which raised the indignation of the Chambers to its height, but gained the orator a diplomatic appointment.

The law of success works backwards, similarly to the law of nobility in China, and embellishes and brightens with its rays the doubtful antecedents of the favourite of fortune.

It would only be to confuse all historical perspective to say that in M. de Bismarck could be foreshadowed, from 1847 to 1850, any tokens of the important part he was to play fifteen years later. The truth is that the part he thus played during this early period was neither sufficiently important nor sufficiently conspicuous to have tempted anyone to draw any inference at all from it. As an active and restless member of the *Junker party*, in 1847, and of the important body of the *Party of the Cross*, which was formed after the revolution of February, the squire of Schœnhausen was very far from occupying the position of a Gerlach or a Stahl, or the proud position of a feudal lord of Silesia or Pomerania.

In spite of his audacity, his impetuosity, and coolness—in spite of many striking outbursts of an eloquence which was far rougher and more embarrassed than it is to-day, M. de Bismarck was at that time only the Hotspur, or *l'enfant terrible*, of the sacred ranks which defended the throne, altar, and conservatism. He was, in some sort, a kind of Général du Temple of the skirmishers of Borussia—a Général du Temple with a dash of a Marquis de Piré.

Take him for all in all, he was but a successful edition of Thadden-Triglaff, that heroic M. Thadden-Triglaff who declared that he wished for nothing more than the liberty of the press, but on one condition, "that, side by side with every journal should stand a gibbet, on which to hang its contributors."

The propositions of M. de Bismarck (a friend and neighbour of this ingenious legislator for the press) were often not more reasonable, for did he not publicly exclaim on one occasion "that all large towns should be destroyed and razed to the ground for being, as he termed them, the eternal hot-beds of revolution ?"

The Athenians of the Spree laughed at these sallies, and repeated his humorous saying, especially admiring the argument *ad hominem* of the blow with the beer-mug.

Sometimes also they commented maliciously on the advances made to the democrats by the country squire of Schœnhausen. These advances were made intermittently, and when he was in a good humour. Even twelve years later, and at the moment when returning from France, he was about to assume the reins of government, he amused his surroundings with the well-known olive branch, which he displayed one day to a former colleague in the Chamber, the very radical Doctor d'Ester.

"This branch," said he to the doctor, "was gathered as I passed through Vaucluse, on the grave of Laura and Petrarch. I keep it carefully in my cigar-case, and intend to offer it at some appropriate time to the gentlemen of the Red, "in sign of reconciliation." . . . It is a most singular trait in this extraordinary man's career, that he is only believed to be serious when he becomes terrible. "Mad Bismarck" was his appellative in Germany during 1850. At Frankfort, the Count Rechberg called him disdainfully a *bursche,* and as late even as 1864 he was regarded by a French minister of considerable ability as being a very contemptible person. In the following year, on the historic sands of Biarritz, he pursued the Emperor Napoleon III. with his plans, who, leaning on the arm of the author of "Colomba," whispered from time to time to that academic senator, "He is mad!" Five years later, the visionary of Ham surrendered his sword to the *madman* of the Mark.

"I belong," says M. de Bismarck, defiantly, in one of his early speeches in the Chambers, "I belong to a party that glories in the reproach that its opinions are old-fashioned and belong to a bygone age. I belong to that great multitude which you oppose with disdain by the more intelligent classes of the nation." He wanted a *Christian state.* "Without a religious basis," he says, "the State becomes nothing but a chance conglomeration of interests, a sort of bastion in a war of all against all; without this religious basis, all legislation, instead of seeking fresh strength at the well of eternal truth, becomes tossed to and fro by humanitarian ideas as vague as they are changing."

It was for this reason that he opposed the emancipation of the Jews, and rejected with horror the institution of civil marriage, an institution which, to use his own words, degraded the Church to the position of train-bearer to a subaltern bureaucracy.*

He showed himself as exacting for the throne as for the altar; he denied the sovereignty of the people; and universal suffrage (which he himself introduced later on throughout the entire German empire) appeared to him as a social danger and an outrage on common sense!

He denied the rights of the nation, the crown alone had any rights: the old Prussian spirit recognised none other; "and," he added, "that old Prussian spirit is a Bucephalus, docile enough in the hands of his legitimate master, but who would fling to the ground any audacious cockney-rider (*sonntagsreiter*)!"

As the resolute adversary of modern ideas, of constitutional theories, and of every item which was contained in the programme of the then Liberal party

---

* Sitting of the Chamber on the 15th November, 1849. It is well known that since then the German Chancellor has lately instituted a law which introduces civil marriage into Prussia. It may be added that none of the speeches which we are about to quote will be found in the official collection of M. de Bismarck's speeches published at Berlin.

in Prussia, the deputy of the Mark combated with energy the two great national passions of this party; the "deliverance" of Schleswig-Holstein, and the unity of Germany. He regretted that "the royal Prussian troops should have been employed to uphold the revolution in Schleswig against its legitimate sovereign the King of Denmark;" and affirmed that they were provoking a regular old wives' quarrel, a squabble "*à propos* of nothing;" and finished by declaring, in the midst of an indignant Chamber, that the war they were stirring up in the duchies of the Elbe was "an eminently iniquitous, frivolous, disastrous, and revolutionary enterprise."* . . .

As for the unity of Germany, the young orator of the Ultras rejected it in the name of justice, in the name of the sovereignty and of the independence of its princes, as well as in the name of real patriotism. He was a Prussian—a Prussian of the old school (*stockpreusse*)—and had little wish to see, grafted on to the old and steady Borussian tree, "the shifty, changing growths of the South." He appealed to the army. Did it ask to exchange its old national colours, black and white, for that German tricolour, which had ever been the emblem of revolution? Did it wish to exchange the old Dessauer march for some song composed by Professor Arndt on the "German Fatherland?" We have already mentioned his speech in opposition to the offer of the imperial crown by the Frankfort Parliament, and his in-

---

* Sitting of the Chambers on the 21st April, 1849. See also the interpellation of M. de Tomme in the sitting of the 17th April, 1863.

genious quotation from the libretto of the "Freischütz." Although Frederick William IV. refused the imperial crown, he nevertheless strove during 1849 and 1850 to save a few spars from the wreck of the plan of German unity, and with the help of the German Liberals he succeeded in grouping around him a notable portion of the Germanic body, and in creating a sort of Northern Confederation. "The restricted union" became for a time the watchword of a programme which General Radowitz was empowered to realise by the aid of the Parliament of Erfurth. M. de Bismarck condemned without pity or hesitation all these vain efforts, and, in common with the great theorist of his party, the celebrated Professor Stahl, pleaded for the return to the *statu quo* which preceded 1848. These two demanded " that the broken column of justice in Germany should be raised up anew ;" that the Bund should be replaced on its legal basis, according to the terms contained in the Treaty of Vienna ; and unceasingly warned Prussian politics from taking any "Phæton-like flights" into regions of clouds and storms.

The storms, indeed, did not fail to burst, and "Phæton's course" was brusquely arrested by the hand of that great Austrian minister, who himself only flashed like a meteor through the most elevated regions of power to disappear as suddenly, leaving behind him the most enduring regrets. The Prince Felix of Schwarzenberg calls to mind in many respects the school of statesmen of whom England has shown the most surprising examples—the Peterboroughs, the

Bentincks, and others of a similar type—who, suddenly abandoning a life of pleasure and the vanities of society, appeared before the world as political marvels, only to die in their prime, after having drained to the dregs the very different cups of happiness and glory.

We know with what a firm and daring hand the prince grasped the helm of public affairs in Austria, and in how short a space of time he succeeded in re-establishing a monarchy that was tottering on the brink of an abyss. Was his conduct irreproachable on every point? Was it clear-sighted to the end? These are questions on which we cannot at present dilate: we must restrict ourselves to the statement that rarely has any minister met with more good fortune in so short a career, been more confident in his own success, or assumed a prouder or more disdainful tone when placed in the most painful straits.

On this occasion Prince Schwarzenberg spoke with all the authority with which he was invested—spoke, perhaps, too harshly—and for a time Prussia seemed on the point of picking up the gauntlet. Frederick William IV. asked the Chambers to vote fourteen millions of dollars, with which to place his army in readiness for war, and delivered a warlike speech. Europe became attentive; the National Assembly of France was on the point of levying fresh troops; and —like a prophetic prelude to a tragedy which was not to be performed till fifteen years later—in 1850, as in 1866, Louis Napoleon thought fit to encourage the Cabinet of Berlin, to encourage it secretly, and in direct opposition to the sentiments of his country.

While the French National Assembly was declaring itself most emphatically in favour of neutrality, and the Minister for Foreign Affairs seemed even to incline towards Austria, the President of the Republic was, sending a confidential envoy, M. de Persigny, to Berlin, charged with the mission of encouraging the King of Prussia as much as possible to engage in war. War seemed inevitable; the troops on both sides had already taken up positions; there had even been a few skirmishes at the outposts. Suddenly, and in consequence of a menacing ultimatum on the part of Vienna, backed up by some friendly advice from St. Petersburg, M. de Manteuffel, the President of the Prussian Council, proposed a meeting on the frontier at Oderberg to the Austrian Premier. A few hours later he telegraphed to him (a most unusual proceeding in those days) that, in accordance with the positive orders of his king, he would start for Olmütz without awaiting his reply. He went there, and on the 29th of November, 1850, signed the preliminaries of peace—the celebrated "punctuations," in which Prussia agreed on every point to the demands of Austria.

It was not surprising that such a profound humiliation—preceded by an act so indicative of distress, until then unheard of in the annals of diplomacy, and followed by an Austrian despatch which needlessly envenomed the wound*—filled the Liberals in

---

* A circular of Prince Schwarzenberg's, published by an intentional mistake, after setting forth the incident of the telegraph, and the truly desperate pursuit of the Austrian Minister by M. de Manteuffel, added, "H.M. the Emperor could not refuse the wishes of the King of Prussia, when they were so modestly expressed."

Prussia with pain and indignation. It was in vain that M. de Manteuffel tried to justify his conduct before the national representatives, declaring that he would rather "face conical balls than such sharp speeches" (*lieber spitzkugeln als spitze reden*); the Chambers of Berlin passionately re-echoed the complaints of the country, and M. de Vincke concluded a most vehement philippic with the words, "Down with the Ministry!"

Only one orator had the courage to defend the minister, and at such a time to exculpate Austria. In the preceding year M. de Bismarck had already coveted for his country the part that was played by the Emperor Nicholas in Hungary, and since then had never neglected an opportunity of revenging every insult offered to the Hapsburgs by the German Liberals; he remained faithful to this line of politics amidst the extraordinary circumstances of the hour, and face to face with the tumultuous clamour of the Assembly. He maintained that in Germany there was no possible or legitimate Federation outside of Austria.

One of the greatest grievances of the Teutons against Austria has always been that it does not form a purely German state, but is composed of different populations, and partly of an "inferior" race. These were the first arguments brought forward in the Frankfort Parliament in favour of a German Constitution which was to exclude the empire of the Hapsburgs; and M. de Bismarck did not fail to reproduce them in a well-known circular of the year 1866.

In 1850 the deputy of the Mark did not hold these opinions. He was convinced that "Austria was a German power, in every sense of the word, although fortunate enough to have alien nationalities under its dominion;" and concluded boldly that "Prussia ought to submit itself to Austria, in order to combat in union with her a menacing democracy."

Certes, in calling to mind this session of the Prussian Chambers of the 3rd of December, 1850, one is enjoying, to use the words of Montesquieu, the spectacle of the extraordinary vicissitudes of history: but the irony of destiny assumes truly fantastic proportions when we consider that it was precisely this discourse of the 3rd of December, 1850, which decided the vocation of M. de Bismarck, and opened to him the career of foreign affairs. Forced to consent to the restoration of the Bund, and resigned to the preponderating influence of the empire of Austria, the Prussian Government considered that it could not give a better token of its dispositions than by appointing as its minister plenipotentiary to the German Confederation that fiery orator whose devotion to the house of Hapsburg had resisted even the humiliation of Olmütz ; and it was as a most decided partisan of Austria that the future conqueror of Sadowa made his entry into the arena of diplomacy. . . .

The Chamber was prorogued after this stormy discussion. The rupture with the national party was consummated, and M. de Manteuffel, whose cold and bureaucratic mind had in reality very little sympathy with the Ultras, still judged it to

F

be advisable to make them a few concessions in order to consolidate the Government.

Several important posts in the Civil Service were confided to members of the extreme right: M. de Kleist-Retzow, among others, received the presidency of the Rhine provinces. To employ the talents of the whilom barrister of Potsdam and Greifswalde in a similar manner was, however, not to be thought of; he had already shown too little taste or aptitude for an administrative career, and, for reasons already mentioned, it was decided to send him to Frankfort as first secretary of legation, but with the assurance of being promoted to the post of representative after a while. This selection naturally caused some surprise, as it was quite a novel proceeding (they became used to it in time) to reward a deputy by a diplomatic mission for any vote he might have given, or for any attitude he might have assumed in the Chamber. It was also generally questioned whether the eccentric and impetuous knight of the Mark could possibly be the right man in the right place in the midst of such delicate circumstances. The timid and scrupulous M. de Manteuffel was not without some apprehensions on this point, and the eagerness with which M. de Bismarck accepted the post only increased the discomfiture of the premier. The king, Frederick William IV., who personally was much attached to the fiery "Percy," of the faction of the Cross, was himself not without his doubts.

"Your Majesty can but try me," said the aspirant to diplomacy, "and if it won't do, your Majesty is at liberty to recall me at the end of six months, or even sooner."

Eight years were to elapse before he was recalled, and then it was by the successor of Frederick William IV.

This is, however, the manner in which he expresses himself during the early days of his mission (June, 1851), in a confidential letter speaking of the men and things he had to deal with:—

"Our relations here are full of suspicion and mutual espionage. And had we but something of consequence to hide or to find out! but it is on the score of the veriest trifles that these people torment themselves.

"These diplomatists, retailing their *bric-à-brac* with such airs of importance, seem to me to be even more ridiculous than deputies of the second Chamber standing on their little dignity. Unless we are pompously stirred up by some outside events, I can check off on my fingers all that we shall do during the next two, three, or five years, and which might all be done in four-and-twenty hours if we could only be sincere and reasonable for one whole day. I never doubted but that these gentlemen mixed a good deal of water with their *cuisine*; but anything so thin and poor as their soup it is impossible to imagine—such a thing as a globule of fat on the surface is not to be seen. . . .

"I am making the greatest progress in the art of saying nothing in a great many words. I fill several pages with reports, as neat and as well rounded as leading articles; and if, after having read them, Manteuffel understands one word, his intelligence is greater than mine. . . .

"No one, not even the most spiteful democrat, can form an idea of the amount of nullity and charlatanism that is concealed under the name of diplomacy."

A few years later on, during the Eastern complications, he writes to his sister Malvina :—

"I am at a session of the Bund; a much-esteemed colleague is reading a very tiresome report on the disturbed situation of the Upper Lippe; and it seems to me that I cannot employ my time to greater advantage than by pouring forth the sentiments of my brotherly love.

"These Knights of the Round Table, surrounding me at present on the ground-floor of the Taxis Palace, are most honourable men, but certainly not very amusing; the table is twenty feet in diameter, and is covered with green cloth.

"Think of X . . . and of Z . . . in Berlin; they are just the style of these Bundestag gentlemen. I conform to everything with a delightful sensation of languid innocence. My mind is in a state of the completest tranquillity (*gänzliche wurschtigkeit*), after having brought the Bund little by little to a despairing consciousness of its own utter nonentity. Do you remember Heine's song, 'O Bund, O dog, thou art not well,' &c. ? Well, this song will soon be raised, and by an unanimous vote, to the post of the German national anthem."

The lassitude, the disgust, as well as the contempt which he feels for the Bund increase from year to year. In 1858 he almost decides on giving up the diplomatic career. He has had enough "of this diet of truffles, despatches, and grand crosses;" he speaks of retiring under the cannons of Schœnhausen, or, better still, of growing young again by ten years and taking up the post of attack he had held in 1848 and 1849. He would like to fight without being hampered by official laws and rules, to lay down his uniform, " and lay about him in political swimming-drawers" (in *politischen schwimmhosen*) . . . And was it surprising? Of all political men, M. de Bismarck was certainly the least likely to feel any respect or taste for a deliberative body that was essentially moderating and moderate, where everything took place privately, with long and elaborate reports, lengthily justified and still more lengthily debated, and where thrusting and parrying were utterly unknown. A great peace congress can scarcely offer much attraction to the fiery Percys on whom the smallest conference of Bangor has such exciting effects,[*] and the Bundestag, we have already said, was a permanent peace congress whose mission it was to maintain the *statu quo*, and to turn aside any cause of conflict.

Small incidents — the petty manœuvring, the puny struggles for influence—were, it is true, not wanting in this community, any more than in others; they served to maintain the good temper of the ordinary diplomatists, and were generally considered

---

[*] Shakespeare (Henry IV., Part I., Act iii., Scene 1).

as useful stimulants to the better digestion of their affairs and their dinners ; but no doubt they appeared contemptible in the eyes of a man of action and of war—no doubt they must have irritated and at times exasperated him.

To observe the workings of the world from this post on the Main, from whence they could be grasped in their entirety ; to profit by the abundant sources of information to collect and compose despatches fit to instruct and especially to amuse his august master ; to discover now and then a witticism full of malice ; to enjoy it himself and share it with others ; to carry it, still fresh, to Stuttgart, and confide its further extension to a gracious Grand-duchess ;— these were occupations which could content a Prince Gortchakof and charm the leisure hours of a man brought up in the school of Count Nesselrode, and grown old in his career.

But how to render such an existence bearable to the knight of the Mark suddenly turned into a plenipotentiary—to find the means of enclosing in so narrow though so enchanting a circle " a betrothed of Bellona," all quivering yet from battles fought during four years without cessation on a resounding battlefield ! In order to find some kind of compensation in the new sphere where he had just been placed he wanted at least some intricate European combination, or some great negotiation capable of straining his faculties and proving their worth ; and instead of these, all that saluted his ears was the " tittle-tattle " from the Upper Lippe ! Such an insignificant negotiation as that which took place with the unfórtunate Duke of Augustenburg, and which ended in the year 1852, certainly cannot be reckoned among the triumphs worthy of a Bismarck;* and yet this affair was the only miserable globule of fat ever discovered by him in all the soup set before him, during the years he spent at Frankfort ! . . .

It is true that before long the Eastern question burst over them, and seemed for a while to open out a vast field of enterprise. Prussia showed herself favourable to Russia ; the secondary States were even more demonstrative, and gave themselves the most warlike airs ; so much the worse for Austria, if she persisted in making common cause with the Allies; her doing so might bring about the most important territorial alterations, and be of the greatest advantage to the House of Hohenzollern ! . . . And, indeed, the Prussian representative at the German Confederation ("his Excellency the Lieutenant," as he was then called, on account of

* And yet this negotiation is not without interest, and even great piquancy. Full of the conviction that the war which had been made against Denmark was "eminently iniquitous, frivolous, and revolutionary," the Prussian plenipotentiary at the Bund worked very actively, in 1852, to set aside for the future any possible cause of disturbance, and negotiated an Esau-like treaty with the Duke Christian Augustus Augustenburg, the former abettor of Schleswig-Holsteinism, and eventual pretender to the Duchies. Thanks to the intervention of M. de Bismarck, for the sum of one and a half million of rix dollars, given by the Government of Copenhagen, the old duke signed a solemn deed, by which he bound himself and his family, on his word and honour as a prince, never to undertake anything which might disturb the tranquillity of the Danish monarchy. That, however, did not prevent the son of Christian putting forward his pretended claims in 1863, nor did it prevent M. de Bismarck from supporting them during a certain period, until the moment when the famous syndics of the crown threw a doubt into the soul of the first minister of Berlin, and proved to him that as the Duchies legally belonged to no one, King William was entitled to them by right of conquest.

the *landwehr* uniform he was so fond of wearing) lent during the crisis the warmest and most faithful support to his Russian colleague, then his most intimate friend. Discovering, however, before long, that the German Confederation had no intention of changing its neutral position, that the secondary States, in spite of all their agitated conferences at Bamberg, were not going to take any active part either on one or the other side, and that the seat of war would be confined to the Black Sea and to the Baltic, he conceived the most profound contempt for the Bund, feeling convinced " in his inmost soul of its utter nullity," and while seated at the green table in the palace of Taxis hummed Heine's song on the Diet of Frankfort.

Moreover, he had to pass through a very mortifying phase at this period which he never forgot, and which he alluded to years afterwards in a confidential despatch now become famous. In 1859 he wrote as follows to M. de Schleinitz : "During the Eastern crisis Austria outweighed us in everything at Frankfort, in spite of our sympathy and community of ideas with the secondary States. These States, after every oscillation, return with all the persistence of the magnetised needle to the same point of attraction." . . . And what could be more natural. It was not from the empire of the Hapsburgs that Hanover and Saxony had to dread annexation, as later events have only too clearly proved; but the man who could condemn all great towns to utter destruction for being the hotbeds of revolutionary spirits, would not hesitate in condemning little States for being the hotbeds of Austrian sympathies.

As will be seen, Austria soon became the obnoxious object, and filled the space once occupied in the mind of the Knight of the Mark by the hatred of democracy; and the valorous champion of the Hapsburgs in the Berlin Chambers became by degrees their most implacable, most untiring enemy in the Bund. But it is a notable fact that all Prussia's great men—to begin with the Great Elector and Frederick II., not excluding William I.—have at all times held two opinions with regard to Austria; have, on this point, had, like Faust, "two souls in their bodies;" or, like Rebecca, "two children struggling in their bosom;" two principles, in fact, one of which bound them to respect the ancient and illustrious imperial house, whereas the other goaded them on to its spoliation and conquest.

In the month of May, 1848, the honest and poetical King Frederick William IV. declared to a deputation of German statesmen[*] that he should "reckon that as the happiest day of his life on which he should hold the ewer (*waschbecken*) at the coronation of a Hapsburg as Emperor of Germany;" which sentiment, however, did not prevent him, later on, from quietly encouraging the work of the Frankfort Parliament, nor from attempting the "restricted union," under the auspices of General Radowitz.

M. de Bismarck was, no doubt, perfectly sincere in his attachment to Austria when, as Prussian deputy, he rose, and, in the name of Conservatism,

[*] At the head of this deputation was Baron Max de Gagern, the Nassau Minister.

energetically defended the house of Hapsburg against the aggressions of the German Liberals. But now he was the representative of his government in the Palace of Taxis; Austria stood in his way, disputed his influence over the secondary States, and disagreed with him on the Eastern question; and now, slowly but surely, began the growth of those feelings which reached their climax when he dealt Austria its "death-blow."

Thus arose, at the time of the same Crimean war, and in the same town of Frankfort, a hatred of Austria in the hearts of the two future chancellors of Russia and Germany, that hatred of Austria which was to bear such fatal fruit; for most undoubtedly it was the connivance of these two men, assisted by the fatal ideology of Napoleon III., which brought about the terrible catastrophes we have witnessed in our day—the calamity of Sadowa, the destruction of the Bund, the dismemberment of Denmark, as well as that of France! With Prince Gortchakof this sentiment of hostility was conceived with the rapidity of lightning, in consequence of the erroneous view he took of Austrian politics, and was shared by his whole nation.

M. de Bismarck's hatred of Austria was of a slower growth; it did not spring, for example, from the humiliation at Olmütz, for the deputy of the Mark had triumphed lightly over that; it was long in coming, slow in its development, became solidified after a daily course of lengthy disputes in the Bund, and in consequence of a conviction acquired, after years of wasted efforts, that the house of Hapsburg would never voluntarily desert the secondary States, and would defend them against any attempt at annexation.

Summing up the teachings received during his eight years' sojourn in Frankfort, the representative of Prussia to the German Confederation writes in 1859, in his well-known despatch to M. de Schleinitz, "I see a vice in our Federal relations that must, sooner or later, be extirpated by *ferro et igne.*" *Ferro et igne!* This is the first known version of the text "blood and iron," given out officially, however, in later years by the President of the Council in a speech to the Chambers. At the same time that M. de Bismarck's devotion to Austria was being so radically effaced, a change no less singular was taking place in his mind with regard to the other articles of his party's faith.

Removed from the thick of the fight, and no longer participating in any parliamentary battles, he began to consider more coolly questions on which he had once debated with the greatest heat, and to be more temperate than in former days in some of his old antipathies. "There is," he writes, on his return from a trip to Berlin in 1852, "something demoralising in the air of the Chambers; the best of men become vain there, and as fond of the tribune as a woman is of her toilet. . . . I consider those parliamentary intrigues to be hollow and base beyond all belief. So long as we live in their midst we are deluded by them, and consider them to be of importance. . . . Whenever I come back from Frankfort, I experience the feelings of a man who has been fasting and comes suddenly into the midst of drunkards."

Many things and persons that were formerly despised and abhorred now took a more pleasing form in the eyes of the statesman occupied in forming vast projects for the future. "The Chamber and the press might become the most powerful weapons of our foreign policy," was, in 1858, the opinion of the man who once so strongly despised parliamentary rule, the friend of M. Thadden-Triglaff; and similarly we find, in his correspondence at this time, the vague idea of a national representation of the Zollverein, and even an inclining towards universal suffrage, so long as these institutions could be used as *instrumenta regni*. The example of the second empire was then diffusing an influence which the historian will do well to note. That system of absolute power, interwoven with popular passions —" striped with red," to use one of M. de Bismarck's characteristic remarks—seduced the imagination of more than one aspirant to *coups d'état* and to political thunderbolts; and the former colleague of Doctor d'Ester must have thought more than once that Hanover and Saxony were well worth "a brief plunge into the muddy waters of democracy."

But how far off was still the distant goal; how veiled in obscurity the half-seen future! It was not under Frederick William IV., whose intelligence was becoming daily more clouded, that any action was to be thought of; even the advent of the regent (now the reigning king) seemed at first to bring with it but little hope of change. The ministers of the regent—ministers of the new era, as they were then called—were honest philosophers, who talked about the development of existing liberties and the solidification of representative government; good and simple creatures, who allowed King William I. later on to proclaim solemnly "that Prussia's conquests over Germany should only be of a moral nature!" Evidently this "new era" was not exactly that of M. de Bismarck. During the years that elapsed from the time of the Crimean war until his embassy in Russia, we find M. de Bismarck in a constant state of agitation, travelling continually through Germany, France, Denmark, Sweden, Courland, and Upper Italy; seeking for entertainment, perhaps also for information; and returning each time to Frankfort, only to raise a storm, or to break through some "tittle-tattle," and to drive the nervous and bilious Count Rechberg, the Austrian representative and the President of the Bundestag, almost to desperation.

His frequent excursions to Paris opened his eyes to the coming events in Italy, and made him still more aggressive, till at last his recall to Berlin seemed indispensable for the maintenance of peace. It was then that he seriously contemplated abandoning the diplomatic career, throwing aside his uniform, and carrying on his political warfare "in swimming-drawers."

He consented, however, to carry it on a little longer "on caviare and in bearskins," as he expressed it in one of his letters; to speak more clearly, he consented to exchange his post at Frankfort for a similar one at St. Petersburg.

It was hoped thus to remove him to a cooler sphere—" to put him in ice " (another expression of M. de Bismarck) ; but he himself, perhaps, conceived very different hopes of his change of office, and, at any rate, found much consolation in the society of his former colleague at Frankfort, now become Prime Minister of the great empire, and with whom he had always agreed so well. On the 1st of April, his natal day, M. de Bismarck presented his letters of credit in the capital of Russia.

CHAPTER III.

A NATIONAL MINISTER IN RUSSIA.

Prince Gortchakof's Predecessors: Panine, Bestoujef, Nesselrode—Secular Traditions and fundamental Principles of Russian Foreign Policy until the Retirement of Count Nesselrode—New Style of Politics inaugurated by Prince Gortchakof—His personal Popularity—His Endeavour to promote it—His Hatred of the Germans and his French Sympathies—The Emperor Napoleon III. prepares the War in Italy—Unity of the two Cabinets of Paris and St. Petersburg on the Questions of Montenegro, Servia, and the Principalities of the Danube (1856-59)—Italian Complications: Services rendered to France by Russia during the War in Italy (1859)—Annexation of Savoy and Rupture of the Anglo-French *entente* (1860)—Profits derived by Russia from this new Situation—Circular of the 20th May, 1860, on the Subject of the Christians in the East—Isolation of France—Interview of the Sovereigns of the North at Warsaw and Embarrassment of the French Diplomatists (1860)—Russia becomes more friendly but at the same time more exacting—Marked Ability shown by Prince Gortchakof during this early Period of his Ministership—He takes Advantage of the French Alliance without compromising the Conservative Principles of his Government.

DURING the period of immense development which followed the impulse given by Peter the Great to the Russian empire, we meet with more than one Minister of Foreign Affairs whose name is worthy of a place in history.

For instance, Count Panine could have been a man of no ordinary stamp to conceive the idea of an "armed neutrality at sea," and get it accepted by various States, at a time when Russia barely held a second or third-rate place among the maritime powers.

If in this daring undertaking, as well as in his more interesting attempts to limit the absolute power of the Czars by the establishment of aristocratic institutions, we trace the influence of an Italian origin (the Panines are descended from the Pagnini of Lucca), we cannot deny the pure nationality, the grandly primitive character of another celebrated minister of the same century—of the Chancellor Bestoujef, of whose character Rulhière gives us a most original outline.

Bestoujef, who was a perfect speaker, feigned to stutter, and had the persistence to simulate this defect during seventeen years. In his conversations with foreign ambassadors he stuttered in such a manner as to be unintelligible; he complained in the same way of being deaf, and that he was not able to grasp or understand all the subtleties of the French language, causing the same thing to be repeated to him again and again.

He was in the habit of writing his diplomatic notes himself in a totally illegible hand: they would be returned to him, and at times he has been known to alter their contents. Falling into disgrace, Bestoujef immediately recovered his speech, hearing, and, in fact, all his senses. Very different is the type presented to us during the first half of this century by the immediate predecessor of Gortchakof, the Chancellor of the Emperors Alexander I. and Nicholas. Attached to Germany by his origin and the interests of his family, never even having acquired the language of the country whose international relations were confided to his care, Charles Robert de Nesselrode, however, fulfilled a long and laborious career to the satisfaction of both his august masters, and figured with honour at all conferences and congresses side by side with Talleyrand and Metternich. Without adopting the too Asiatic subterfuges of a Bestoujef, Count Nesselrode knew and practised all the known tricks of the trade; and few men could equal him in the art of maintaining his dignity and ease of manner under the most trying and embarrassing circumstances.

He understood how to change his line of conduct without too great a change of tone, and among other achievements most delicately softened the transition from the anti-Greek politics of Alexander I. to the frankly expressed sympathy for the Greek cause shown by his successor. During the Eastern crisis he exerted all the powers of an astute and subtle understanding in the service of a cause whose most serious dangers alone, however, he foresaw, and to whose national and religious side he was completely blind.

In contrast to Bestoujef, and more European in this respect as in every other, M. de Nesselrode lost in his disgrace, or rather his retreat, the greater part of his faculties and his virtues; in consequence of which his posthumous memoirs, composed in the decline of life, and painfully wanting in importance, caused great disappointment. But who can tell?

Perhaps these memoirs were the last stroke of his cunning and of his diplomatic malice, and were written with the intention of disappointing all profane curiosity, by leaving behind him as empty and as little instructive a record as could well be penned of a life so crowded with stirring events.

Yet none of those Russian statesmen, whose names we have just mentioned, were actually great ministers in the Western acceptation of the term. None of them (to confine ourselves to comparisons drawn only from absolute monarchies) occupied the position of a Duke de Choiseul in France during the last century, or wielded the authority of a Prince Clement de Metternich in Austria during the present century, or even were as celebrated and as popular as Prince Gortchakof is at this present moment in Russia.

Bestoujef, Panine, and Nesselrode were, so to say, better known abroad than in their own country, and their contemporaries never attributed to them those qualities which posterity (thanks to the revelations of posthumous archives) awards them. Not one of them was ever raised to power by the current of public opinion, or sustained in his post by public favour; not one of them ever attempted to give a personal direction, or to stamp with his own individuality the affairs over which they had control. The truth is that, from the time of Peter the Great until the present reign, the splendour of the imperial name in Russia threw all others into the shade, and, unless occupying the position of chief favourite or that of a great warrior, all the servants of the State were passed over in obscurity, as the humble executors of an absolute and solitary will.

Foreign policy in particular was considered to be the sovereign's exclusive domain, and the unalterable fixity of its system made the person chosen to fulfil the work a matter of secondary importance.

Since the days of Peter the Great we notice in effect that, in its relations with Europe, Russia has always maintained certain traditions which have been well tried by experience, and certain sacred principles from which it has seldom deviated.

Whoever the Foreign Minister at St. Petersburg might be, he had always the same programme to fulfil. His duty was to foster the growth of Russian prestige among the Christian populations of the East, to maintain the balance of power between Austria and Prussia, and to increase the influence of his Government among the secondary States of Germany.

To the few rules, which we may designate as the elementary and invariable axioms of Russian foreign policy, were added, in 1815, a principle of international conservatism—a sort of coalition among the various governments for the defence of public order—a sentiment of self-preservation, inspired in all representatives of monarchical authority by the sight of the overwhelming and destroying passions born of the Great Revolution; and it was this outcome of the views and convictions of the Emperors Alexander I. and Nicholas, that Count Nesselrode had to disseminate through all the acts and documents that issued from the Russian Foreign Office.

Destiny reserved for the successor of Nesselrode the task of breaking loose, by degrees, from all these traditions and principles, and of inaugurating in the empire of the Czars a completely new style of foreign policy. We may dispute the merits of this new policy; dispute it the more as it is far from having borne all its fruit; but one fact is indisputable, and strikes us at a glance, that Prince Gortchakof knew how to attach his name to an historic change in the annals his country's diplomacy, to put forward his own individuality as Russian Minister for Foreign Affairs, and to occupy a position of importance such as none of his predecessors ever held. Alexander Mikhaïlovitch is not only his august master's faithful servant, he is the real chief of his department, the guiding minister, taking his part openly in all responsibility, and also in the celebrity reflected from the various transactions of Europe.

A phenomenon of an equally startling character to the Russian mind was the sight of a minister depending, not only on the favour of his sovereign, but also on that of the nation; husbanding the public opinion of his country, caring for it, even flattering it at times, and finding it remunerative.

The Russian nation has had its moments of infatuation for Alexander Mikhaïlovitch, as was shown by the burst of enthusiasm after the transactions in Poland; and we might even call him a creation of the people, as its voice was not the least among the elements that raised the Vienna plenipotentiary to the lofty position vacated by Count Nesselrode in April, 1856.

In 1815, after his triumphal return from the Congress of Vienna, Alexander I. had time to select, at his leisure, from among the many celebrated men who then formed the staff of the Russian diplomatic corps, the least known and the most humble member of that illustrious body. Passing over the Capo d'Istrias, the Pozzo di Borgos, the Ribeaupierres, the Razoumovskys, the Stakelbergs, the d'Anstetts, it suited him to confide the direction of his foreign policy to a German gentleman of Westphalian extraction, born at Lisbon, and Russian only by naturalisation. In 1856, after the Congress of Paris, the nomination of Prince Gortchakof to the same post was, we will not say dictated, but was certainly indicated to the Emperor Alexander II. by the voice of the people; or, if we prefer to use another expression, by the voice already pervading the *salons* of the nobility, and which was but the faithful echo of popular opinion.

We see in effect that, immediately after his *début* in the Hôtel de la Place du Palais, the former pupil of Tsarskoë-Selo distinguished himself by his liberal opinions and the advances he made to the public spirit of the times—advances that must often have astonished his still living predecessor, who yet enjoyed the honorary title of Chancellor. For the first time a Russian Minister arranged his speeches not only to satisfy the *salons*, but also the lecture-halls and the newspaper offices; speeches which touched alike the heart of the great lady and the country gentleman, the humble student and the haughty officer of the Guards.

His saying about Austria was known over all Russia.*

Another aphorism, borrowed from one of his circulars, enchanted the nation: the celebrated sentence, "Russia does not sulk, she meditates," seemed to be dictated by the very heart of the nation, and drew from it a cry of enthusiasm.

It was at this period, it will be remembered, that the Russian spirit roused itself, after a long period of compression; the newspapers, the periodicals, began a new life, and writers and scientific men assumed an importance hitherto unknown. Alexander Mikhaïlovitch, the former companion of Pouchkine, the diplomatist who had at all times shown great taste and sympathy for Russian literature, appeared in the light of a patriotic statesman to such men as Pogodine, Axakof, Katkof, &c. His hatred for Austria was well known, as also his leaning towards a French alliance; and the nation, which shared both these sentiments in the highest degree, hailed him as a genuinely national minister.

What a strange coincidence, and how strikingly formed to show us the instability and hollowness of all earthly things, it is to consider that it was, as the warmest partisan of the house of Hapsburg, that M. de Bismarck, the future conqueror of Sadowa, made his entry into the diplomatic circle; and that it was the implacable enemy of the Germans and the warm friend of France that the Russians particularly

---

* "Austria is not a state, it is only a government."

cherished in 1856, in the person of their Vice-Chancellor, of that statesman who later on, by a policy of omission and commission, favoured more than any other the dismemberment of France, and the constitution of a greater, a more powerful Germany than had ever been known in past history.

It is true that by "the Germans" the Russians of 1856 especially meant the Austrians,* and that in the France of that day they especially admired a certain democratic absolutism which had shown such sympathy for the misfortunes of Italy, for those of Roumania, Servia, and Montenegro, and which had not yet pronounced the ill-fated name of Poland.

"Be satisfied," said the Emperor of the French to M. de Cavour, in the month of April, 1856, after the dissolution of the Congress of Paris, "be satisfied, I have a presentiment that the existing peace will not be of long duration."†

Prince Gortchakof no doubt shared this presen-

---

* It is well known that many of the different branches of the Russian service were encumbered by large numbers of Germans, who were either naturalised subjects or born in Russia, and who exercised a very important influence over the administration of the empire. On his accession to the post of Minister, Alexander Mikhaïlovitch declared his intention of purging his department of all these intruders. He found, however, that official routine and Slavonic laziness (which willingly leaves all work that demands any perseverance or application to "intruders") did not fail to triumph over any principle of nationality; and the Minister's regenerative plans, which were announced with so much noise, evaporated quickly in a very insignificant change which took place among the inferior officials. It was precisely from among the Germans that he found his two most capable and devoted *aides*—M. de Westmann, who died last May (1875) at Wiesbaden, and M. de Hamburger, recently appointed to the post of Secretary of State.

† Letter of M. de Cavour to M. Castelli. Bianchi, "Storia Documentata," t. vii., p. 622.

timent, and, perhaps, was in possession of still more positive facts. The thought of "fighting for an idea," of liberating Italy, was fixed from that time in the mind of Napoleon III.; and when he signed the Treaty of Paris with "a pen torn from an eagle's pinion," his veiled and dreamy glance was already wandering over the classic plains of Lombardy.

But in order to carry out the enterprise which France contemplated against Austria, it was necessary to secure the friendship of Russia and Prussia; for at that time England's neutrality was scarcely to be relied upon. Prussia had come forth sadly shorn of political influence after the Oriental crisis; England, Austria, and Turkey scarcely cared to admit it to the honours of the congress. The Prussian Prime Minister, M. de Manteuffel, was kept out in the cold long after the plenipotentiaries of Europe were already in full deliberation, and it was only at the request of the Emperor of the French that the Prussian envoy was finally admitted.

Napoleon III. insisted in 1856 in aiding Prussia in the resumption of its former rank in Europe —that same Prussia which fourteen years afterwards was to dethrone him. As for Russia, we have already spoken of the cordiality and politeness which Count Orlof received from the French during the time of the congress.

Since then,* it is also noticeable that in the

---

* See, in reference to this and to all that follows concerning the relations of France with Russia in the years 1856-63, our "Studies of Contemporary Diplomacy," Part I., chaps. i.—iii. Paris, 1866.

arranging of the various difficulties which arose in the fulfilment of certain clauses in the Treaty of Paris (Bolgrad, Island of Serpents, Navigation of the Danube, &c.), the suggestions or explanations made by the Russian plenipotentiary were invariably seconded by the plenipotentiary of France.

In the various and numerous conferences and commissions which followed each other during 1856-59 for the purpose of regulating divers impending questions, the distribution of voices was almost invariably as follows: on one side, England and Austria; on the other, France, Russia, and Prussia. Prince Gortchakof graciously received all the cordialities of the Cabinet of the Tuileries, though he was not so complaisant as to join it in a wordy campaign of remonstrances directed against the government of Naples—a campaign which was undertaken in concert with the Cabinet of St. James in consequence of well-known letters addressed by Mr. Gladstone to Lord Aberdeen respecting the rule of King Ferdinand II.

Such an interference with the internal affairs of an independent State seemed scarcely correct in the sight of Count Nesselrode's successor; but he was all the more eager to second the Emperor Napoleon III. in his generous designs, whenever the question arose of improving the state of the Christian subjects in the Ottoman Empire, of enlarging their privileges, and, as it was then expressed, "of reforming the Turk."

In order to reform the Turk it would be necessary, according to the malicious opinion of M. de Thouvenel,

French ambassador at Constantinople, "first of all to impale him;" and, indeed, he was put to the torture of the *hatt-houmayoum*, was interrogated as to his intentions in favour of the *raïas* of Bosnia, of Bulgaria, and of Herzegovina; causing thus an infinity of trouble to the Cabinets of Vienna and London. Naturally, even a much greater solicitude was expressed for the vassal States of the good Padishah— for Moldavia, Wallachia, Servia, and Montenegro; these States were already in the enjoyment of a semi-independence, and everything was done to render that independence complete.

The petty Prince of Montenegro, the former salaried *protégé* of the Emperor Nicholas, visited the sovereign of France, after the conclusion of peace, in Paris; and, indeed, raised such disturbances with the Sultan on his return, that two vessels, the *Algésiras* and the *Impétueuse*, appeared before Ragusa.

French vessels in Eastern waters, menacing Turkey —a great mortification to England and Austria, and a great source of satisfaction to Russia, more especially as it occurred scarcely two years after the Crimean war! . . . The sight was certainly an original one, and prepared the world for a series of surprises.

About the same time, Servia dethroned Prince Alexander Kara Georgevitch, and appointed in his stead the old Miloch Obrenovitch. The Porte protested, England and Austria joined in the protestations, but, thanks to the united efforts of Russia and France, the Servian Assembly were able to persist in their choice, and dethrone a prince whose chief error in the eyes of his people was having shown too much sympathy for the Allies in 1853 !

The question of the Danubian Principalities was far more interesting and of greater importance. In the Congress of Paris, France and Russia pleaded for the complete union of Moldavia and Wallachia, to which the other powers were opposed. At last, weary of the contest, it was decided to accept a combination, which, though assimilating the administration of the two countries, yet allowed the countries themselves to remain separate. It was, as might be seen later on in July, the plan of confederation opposed to that of union ; and the first example of that kind of national strategy was shown us on the banks of the Danube, that was soon to be repeated on a vaster scale on the plains of Tuscany. The double election of Prince Couza was the first act of this style of popular diplomacy, which at a later period, in Italian matters, so often confounded the combinations of plenipotentiaries and powerful statesmen, and offered to the world the spectacle of deeds accomplished solely by the suffrage of nations. To see popular voting reversing the decisions of diplomatists, and to see France and Russia agreeing to respect these votes, were among the most marked features of the politics of 1856-59— politics which the liberal opinions of Europe received with favour, but not without being surprised at the sight of such a harmony in the views of the Cabinets of the Tuileries and St. Petersburg, on that same

Eastern ground yet reeking with the fumes of war—that ground from which the Allies had thought, in 1853, Russia was for ever to be excluded, but where she was again taking root and gaining influence, as yet but modestly it is true, and under the protecting shadow of France.

When, at last, the complications in Italy reached their climax, the Government of the Czar redoubled its expressions of goodwill towards the Cabinet of the Tuileries. "Our relations with France are *cordial*," replied Prince Gortchakof to Lord Napier on being sounded by him as to the intentions of Russia in such serious circumstances. England at that time was making the most vigorous efforts to prevent the outburst of the Italian war. Lord Cowley was despatched somewhat noisily on a mission to Vienna, and tried by every possible means to discover a basis on which to found some sort of reconciliation; and the Cabinet of St. James was already flattering itself that it had succeeded in allaying the tempest, when Prince Gortchakof suddenly proposed a *congress*, pronouncing that fatal word which then, as on many other occasions, has been but the signal for a rupture.

A congress! A treaty of peace preceding all hostility; the glory of triumph without the peril of victory! This was the eternal *hysteron-proteron* of Napoleonic theory, the chimera pursued by the dreamer of Ham in the Papal question, in the questions of Poland and Denmark, even in the catastrophe of 1870, after the declaration of war; and it is curious to see Prince Gortchakof as the first hawker of a remedy that imperial France was so often to recommend for all the chronic ailments of Europe.*

The head of the English Government, the late Lord Derby, complained bitterly of the trick played him by the proposition from St. Petersburg; and in London it has always been suspected that it was prompted by a telegraphic hint from Paris. Again, in his circular of May 27th, 1859, the Russian Vice-Chancellor proved himself equally useful to France by calming the warlike ardour of the German secondary States; and it is in this celebrated despatch that he pronounces a wise judgment, and at the same time a well-deserved eulogium, on the "purely and exclusively defensive combination" of the Bund, a salutary combination which could enforce the *localisation* of an inevitable war, "instead of allowing it to spread and to assume proportions exceeding all human anticipation."

Napoleon III. descended into the plains of Lombardy; Austria was beaten at Magenta and Solferino; and Russia enjoyed her first taste of vengeance on that

* It is true that, in a circular of May 27th, 1859, the Russian Vice-Chancellor was careful to offer some comment on his proposition, and to prove to the world that the congress which he had proposed had nothing chimerical in its nature. "This congress," he says, "*does not place any Power in the presence of the unknown*: its programme has already been considered. The fundamental idea which forms its basis *is not prejudicial to any essential interest. On the one hand the present status of territorial possession is maintained*, and on the other this congress may *bring forth results neither exorbitant in their demands nor unusual in international relationship*." It is worth while to read over this remarkable circular, and to weigh well its every word. In it will be found the most peculiar criticisms, made as it were in anticipation of the various projects for congresses which Napoleon III. presented in later years to the gaze of Europe, notably the eccentric project which astonished the world in the imperial speech of November 5th, 1863.

ungrateful House of Hapsburg which had "betrayed" her under the walls of Sebastopol. The following year, in consequence of the annexation of Savoy, Lord John Russell declared solemnly in Parliament that his country "ought not to separate itself from the rest of the European nations; that it ought always to be prepared to act in concert with the other States if it did not wish to hear of such or such an annexation taking place to-day, and such another to-morrow."

This proved to be the funeral oration of the Anglo-French alliance. Four years after the Crimean war France had lost both the great allies she had possessed during the Eastern crisis, and, as we may well imagine, Russia was not the one to regret it.

Russia never protested against the annexation of Savoy, declaring it even to be a "perfectly regular transaction;" but she took advantage of the moment to resume her place in European politics, and again to bring before the world the question of—the Ottoman Empire! On the 4th of May Prince Gortchakof called together the various ambassadors of all the great Powers, in order to examine with them the "painful and precarious position in which the Christians of Bosnia, Herzegovina, and Bulgaria were placed;" and soon after a circular from the Vice-Chancellor (May 20) insisted on the assembly of a conference in order to re-negotiate the stipulations agreed upon in the Treaty of Paris. "The time for illusions is past," are the words of Alexander Mikhaïlovitch; "any hesitation, any adjournment, might now bring about the most serious results;" and he used even the recent emancipation of Italy as an argument in favour of the future independence of the populations for whose welfare he showed himself so solicitous. " The events which have occurred in the west of Europe have re-echoed in the east, *awakening hope and bringing encouragement !*"

Thus, barely four years after the Treaty of Paris, Russia was again drawing the attention of the world to the state of the " Sick Man ;" but no longer, as in the conferences and commissions of 1856-59, under the protection of France, but acting alone, and taking the initiative in the debate.

This, however, was not all. In that one year of 1860 the Cabinet of St. Petersburg was to regain nearly all the ground it had lost during the Crimean war. It was a peculiarly fortunate year for Russia, for it was also a year of universal distrust towards France.

The acquisition of Savoy, the strange and profoundly immoral spectacle afforded by the negotiations of the Treaty of Zurich—a treaty which was rent before it was even signed—the Piedmontese annexations in Italy, the expedition of Garibaldi into Sicily, the " new right " of which the French official journals were speaking, and the famous pamphlet on " The Pope and the Congress," had alarmed and roused in the highest degree the anxiety of Europe.

Lord Palmerston declared that he would " only offer one hand to his former ally, and that in the other he would grasp the buckler of defence," and at once organised his volunteers. Switzerland was in a tumult; the *National-Verein* swore to die in defence of the Rhine; and even the honest and peaceful Belgians thought it necessary to declare, in an address to their king, "that if their independence was threatened, they would know how to endure the hardest trials."

High above all these popular alarms rose the murmur of kingly meetings. The German princes assembled at Baden, and the Emperor of the French thought fit to surprise them, so to say, in the middle of their deliberations by making that "rapid journey" which, according to the *Moniteur*, "was to have such happy results."

"The spontaneousness of such an important action," added the official paper, "was just what was required to put an end to this unanimous concert of malevolent reports and misapprehensions. The very fact of the Emperor going in person to explain frankly to the sovereigns assembled at Baden that his policy had never deviated from the paths of rectitude and of justice, was sufficient to convince minds so superior and so free from prejudices — as, indeed, statements of truth loyally explained never fail to do."

It would appear, however, that the conviction was not sufficient to eradicate prejudice, for, after the meeting at Baden, there followed a second at Tœplitz, between the Emperor of Austria and the Prince Regent of Prussia; where yet a third was agreed upon, to take place at Warsaw, with the Emperor of Russia; and the Czar accepted the rendezvous.

"It is not coalition, it is conciliation, that I wish to bring about at Warsaw," were Alexander II.'s words to the French ambassador, the Duke de Montebello; and at the Tuileries there was naturally much agitation, in consequence of the turn affairs were taking.

In truth there was no lack of conciliatory forms in the despatch in which Prince Gortchakof "invited the French Government to inform him how far they could assist Russia in the efforts it was about to make to avert the crisis with which Europe was menaced;" but however polite these forms might be, they nevertheless concealed a slight demand for explanation.

The Cabinet of the Tuileries replied by a memorandum, in which it pledged itself first of all "to abstain from offering any assistance to Piedmont in case of Austria being attacked in Venetia." The Cabinets of Vienna and Berlin made several remarks on the French memorandum, and addressed them to the Russian Vice-Chancellor, who transmitted them to Paris, demanding at the same time fresh explanations of a more reassuring and more explicit nature. In a word, after all these discussions no positive results were arrived at in this meeting of the three Northern potentates, which at one time had caused France such serious apprehensions; and the reason of this was that the Emperor Alexander had, in reality, gone to Warsaw with but one special object. He wished neither to coalesce nor to conciliate: he simply wished to show his influence and his power. It flattered him to see these sovereigns, these German princes, assembling in the ancient capital of Poland in order to deliberate on the situation of things in general, and to receive from him the word of command. It reminded him of the glorious days of the Emperor Nicholas. Again, Russia was only too pleased to make France sensible of the value of her friendship; to make her understand how high the value of Russian services now stood—how high, perhaps, their price. The successive skilful diplomatic despatches which issued during 1856-60 from the Russian Foreign Office indicate very distinctly the gradual rise of Russian power ever since the Peace of Paris. In the first of these celebrated circulars Russia declares herself to be "meditating, and not sulking;" in the second, on the occasion of the Italian complications, she was already "shaking off the reserve which she had imposed on herself since the Crimean war." After the annexation of Savoy, "her conscience reproached her for keeping silence so long on the unfortunate state of the Christians in the East," &c. Lastly, in the month of October, 1860, she became the mouthpiece of the combined interests of Europe—the intermediary who demanded explanations from the Tuileries. From being the modest *protégé* of France, and enveloped in "reserve" up to the time of the war in Italy, she rose in 1859 to the rank of "confidential friend;" and became, after the interview at Warsaw, an important and almost indispensable ally—an ally who would no longer play a secondary part, but who intended to assume a position of the most marked influence, and to take a large share in all future combinations. Most assuredly, Napoleon III., by his disconnected, undecided, and contradictory policy, played incessantly into the hands of Russia; and it is only just to recognise that Prince Gortchakof never allowed the slightest turn of fortune to escape him; and, without creating events, well knew how to profit by them. The superiority of the statesman shows itself especially in the moderation which he preserved alike in his "cordiality" and in his vengeance—by the wary spirit which never deserted him even in the midst of success.

It does not admit of a doubt, for example, that the warnings of Russia, subsequent to the battle of Solferino, the fears which she suddenly expressed as to her incapability of restraining Germany any longer from succouring Austria, contributed greatly to the hasty Peace of Villafranca; and however fatal this event proved to the interests of France, and even to those of Austria, we cannot deny that Russia found it admirably suited to her own plans. In truth, had the programme been completely carried out from the "Alps to the Adriatic," it would probably have given a very different aspect to Italian affairs, and might have rendered a sincere reconciliation between France and Austria possible at some future time; whereas the partial solution afforded by the Peace of Villafranca, which left so many questions undecided, could have no other result than to envenom the relations between the two belligerents, and render the Russian friendship all the more precious to France. From another point of view, the campaign in Lombardy, while satisfying the rancorous Muscovite feelings born of the Crimean war, was yet very far from destroying one of those fundamental elements of traditional policy which the Czars always pursued with regard to Germany. In spite of the loss of Milan, Austria still preserved her situation intact in the centre of Europe, as a counterpoise to Prussia; and the meeting at Warsaw only tended to show that Russian influence had not diminished in the German states.

The Russian Chancellor also showed himself no less astute than circumspect in avoiding, during his connivances with Napoleon III. in 1856-60, any compromise of certain general principles of conservatism, which had formed the grandeur and the strength of Nicholas's reign.

Doubtless, in Servia, in the Danubian Principalities, Alexander Mikhaïlovitch did not show such rigorous orthodoxy, and suffered popular votes to annul arrangements that had been agreed upon in treaties; but with regard to these Eastern countries, Russia has always allowed herself a certain political licence.

With respect to Western matters, Prince Gortchakof was careful to remain as much as possible within the boundaries of tradition, and not to use the "new right" too freely. He allowed the journals and periodicals of Moscow and St. Petersburg to glorify at their leisure the power which Russia was displaying in the deliverance of nations, and in triumphing over nationalities. For himself, and in all documents dating from the Foreign Office, he carefully avoided any affectation of words, or any use of new forms of speech, preserving steadily the formulas in use with the old style of diplomatists. In these documents, when Milan and Savoy changed hands, there was no mention made of patriotic aspirations, nor of popular voting: in the eyes of the Russian Vice-Chancellor, these events were only the natural results of war, "most regular transactions." Still less did he take upon himself the character of a revolutionary missionary abroad, or associate himself with the traffic of exportation which, according to a spiteful remark made at the time, Napoleon III. had undertaken, along with other liberal ideas. He declined categorically to participate in any form whatever in the remonstrances addressed to the King of Naples, and declared in his circular of September 22nd, 1856, "that to endeavour to obtain concessions from a sovereign respecting the internal arrangements of his States by condemnatory means or by menacing demonstrations, was simply a violation of that sovereign's authority—an endeavour to usurp his place, and to plainly assert the right of the strong over the weak."

Lastly, in his famous note to Prince Gagarine, of October 10th, 1860, he smartly rebuked the Sardinian Government for its conduct with regard to Tuscany and the Duchies of Parma and Modena, and most forcibly expressed his disapproval of those dispossessions of princes and those annexations of provinces which six years later on he tolerated and even approved of in Germany.

"This is no longer," he wrote in his despatch to Prince Gagarine, "a question of Italian, but one of general interest, to every government; it is a question bound up in those eternal laws without which neither order, nor peace, nor security can exist in Europe."

He slyly rallied those political Jenners, who recommended the vaccination of anarchy in order to deprive it of its pernicious nature, and who stole the baggage of the republicans under pretence of depriving them of their weapons :—

"The necessity which the Sardinian Government feels of subduing anarchy does not justify it, as it is only keeping pace with the revolution in order to enjoy its inheritance."

In one word, the Russian Vice-Chancellor took advantage, with the most marvellous dexterity, of all the favourable dispositions of France, and still more of its faults; and while avoiding any sacrifice to it of the will, of the usages, or of the principles of his own Government, he made use of the Emperor Napoleon III. without ever being much used by him, or without ever having lent himself to any order of ideas which could possibly have made Russia a victim of deception. For the good of Russia and the welfare of Europe, it might have been desired that Prince Gortchakof had retained a little later, in his intimacy with Prussia, some of that measured conduct and that intelligent egotism of which he gave us so brilliant an example during his intimacy with France. "In order to feel love you must remain separate," said the great theologian of the middle ages in reference to what centuries of faith have called "divine love," or the relations of the human soul with its divine Creator;

and the precept is still more to be recommended with regard to the far less mystical relations existing between earthly powers. The Russian Vice-Chancellor always kept this precept in mind during his years of "cordiality" with the Tuileries. It was only later on in the second period that the heart of Alexander Mikhaïlovitch began to triumph over State reasons, and that his love for M. de Bismarck proved stronger than the rest of the world—stronger even than Russia and her interests.

CHAPTER IV.

A "FRONDEUR" DIPLOMATIST AT ST. PETERSBURG.

M. de Bismarck at the Court of St. Petersburg—Italian Complications—Pious Desires and patriotic bitterness of Heart of the Prussian Envoy—Private Letters during 1859-60—The Courland Nobility—Affection for everything Russian—M. de Bismarck a Favourite in Russian Society—Slow Tendency of the Court of Berlin towards a Policy of Action—Effect of the Mobilisation of the Army in 1859—Military Reform—The Prince Regent—His reactionary Antecedents—His long Unpopularity—The Princess Augusta—Reconciliation with modern Ideas and the Cause of Progress—The Regency and "the New Era"—The Moral Conquests in Germany—Opposition of the Chamber and the Country to Military Reform—Serious Constitutional Conflict—The "New Right" and the "Piedmontese Mission" of the House of Hohenzollern—The Prince Regent becomes King of Prussia under the Name of William I. (January, 1861)—His Visit to Compiègne (October, 1861)—Reports as to an Alliance between the three Courts of the Tuileries, of St. Petersburg, and of Berlin—M. de Bismarck Master of the Situation—His attentions to William I.—A Review at Berlin and the "Polignac of Prussia" (May, 1862)—Mission to France (June—September, 1862)—The Diplomacy of Frankness—Language of M. de Bismarck to the French Statesmen—A Visit to M. Thiers—Journey to the South of France—Appointed Minister of Foreign Affairs (September, 1862)—An Olive Branch gathered on the Tomb of Laura, and a Word of Farewell to the Office on the "Quai d'Orsay."

WHILE Prince Gortchakof was gathering the fruits of his "French" policy, the sweetest among which was assuredly the vengeance he had wreaked on Austria, his former colleague of Frankfort, having become the representative of Prussia at the Russian court, was being consumed by the restless fever of a man of action condemned to forced idleness. He arrived at St. Petersburg in the spring of 1859, three months after the famous New Year's Day reception given by the Emperor Napoleon III. to M. de Hübner.

The Italian complications were coming to a climax, and the Russian Vice-Chancellor was lending himself to all those diplomatic subtleties which, according to the wishes of the Tuileries, were to force the Emperor Francis Joseph to declare war. The new Prussian plenipotentiary at the Court of St. Petersburg was not for one moment in doubt as to the course which his Government ought to pursue under the circumstances. It was at this time (May 12, 1859) that he wrote his confidential despatch to M. de Schleinitz, in which he recommended a rupture with the Bund, by the radical means of sword and fire—*ferro et igne*. In the previous year he had been to Paris, and had had an interview with the Emperor of the French, during which he had listened to his good intentions towards Prussia, and to the astonishing good wishes prevailing at the Tuileries for the prosperity of the land of Frederick II. and of Blücher. In the month of November of the previous year (1858) Napoleon III. had enjoined the Marquis de Pepoli, then *en route* for Berlin, to represent in their most favourable aspects all the advantages which would accrue to the Hohenzollerns from a rupture with Austria. "In Germany," said the Emperor of the French, "Austria represents the past; Prussia represents the future. In binding herself to Austria, Prussia becomes condemned to a state of inaction which cannot satisfy her; for a higher destiny awaits her, and Germany expects her to fulfil it." *

These were the thoughts of the future prisoner of Wilhelmshöhe on the eve of Magenta and Solferino, and "His Excellency the Lieutenant" certainly found nothing to object to in so splendid a programme; but the worthy ministers of the "new era" in Berlin had unhappily not the slightest notion of the "new right," and the Prince Regent himself was contented with visions of purely moral conquests. At Potsdam it was even asked whether Austria ought not to be assisted—whether they were not under Federal obligations to the Emperor Francis Joseph! The Samson of the Mark struggled in vain to burst the withes wound round him by the "Philistines of the Spree," and the war in Italy became his Delilah. It is in truth from this period that dates the notorious baldness of the Chancellor of Germany.

It is interesting to study the state of mind of M. de Bismarck as depicted in his private letters to Malvina during 1859-60. At the commencement of hostilities, evidently despairing of seeing his Government adopt that line of conduct which he had never ceased to recommend to them, he leaves his post, and visits Moscow and the Kremlin, passes a short and agreeable time at a villa—all the more agreeable as "he is out of the reach of the telegraph." The news of a great battle fought in Lombardy (Magenta) brings him back to St. Petersburg. "Perhaps there will now be something for diplomatists to do." At St. Petersburg

---

* Massari, "Il Conte Cavour," p. 268.

he is informed of the strange weakness which is prevailing at Berlin in favour of Austria; that the mobilisation of the Federal armies is under consideration; and he is filled with the greatest apprehensions for his country. He falls ill, and a serious attack of liver complaint places his life in danger. "They covered my body with innumerable cupping-glasses as big as saucers, with mustard poultices and enormous blisters; and I was already half-way to a better world when I succeeded in convincing my doctors that my nerves were shattered by eight years of ceaseless worry and trouble (the eight years at Frankfort), and that in continuing to enfeeble me in this way they were driving me into a typhus fever or into imbecility.

"My good constitution triumphed in the end, however, thanks especially to several dozens of good wine."

Nevertheless his "good constitution" did not enable him to shake off all his cares, and he remained sad and morose, confessing two months later that he would not have regretted having done with life altogether. Austria was vanquished, it is true; she had lost two great battles and one of her wealthiest provinces to boot, but Prussia had reaped no benefit from these disasters to the House of Hapsburg, and the knight of the Mark was not the sort of man to cherish a purely Platonic hate, such as his friend Alexander Mikhaïlovitch indulged in. He consoled himself, however, with the thought that the Peace of Villafranca was but a truce. "To try and reconcile Austria with France, under existing circumstances, is to attempt to square the circle. I shall try," he writes in the beginning of the autumn of 1859, " to hide myself in my bear-skins and to allow the snow to cover me ; and, when the thaws of spring return, I shall see what is left of me and of our affairs, and if there is too little, I shall close my account for ever with political life." The following spring brought with it several important events. The annexation of Savoy spread that universal distrust throughout Europe of which we have already spoken; but the Cabinet of Berlin still persisted in its former errors, and the Prince Regent held an interview, in July, with the Emperor Francis Joseph at Tœplitz. " I hear," writes the Prussian representative at the Court of St. Petersburg, with scarcely disguised anger, "that we have been nicely humbugged at Tœplitz, and that we have allowed ourselves to be taken in by Viennese good-humour; and all for nothing—not even for a tiny dish of lentils."

Finally, in the month of October, after Castelfidardo and the conquest of the kingdom of Naples, the Cabinet of Berlin addressed an energetic note to M. de Cavour, on the conduct of the House of Savoy in the Italian Peninsula. The note declared that " it is only by the legal road of reform, and by respecting existing rights, that a regular government can pretend to realise the legitimate desires of nations," and terminated with the following passage : " Called upon, as we are, to pronounce our opinion on the actions and principles of the Sardinian Government, we cannot but deplore them profoundly; and we consider that we are only fulfilling a necessary duty in expressing as explicitly and as formally as it is possible, our entire disapprobation of these principles and of the application which has been made of them."

We can well imagine what an access of ill-temper these innocent simplicities must have caused the future destroyer of the Bund, the coming despoiler of Denmark, of Hanover, and of so many other States. He again thinks of abandoning his career, and is resolved, at any rate, "to retire to the position of a philosophic observer" of the monstrous policy in favour at Berlin. He is quite surprised at the scandal caused by the publication of M. de Varnhagen's posthumous diary, a diary filled with piquant disclosures about the Court of Prussia. "Why so much indignation? is it not all perfectly true? Varnhagen was vain and spiteful, but who is not? Does not everything depend on the manner in which nature has ripened our life? Some of us get worm-eaten, some drift into damp places, some bask in the sun, and so we turn out sweet, bitter, or altogether rotten."

All this, however, did not hinder him from cultivating his intercourse with the political world of St. Petersburg with the greatest care (1859-60), from taking root there, or from attaching the fortunes of his country, by a thousand ties, to that Russian friendship whose value he understood so well. The position of the Prussian representatives at St. Petersburg has at all times been quite an exceptional one; thanks to the bonds of close relationship existing between the two courts, they enjoy the confidence and the intimacy of the Winter Palace to a degree unknown to the envoys of other States.

M. de Bismarck knew how to increase these favourable conditions by the influence of his personal merits, and by the good name he had earned in the eyes of the Russians during his long sojourn in Frankfort. His former travels in Courland had made him acquainted and beloved by the German nobility of the Baltic provinces, by the Keyserlingks, the Uxkülls, the Noldes, the Brewerns, &c., families who had always possessed influence at Court, at the Foreign Office, and in Russian diplomacy.

"The first prophets of the future grandeur of M. de Bismarck," says a writer well versed in Russian society, "the first to predict the mission reserved for him in Germany, were, perhaps, those barons of Courland and Livonia with whom the present Chancellor of Germany used to spend many a hunting season, sharing their banquets, their amusements, and their political discussions."*

The Prussian representative at the Court of St. Petersburg was, however, very careful not to abandon himself too freely to his liking for the Courland and Livonian nobles; he was careful to allot the largest half of his affections, or at least of his caresses, to Russian Russia, to aboriginal (*nastaïastchaïa*) Muscovy.

Was this enthusiasm for the manners and peculiarities of the "Scythians," this love of "bearskins and caviare," genuine? We may be permitted to doubt it; we may be permitted to suppose that the man who, in

* "Aus der Petersburger Gesellschaft," t. ii., p. 90.

virtue of his German superiority, had so often and so loudly expressed his disdain for the Latins and the Wallachians, felt in reality a still greater contempt for that Slavonic race which every good German despises as a race of slaves.*

But however this may have been, never had any previous ambassador shown so much devotion for the Polar Star as M. de Bismarck, nor carried to so great an extent his love for everything Russian.

He pushed his admiration so far as to have several little bears in his house, which (like the foxes at Kniephof) would rush into the dining-room during dinner, causing a delightful commotion among the guests, would lick their master's hands, and nip the calves of the servants.†

A devoted Nimrod, he never missed any expedition against the black king of the northern forests, and was always careful on these occasions to adopt the Muscovite hunting costume; the Russian style of driving, indeed, is still dear to him, even in the streets of Berlin. He affected a similar interest in the literary efforts of the country; he kept a professor of Russian in his house, and learnt sufficient of the

---

* In 1862, when he was finally about to quit his post at St. Petersburg, M. de Bismarck received the visit of a colleague, a foreign diplomatist. Russia being mentioned, the future Chancellor of Germany said: "I have the habit, when I leave a country in which I have sojourned for any length of time, to dedicate to it one of the trinkets on my watch chain, on which I cause my final impression of the country to be engraven; would you like to know my final impression of Russia?" And he showed to the somewhat puzzled diplomatist a little trinket on which were engraven the words: "*La Russie, c'est le néant!*"

† M. de Bismarck has since then presented these quadrupeds to the Zoological Gardens of the ancient free town of Frankfort.

language to enable him to give his servants their orders in their native tongue, and even to surprise the Emperor Alexander one day by a few sentences spoken in the language of Pouchkine. The Russians could not do otherwise than give a most cordial reception to a diplomatist who showed himself so enamoured of their customs, pleasures, and "peculiarities;" and who, moreover, had the advantage of succeeding the worthy M. de Werther, whose reputation there and elsewhere was not that of being an uproariously cheerful individual.

Indeed there had never been known on the banks of the Neva so charming a Prussian as M. de Bismarck —such a capital boon companion, so lively, cheerful, good-natured, and witty.

There was no limit to his jokes about the " Philistines of the Spree," about the "periwigs of Potsdam;" and all these jokes met with the greatest success. A plenipotentiary speaking ill of his own Government, a diplomatist quarrelling with and grumbling about the very policy which it was his mission to represent and to forward, was a novel spectacle, and exactly to the taste of a circle always seeking something piquant and highly flavoured. He won the good graces of the Empress-mother, and also those of the Grand Duchess Helena, whose influence at Court was considerable, and whose warm friendship never afterwards failed him, even during some of the most critical moments of his ministerial career. The Emperor showed a great liking for him, invited him regularly to his bear-hunts; and did him the honour of including him in his suite, during his journeys to Warsaw and Breslau, to meet the Prince Regent of Prussia. As for Prince Gortchakof, he enjoyed more than ever the society of his former colleague of Frankfort, and many a malicious saying, many a spiteful joke, generally at the expense of Austria, circulated through the St. Petersburg saloons, which were attributed indifferently to one or the other of these two inseparable friends—friends whom unkind intriguers were striving to separate! As early as the end of 1859, M. de Bismarck wrote in a private letter : " Austria and her dear confederates are intriguing to have me recalled to Berlin ; yet I have been very good, but the will of God be done !" Meanwhile, in Berlin, Prussian politics had begun little by little to slide down the rapid descent which was to bring them from the cloudy regions of the "new era" to that land of reality and action where the friend of Alexander Mikhaïlovitch had so long wished to see them ; and, singular to relate, it was precisely the mobilisation of the Prussian army in 1859—the same mobilisation so much condemned by M. de Bismarck—which became the immediate cause of the change which led to such incalculable consequences. It is now the fashion in France to represent the Prussian Government as meditating, during half a century, on a war of revenge and conquest ; slowly brightening her arms, and training successive generations to meet the decisive hour. Nothing, however, can be more erroneous.

Neither the Government of Frederick William III., nor that of Frederick William IV., ever nourished warlike projects, and even the humiliation of Olmütz failed to sting the Minister of War at Berlin. The two predecessors of William I. sacrificed only just so much to their army as was necessary to keep pace with the other great Powers—just enough to hold reviews and to be able to speak of their faithful troops and their ever valorous swords; in reality they were inclined to exclaim, with the Grand Duke Constantine, brother of the Emperor Nicholas: "I hate war; it spoils one's armies!"

The swords of Blücher and of Scharnhorst had grown rusty since 1815. Even the adoption of the needle-gun, in 1847, was merely an incident—a scientific experiment; and in 1848 and 1849 the Prussian troops did not shine with any very great splendour during the war in the Duchies, and were even miserably disconcerted by the undisciplined bands of the insurgents of Posen and Baden. The brother of the king, who commanded the troops in Baden, was painfully moved by the spectacle presented by his soldiers; and after his accession to the regency of the kingdom, in October, 1856, turned his thoughts incessantly to the reformation of the army. It was, however, only during the attempted mobilisation, which was essayed in consequence of the Italian complications (in the summer of 1859), that all the deficiencies and incoherencies till then existing in the Prussian military organisation became palpable. Two men of superior ability, MM. de Moltke and de Roon, then joined the Prince Regent in reforming the military system from its very foundation. They showed an intelligence, an energy, a rapidity without equal in history; they knew how to take advantage of every scientific discovery; and, above all, they did not allow the precepts to escape them that were soon to be taught to the world by the formidable civil war in America—precepts rich in experiences and in inventions of every kind.

In spite of the opposition with which they were met on every side, these two men created, in the short space of six years, an armed force on a totally new system — powerful, invincible — and "the instrument,"* as yet but in a rough and rudimentary stage, that was to give proofs of its terrible "perfection" on the fatal day of Sadowa! No less erroneous is also the opinion, widely spread nevertheless, that the Prussians demanded victories and aggrandisements of their Government. In order to refute all these gratuitous suppositions, it will suffice to remember that the several Parliaments of Berlin never ceased opposing the plans of army reform, and that they had with them the unanimous voice of the people. Ideas of German grandeur, of German power, of German influence, haunted the minds of professors and writers far more than those of the people. They formed the subjects of academical themes, of fine pieces of rhetoric, of grandiloquent essays, and even these opinions were more frequent south of the Main than to the north of that river. Here, indeed, we have a

* "In order to come out victorious from this war (against Austria) I wanted two things: a conviction of the justice of my cause and 'the instrument' capable of ensuring my triumph. I mean by this the Prussian army. I had no doubts 'as to the perfection of the instrument.'"—*Reply of William I. to the Hanoverian deputation, August 17th, 1866.*

striking proof of the astonishing art of M. de Bismarck in having, to use the words of Münchhausen, " changed fogs into stones, and reared up with them a solid and gigantic edifice," in having turned the dreams and aspirations of philosophers into an overwhelming popular passion. Strength of will, strength of character—genius, in fact—can still, in this century of democratic equality, play a part of which our poor philosophy has but little suspicion, when it lays every responsibility and every initiative on the blind fatality of the " masses," and, as the German proverb has it, "can no longer distinguish the trees from looking so long at the forest." Take away from the recent history of Prussia the three or four men who answer to the names of William I., Moltke, Roon, and Bismarck, and old Barbarossa might still be sleeping his sleep of ages in the caverns of the Kyffhäuser.

Nature is as fond of analogies as of contrasts, and thus we find that the antecedents of the Prince Regent, who bears to-day the name of William I., Emperor of Germany, are not without some parallelism to the past life of the extraordinary man who, at the appointed hour, was to forge for him, *ferro et igne*, the imperial crown of Barbarossa. In order to throw light upon these antecedents we must refer to the posthumous diary of M. von Varnhagen of Ense—the liberal, biting, compromising, yet amiable *Dangeau* of the Court of Berlin—the same diary which M. de Bismarck defended in a private letter, in which he expressed his surprise at the clamours which the publication had given rise to in Berlin. There is no doubt that Prince William strenuously opposed the liberal weaknesses which distinguished the early period of his brother Frederick William IV.'s reign. He caused certain elaborate memoranda to be drawn up in which his right to interfere in all the fundamental changes taking place in the State was asserted. The rumour that a formal protestation had been put forward in his name and in that of his descendants, against any fresh constitutional projects, obtained some credence even in the bosom of the Ministry; at all events he only gave his consent to the "feudal" charter granted by his brother on the 3rd February, 1847, on the express conditions that the States were not to interfere in the budget, and were never to meddle with foreign affairs.

Thus the unpopularity of the heir-presumptive was very great before the revolution of 1848; and during the fatal month of March of that year it was more especially against him that the fury of the Berlinese was directed—they attributed to him (and wrongly) the order which had been given to fire upon the people. He was obliged to quit the country, to undertake a "mission" to London, and the populace satisfied their malice by inscribing on his palace "national property." On his return from England after the revolutionary effervescence had subsided, he placed himself at the head of the army (1849), in order to subdue an absurd insurrection in Baden, and gave out that "important military operations" were keeping him in the South of Germany, in order to avoid being present at a solemn sitting of the 6th February, 1850, when King Frederick William took the oath to the statutes of limitations.

After a while, however, and towards the close of the disappointed and morose reign of his brother, the Prince of Prussia relaxed in his reactionary rigour, and opposed with vigour the "pietist" influences pervading at that time the Court of Potsdam. Family affections and interests all combined to isolate the prince, and create for him a place apart. The esteem and tenderness which the King Frederick William IV. lavished on his queen scarcely consoled her for the barrenness by which she was afflicted; and the sight of her more fortunate sister-in-law, mother of several children, heirs to her husband's crown, inspired her with feelings of irritation and jealousy, which were keenly resented by the wife of the heir-presumptive.

The Princess Augusta was not one to submit tamely to any slight. A descendant of that House of Weimar which has always been distinguished for its love of art and pleasure, she had early collected round her a circle of her own, and had assumed an attitude which contrasted sufficiently with that of the court to make the contrast seem intentional. These tendencies of the Princess Augusta were not without their influence on her princely husband; and even the project so long contemplated by the royal couple, of uniting their son to the daughter of Queen Victoria, which was finally carried out in 1857, was considered an advance made towards gaining popular opinion. There were, however, not wanting at Potsdam certain courtiers who, according to the terrible M. de

Varnhagen, were asking themselves whether it was not beneath the dignity of the House of Hohenzollern to ally itself with a dynasty which held but a divided sceptre, and which was subject to a House of Commons! How greatly must the times and the habits at the Court of Potsdam be changed, when we hear of the presumptive heiress to the throne of Prussia—that same daughter of Victoria—sending affectionate telegrams to the dying Doctor Strauss, rendering to the author of "The Life of Jesus" an homage *in extremis* that filled with enthusiasm all the valiant knights of the "battle of civilisation." Grown accustomed, as it were, for some years past, to see in the brother of the king a disciple of modern ideas and a champion of the cause of progress, the Prussians were not surprised, but were none the less pleased, to hear him, on his accession to the regency, express himself liberally and constitutionally. A "new era" was about to dawn for Prussia, and this expression was almost officially adopted, in order to express the change which had taken place in the system; and in a noteworthy address of November 8th, 1858, which the Prince Regent delivered to the cabinet which he had just formed, he traced the programme of a healing policy, and recommended his councillors to ameliorate all that was arbitrary or contrary to the wants of the times.

While on one hand he restrained himself from inclining too much towards liberal ideas, and expressed the will " to withstand courageously any demands that have not been agreed to," on the other hand he proclaimed his intention of loyally keeping any engagement he may have contracted, and of not repulsing useful reforms. The address ends with the sentence, since become famous and often quoted, "that Prussia was only to make moral conquests in Germany."

The good understanding between the regent and the nation was not, however, to be of long duration; the relations between them increased in bitterness and led to a complete rupture, caused more especially by the projected army reforms.

The prince had this reform particularly at heart. The events of 1859 had served to convince him of the urgency of a measure which he had secretly cherished for several years; but the deputies of the nation declined to agree with him on this point, and opposed him in the most tenacious, unshaken manner. They could not understand the obstinacy with which the prince clung to a plan which fulfilled neither the wishes nor supplied the wants of the country; and they laughed at those who pretended that, once in possession of his new "instrument," the Hohenzollern might also in his turn *faire le grand !*

" We resisted," writes a judicious German writer, "the temptations of the Frankfort Parliament in 1849; we resisted the provocation of Olmütz in 1850; we allowed the opportunities of the wars of 1854 and 1859 to pass by us. Love of peace has become absolute; there is a complete want of ambition; all are satisfied with the political situation which we now occupy, and no one can suppose that so peaceful a kingdom can be in danger of being menaced by its neighbours. Considering, then, this state of affairs, any aggrandisement of the army, bringing with it an increase of military and civil taxes already sufficiently heavy, appears to the country as an inconceivable caprice on the part of the Government."*

The Chambers refused the supplies asked for; the Government did without them, and continued to incur expenses. The military question thus grew into a financial one, and soon became a topic of perpetual constitutional conflict. Towards the end of 1861 the only remedy for the dead lock seemed to be a *coup d'état*.

No less great and irresistible was the change which soon took place in the ideas of the Court of Potsdam with regard to foreign politics. As the "instrument" grew more perfect (and its growth was most rapid) questions were asked as to how it could best be employed. As yet no one knew precisely what was wanted; but whatever that want might be, it was desired with vigour—with a vigour drawn from the battalions which day by day were increasing in strength.

Certainly "moral" conquests in Germany could hardly now be the only ones aimed at, but it was thought that a moral activity, supported now and again by the needle-gun, might have the most excellent results. The atmosphere was charged with electricity and with principles of nationality; and it was no longer only the rhetoricians and the professors of the *National-Verein* who recommended "a Germany united by a Prussian needle" (*mit Preussischer spitze*).

---

* Constantine Roessler, "Graf Bismarck und die deutsche Nation." Berlin, 1871.

When, in the month of October, 1860, the envoy of Prussia, Count Brassier de Saint-Simon, read M. de Schleinitz's celebrated note against the Italian annexations to Count Cavour, the President of the Sardinian Council listened in silence; then, after expressing his regret at having displeased the Berlin Cabinet, he declared that he felt himself consoled by the thought that " Prussia would one day be grateful to Piedmont for the example the latter had just set her." In France, the democratic journals—the organs devoted to the "new right"—could not sufficiently praise "the Piedmontese mission" of the House of Hohenzollern ; and we have already mentioned the encouragements that Napoleon III. sent to Berlin in the year 1858. The visit of William I. to the Emperor of the French at Compiègne, in October, 1861, was in this respect a still more significant symptom, as none of the northern sovereigns had as yet paid this mark of courtesy to the elect of universal suffrage. Strange rumours began to circulate from that time as to an alliance of the three courts of the Tuileries, St. Petersburg, and Berlin, which continued until the month of March, 1868. Publications—whose origin was mysterious, but which showed a great fund of information respecting political affairs—spoke of "*great agglomerations of States* to be resolved by the three races —the Roman, the Slavonic, and the Germanic, with which corresponded the three centres of gravitation— France, Prussia, and Russia; alluded also to the definite establishment of the peace of the world by a *triple alliance of these universal monarchies*, whose distinguishing features would be not only the three principal races of the European system, but also its three great Christian Churches!"*

Lord Palmerston declared about this time in Parliament, with his British ingenuousness, "that the situation was pregnant with at least half-a-dozen respectable wars;" and, in spite of the obscurity which still overclouds the transactions of 1861-62, we cannot doubt that Napoleon III. cherished in the recesses of his soul some vague and gigantic combination that should embrace at once the East and the West, and which Prince Gortchakof prepared with his usual dexterity to take advantage of. Whatever may have been the truth of these hidden designs, the Hohenzollern could not but be satisfied with his sojourn at Compiègne, which he remembered with some emotion two years afterwards in his polite reply to the invitation to the congress. In October, 1861, Napoleon III. employed, no doubt, the same language in which he afterwards expressed himself by the mouth of the Marquis Pepoli, a language prophetic of "the great destinies which awaited Prussia in Germany, and which Germany expected her to fulfil."

It was thus that internal difficulties and exterior facilities, internal parliamentary conflicts and external political friendships, combined towards the end of 1861 in impelling the King of Prussia to form ener-

---

* See the remarkable pamphlet entitled "Europa's Cabinete und Allianzen," Leipzig, 1862. It is the work of a Russian diplomatist celebrated in political literature, the same whose book on the *Pentarchie* had so great a success at the time of the July Monarchy.

getic resolutions. A vigorous man was wanted for the vigorous measures that were in contemplation, and all eyes were naturally turned towards the railing (*frondeur*) diplomatist at St. Petersburg, who during several successive years had never ceased criticising the ministers of the "new era," nor ceased condemning their foreign as well as their home policy. In spite of the promise which he had made to himself, "to take up the position of a philosophic observer," M. de Bismarck did not fail to score his points from time to time during 1860-61, and to repeat most untiringly the precept of Strafford "to be thorough" (*à l'outrance!*). We see him making several tours in Germany during this time, seeking to meet the chief of the State, to inform him of his ideas, and to present him with divers memoranda. In October, 1861, on the very eve of the journey to Compiègne, he submitted to the king a small work which he hoped would obtain some success; a work whose tenor it is not difficult to divine, if we take the trouble to read a private letter written by him a few days previously (September 2nd, 1861), filled with opposition to a programme of politics which the Prussian Conservative party had just published. In this curious letter he inveighs most violently against the Bund, "that hotbed of 'particularism,' demands a closer (*straffer*) concentration of the armed forces of Germany, and a more natural outline for the frontiers of the States." But, first of all, he warns his party against *the dangerous fiction of a unity which, it is supposed, would exist between the different conservative interests.* Indeed, to triumph over this *dangerous fiction,* so deeply engrafted in many minds, was the one great difficulty of the future minister of William I.—his *omne tulit punctum*; for it is not easy in such matters to distinguish reality from fiction; it is even sometimes perilous to discuss them; and a Retz would certainly have repeated, with regard to conservative interests, the saying he had so subtly uttered about the rights of the people and those of the king, "that they never agree so well as by keeping silence." M. de Bismarck had yet many times to fight against this "fiction" at Berlin as at St. Petersburg; and if the enlightened and acute mind of his friend Alexander Mikhaïlovitch allowed itself to be convinced without much resistance, it was not so with the Hohenzollern, who, at a later period, and on several decisive occasions, was to be beset by scruples, by shiverings, and by what Falstaff terms "tertian agues of the conscience."

On the return of William I. from Compiègne, the nomination of the Knight of the Mark to the direction of affairs was already regarded as settled. M. de Bismarck arrived immediately afterwards, in order to assist at the king's coronation at Königsberg, and only returned to St. Petersburg in order to take his final farewell. In the beginning of May, 1862, he was again at Berlin, and was present at the great military parade which took place in the capital on the occasion of the consecration of the statue of Count of Brandenburg (May 17th). Politicians, deputies, and great functionaries already looked upon him as the future "Polignac" of Prussia. The hopes and fears that such anticipations were sure to awaken were, however, not so soon to be realised; and society was disconcerted by learning that M. de Bismarck had been appointed to the post of ambassador at Paris. Was it that he still hesitated to lift up the burden of power, or did he prefer to await the results of the new elections to which Prussia was about to have recourse? It is more probable that, before inaugurating his combative government, he may have wished to add yet a few more interviews to those which he had already had at Compiègne, to take once more the measure of a man on whom it was then universally believed depended the destinies of Europe, and to generally prepare French opinion for the new policy he was about to attempt.

He only remained two months in Paris, during the lovely months of June and July; but this short sojourn was more than sufficient to complete his studies and clear up his doubts. He had more than one conversation with the sovereign of France, whose profound ideas, whose least word, whose very silence, furnished topics of admiration to the whole world at this epoch; and whom the future conqueror of Sedan did not hesitate to designate, in his confidential moments, as "the embodiment of misunderstood incapacity." He also associated with the influential men of the government and of society, and tried to rally them round his ideas and his projects. He did not conceal the fact that his sovereign would very soon require his services, and he demonstrated with great openness the line of conduct he intended pursuing under the circumstances. That which history will the most admire in the present Chancellor of Germany is the supreme art with which he makes use of the truth; he is a genius who has known how to give to truth itself all the political virtues of falsehood. Very cunning and very astute as to his means, he has, for all that, always displayed in pursuit of his ends an ingenuousness and an amount of indiscretion that has never had its equal; and it was thus that in Paris, during 1862, he imparted some of those astonishing confidences which only amused when they ought to have caused the most serious reflections.*

"France," said M. de Bismarck then and afterwards, in 1862, in 1864, in 1865—in short, at all his interviews with French statesmen, "France would be wrong to take umbrage at the growth of Prussian influence, or be offended by her possible territorial aggrandisement at the expense of the smaller States. Of what use, of what assistance, are those petty States without a will, without strength, without an army? However wide-spreading the desires and wants of Prussia may be, they must necessarily be bounded by the Main—the river Main is Prussia's natural frontier. Beyond that river Austria will retain, will even increase, its preponderance; so that in Germany there will always be two powers acting as a useful counterpoise one to the other. Public peace will be benefited, and France will certainly lose nothing; she

---

* See " Préliminaires de Sadowa," chap. i.

will even derive immense advantages in her politics and in her transactions with the world.

"Prussia is, in effect, very badly made, and of an impossible shape; on the side of Cassel and Nassau she has 'no stomach,' and on the side of Hanover 'her shoulder is out of joint;' she floats in the air; and this painful situation condemns her necessarily to follow in all things the politics of Vienna and St. Petersburg, and to revolve unceasingly in the orbit of the Holy Alliance. Were she better shaped, more solidly placed, complete in her members, she would be independent, would have more liberty in her movements, 'the liberty to form alliances;' and what alliance could be more desirable for her than that of the French empire? More than one question now undecided, and almost insoluble, might then be entered into with perfect safety—the Venetian, the Eastern question—who can tell? Perhaps even that of Poland!

"Lastly, if the possibly increasing size of Prussia threatened to become excessive and destroy the balance of power, what is to prevent France from enlarging her own territory in her turn? Why should she not take possession of Belgium, and, in so doing, 'stamp out that nest of demagogues?' Certainly the Cabinet of Berlin would not oppose it; *suum cuique*, that is the ancient and venerable motto of the Prussian monarchy."

All this was lightly, attractively, and wittily said, and accompanied by various *bon mots*, more or less ingenious or malicious, at the expense of the men and things of the period; for example, at the expense of the House of Lords at Berlin, composed of respectable *perruques*;* at the expense of the Chamber of Deputies, composed equally of *perruques*, but not so respectable; and at the expense of an august personage, the most respectable, but the most unmanageable, of all the *perruques*.

M. de Bismarck's success in Paris during his two months' stay was almost as great as that achieved during his sojourn of three years on the banks of the Neva.

Men of importance, those occupying high positions, were careful, however, not to rate him too high; they readily acknowledged that he was a clever man, but could not make up their minds that his cleverness had any serious side.

Nor was he better appreciated by a sage who at that time was living in retirement, but who, in the midst of his favourite studies, yet followed with attention, even with ardour, the great events of the world.

One evening in the month of June, 1862, in the well-known *salons* of the Place St. George, where the brilliant and caustic talents of M. Thiers drew around him all the more moderate opposers of the Second Empire, the suddenly-announced name of his Excellency the Prussian ambassador fell like a thunderbolt at the feet of the astonished host and his equally astonished guests, the ambassadors at the Court of the Tuileries being at that time very careful to avoid the marked house of "the illustrious

* Wigs; meaning wigs with no brains under them.

national historian." The general astonishment became even greater when M. de Bismarck, joining immediately in the conversation, began an exposition of his future political plans, should his royal master ever place him at the head of affairs.

The assembly agreed unanimously that the ambassador was very *bizarre*, and his frankness appeared to them "a sort of ironical challenge addressed to their credulity."

A few days later M. Thiers returned the call of the ambassador, who said to him suddenly, in the midst of the interview, in the most good-natured and off-hand manner: "Confess it, you are sulking in your retreat with your friends and your books." "I must respect my opinions," replied the French statesman. "You are right," was the answer; "one ought to entertain strong opinions, but one ought to strive for power to carry them into effect. And having given vent to this characteristic maxim, the Prussian envoy added.: "See here; I will arrange your affair with the Emperor;" and in the look which accompanied this proposition, his listener seemed to read the secret thought, Be minister, and we two will remake the map of Europe.

The former minister of Louis Philippe turned the conversation, setting aside by a gesture both the offer and the idea, and was not long in taking leave of this extraordinary man.

He was not to see him again until he met him, eight years later, at Versailles, conqueror of Napoleon III. and master of France.

During the latter part of July, the new representative of Prussia at the Court of the Tuileries undertook a pleasure trip through the South of France. He successively visited Chambord, Bordeaux, Avignon, Luchon, Toulouse, and made an excursion in the Pyrenees. "The Castle of Chambord," he writes, in a letter dated the 27th July, 1862, "resembles, in its isolation, the destiny of its possessor. Those great halls and porticoes, where once kings and their mistresses held their festivals, are now empty but for a few of the childhood's toys of the Duc de Bordeaux. The porteress, who was my guide, took me for a Legitimist, and squeezed out a tear as she showed me a small cannon that had once belonged to her prince. I paid her an extra franc for the tear, although my sympathies little incline me to swell the subscription lists of Legitimism."

At Bordeaux he was delighted to be able "to study in the original, and at the door of their cellars, the great masters named Laffitte, Mouton, Pichon, Larose, Margaux, Branne, Armillac," &c., who are only known in Germany by means of "very bad translations." He was delighted with his tour in the Pyrenees, but more especially with the baths of Biarritz and St. Sebastian. He "devotes himself entirely to the sun and the salt sea;" he completely ignored all politics, and ignored the very meaning of journals or despatches. It was at this moment (end of September, 1862) that he received an imperative notice from his sovereign to return to Berlin. The elections had produced the most deplorable results; and an immense majority of the new Chamber was composed of *progressists*. They had not been able to come to any decision in Berlin as to the choice of a future president for the Ministry—" a lid for the government saucepan," as M. de Bismarck expresses it. He was to take the portfolio of foreign affairs, filling at the same time the other post for a while.

Burnt by southern suns, and fortified by the waves of the ocean—"browned and salted"—the whilom aspirant to the post of superintendent of dykes in a district of the Mark returned to his country to assume the highest post in the State.

As he passed through Avignon, he gathered that olive branch which has been so often commented on— that sign of his future reconciliation with the democrats which he showed to M. d'Ester on his first entry into the Chamber. He only, so to say, passed through Paris this time, but still remained there long enough to utter a characteristic speech, which defined his whole programme. "Liberalism," said the chosen chief of the Prussian Government, in bidding farewell at the office on the Quai d'Orsay, "Liberalism is but a child, easily brought to reason; but Revolution is a power, and you must know how to use it."

CHAPTER V.

THE CAMPAIGNS OF THE VISTULA AND THE ELBE.

Combination of Genius and Chance in the Achievements of M. de Bismarck—Situation of Europe on his Accession to the Ministry (September, 1862)—Intimacy existing between France and Russia—The Polish Insurrection (January, 1863)—A Nation's Suicide—European Folly—Lord John Russell—Wise Hesitations on the Part of the French Government—Remonstrances in favour of Poland—Exasperation of Russia—Popularity and great Position of Prince Gortchakof—Benefits derived by M. de Bismarck from the Change in the Situation—His first Efforts—Views of Prussia with regard to the Vistula—Singular Conversation with the Vice-President of the Chamber—Saying of M. de Bismarck *à propos* of the *Spectateur profane*—The Duchies of the Elbe—M. de Bismarck simulates Indifference on the Question of the Duchies — Profound Satisfaction of Lord John Russell and M. Quade—*Minute* of the 14th October, 1863—Last Despatches on the Subject of Poland—Withdrawal of England, and Displeasure of France—The Emperor Napoleon III. proposes a Congress (November 5th, 1863)—Anxieties of Lord John Russell, and Rupture of all European Unanimity—M. de Bismarck precipitates the Federal Execution in Holstein—Sudden Death of the King of Denmark, Frederick VII. (November 15th, 1863)—Resolution and Acuteness of M. de Bismarck: he sets aside England, France, Austria, and the secondary States—Revolutionary Europe of 1848, and Monarchical Europe of 1864—The Dismemberment of a Monarchy—Russian Services rendered to Prussia in the Campaign of the Elbe.

However great a share genius may have had in the achievements of M. de Bismarck, it is impossible to deny that much of their success has been due to chance, to a most extraordinary concourse of fortuitous circumstances—in one word, to that goddess

Fortune, whose praises the *minnesingers* of the middle ages were never tired of celebrating, and whom even Dante has not failed to commemorate in his immortal lines as " flashing on its way like a meteor through the skies, its destination ever hid like a snake in the grass.".

We must doubtless admire the wonderful audacity with which the German Chancellor has again and again cast the "iron dice of fate," and we may even suspect, with the witty Abbé Galiani, the presence of at least one loaded die in such a persistent run of sixes. It is nevertheless a fact that, in his long career, the President of the Berlin Council has often met, at the most decisive moments, with extraordinary turns of good fortune which could not have been calculated upon or foreseen by the most astute politician, and where the daring of the player has had but the merit—but that no inconsiderable one—of having taken the tide of fortune at its flood, and of not having missed the smallest eddy of the rushing waters of luck.

One of these splendid turns of fortune, one of these perfectly astounding events befell the minister of William I. on his accession to power in the month of January, 1863. This event laid the foundation of his future grandeur, was the starting-point of his action in Europe—the fulcrum of Archimedes from which he eventually raised a whole world of daring projects, and one we must fully take into consideration.

The idea with which M. de Bismarck was imbued

when first he assumed the reins of government, was the aggrandisement, "the rounding off" of the monarchy of Frederick II. He had already declared his feelings on the subject during his stay in Paris, and he repeated them openly in the first sitting of the Commission in the Chamber at Berlin, barely a week after his accession to the Ministry (September 29th, 1862).

He certainly did not foresee to what extent he was to carry out his ideas, to what extent he was to carry through Germany conquests no longer only of a "moral nature;" but he foresaw from the beginning that Austria would always be his resolute adversary, and he shaped his course accordingly.*

The only question which preoccupied him was the attitude which the other great powers of Europe might assume with respect to certain eventualities. Among these he did not reckon England. With his usual political perspicacity he had seen at an early date to what a state of tameness and gentleness the excellent Manchester schooling had reduced the once fiery lion; and his conviction that "proud Albion" would not rebel, but would even quietly submit to be slighted, was more than justified during the piteous Danish campaign. "England has for many a year been erased from all my political calculations," said he, in course of private conversation a few years afterwards; "and do you know since when I began to reckon without her?

---

* See the celebrated circular despatch of M. de Bismarck, dated January 24th, 1863, in which he describes his curious interviews with M. de Karoyli, the Austrian ambassador, during the closing months of 1862, shortly after his accession.

Since the day on which she renounced, of her own free will, her right to the Ionian Islands. A power which ceases to take, and begins to give up, is an exhausted power." There still remained France and Russia; and he was not without hope that, by careful management, he might bring both of these powers to regard with favour, or at the least not to interfere with, Prussian designs.

On the banks of the Neva the old grievances born of the Crimean war still flourished, but half pacified by the war in Lombardy. There were the still older ties existing between the Gottorps and the Hohenzollerns—ties which had become stronger of late, thanks to the efforts of M. de Bismarck during his sojourn in St. Petersburg. Lastly, there was his friend Alexander Mikhaïlovitch, his former colleague at Frankfort, so attached to the new minister of William I., so at unison with him in his hatred of Austria, so thoroughly aware of the "dangerous fiction" of a combination between all Conservative interests. On the banks of the Seine, at the Tuileries, so much feared in those days, a sovereign held sway who, in striving to accomplish the welfare of humanity, was fast endangering that of France, and whose dimmed and vacillating sight could easily be dazzled by dangling before it the glories of the "new right" and the freedom of Venice.

Besides, since the Congress of Paris there had arisen between the two Cabinets of the Tuileries and St. Petersburg an ever-increasing "cordiality," in which Prussia was beginning to largely share. Were there not, after taking all these things into consideration, strong hopes that these two powers, so friendly to one another, and so antagonistic to Austria, might, if they did not assist, at least maintain a benevolent neutrality towards Prussia in her meditated designs? And yet these designs were profoundly antagonistic to all the interests and deeply-rooted traditions of Russia as well as to those of France. To substitute in the centre of Europe a great military and aggressive kingdom in lieu of a peaceful and "purely defensive" confederation, would be to create such manifest drawbacks, such palpable dangers to the security and the equilibrium of the world, that M. de Bismarck was not able to flatter himself with too much hôpe from these quarters. The bitter animosities of the Winter Palace and the gentle dreams of the Tuileries would scarcely long prevail against geographical realities and stern facts.

Unless at Paris and St. Petersburg there was a complete want of statesmen possessing even the slightest political discernment, or the slightest knowledge of their national histories, it would be impossible for the two governments of Russia and France to witness with indifference so complete a revolution in the balance of the Continent. From benevolent their neutrality would not fail to become watchful and then alarmed—would even change into actual hostility in the face of Prussian success; and the very "cordiality" that existed between the two empires, apparently so favourable to Prussia, would only become one peril the more by facilitating any prompt and decisive measures they might wish to undertake against the House of Hohenzollern. This being the situation of Europe at the beginning of 1863, it naturally ensued that the minister of William I. should ardently desire—should, in his most sanguine moments, invoke some unexpected incident that would irremediably estrange the two emperors Alexander II. and Napoleon III., that would reawaken in St. Petersburg all the old rancorous feelings against Vienna, and permit Prussia to unite herself to Russia by ties of a yet stronger and more indissoluble nature, while yet maintaining her friendly intercourse with the French Cabinet. "Chimeras!" would have been the exclamation of even the hardiest constructor of hypotheses; "such a problem of political alchemy and algebra is not worthy the contemplation of a serious mind!" Yet chance, that Providence of the fortunate ones of earth, was not long before it brought about an event which solved in M. de Bismarck's favour every condition of this problem, fulfilling his seemingly visionary wishes on every point.

"If Italy did not exist we should have to invent her," was the saying in 1865 of the President of the Council at Berlin.* In the month of January, 1863, this was probably his opinion respecting the Polish question. History offers few examples of so rapid, so humiliating a descent from the sublime to the odious and disastrous, as that which was presented to the world in the lamentable drama played out on

* La Marmora, "Un pó più di luce," p. 59.

the banks of the Vistula, which, after running its course full of bitter agonies for two years, ended in a final catastrophe in the month of January, 1863, in celebration, as it were, of the joyous accession of M. de Bismarck to the head of affairs.

Certainly there was much that was elevated and poetical in those first manifestations at Warsaw, when a populace, so long and so cruelly tried, knelt in unison before the palace of the king's lieutenant, in silent appeal, holding nothing in their hands but the symbol of Christ's crucifixion, and asking for nothing "but their God and their country!" The king's lieutenant, who was no other than the old hero of Sebastopol, Prince Michael Gortchakof, shrank with horror from so unequal, so strange a contest; he appealed to St. Petersburg, and—miracle of divine mercy!—from the source from whence during thirty years had issued no other orders than those of blood and torture, now for the first time issued mandates of clemency and moderation.

A generous instinct seemed to pervade the governing and intelligent classes in Russia at this period; ideas of reform and emancipation were abroad; the esteem of Europe and the friendship of France were valued; and there was a sincere desire to conciliate Poland. The Emperor Alexander II. sent his brother to Warsaw, and a patriot of exceptional vigour of mind and character undertook the civil government; education, law, administration, all were invested with the stamp of nationality, and a degree of modest independence was guaranteed to the country.

The precepts of the most commonplace wisdom, the instincts of self-preservation, the fearful lessons of the past, ought to have counselled the Poles to have taken advantage of the friendly intentions of their sovereign, to have given the newly-granted institutions a trial, to have accepted with eagerness the hand of mercy. Everything, in truth, seemed to counsel them to follow this course, but they were under the curse which Holy Scripture has long ago pronounced on every nation which allows itself to be guided by women and children. The women and the youth of the schools resolved to hold out, and to multiply hitherto successful manifestations which, in ceasing to be spontaneous, became theatrical and sacrilegious. The demagogues of Europe made haste to plant their emblems in so convulsed a soil, to bring with them their passwords of disorder, their secret societies, and their *instrumenta regni*; and from afar, from the depths of the Palais-Royal, came the advice "to throw away their Catholic mummeries and up with the barricades." The great Conservative party showed itself as pusillanimous here as elsewhere, as in fact it does everywhere and at all times, and, in wishing to save its popularity, it ruined a whole population.

Solitude environed the brother of the Emperor and the patriotic minister — a solitude soon to be peopled with horror, terror, and crime.

The Government struggled in vain to free itself from the trammels of a mysterious organisation which surrounded it on every side, and adopted contradictory and violent measures. The demagogues were victorious, and succeeded in plunging into futile revolt an unhappy people who for the last century seem to have taken upon themselves the task of astonishing the world by periodical resurrections, and by disappointing it, at the same time, alas! by equally frequent periodical suicides.

The criminal-folly of this nation was only equalled by the no less guilty folly which Europe displayed in encouraging it.

Europe, which had not dared to touch on the Polish question during the Crimean war, thought fit to sympathise and sport with it at this most unseasonable and desperate moment! Lord John Russell was the first to enter the lists. In 1861 he had written the famous despatch to Sir J. Hudson, and had persuaded England, as well as himself, that in doing so he had delivered Italy. In the following year, in the celebrated Gotha despatch, he had invented for Denmark a constitution of the most original description, divided into four parts, with four parliaments; and had thus given the signal for the dismemberment of the Scandinavian monarchy. This time he thought proper to recommend parliamentary institutions for Poland, and on the observation of the Russian ambassador that it would be difficult for the Czar to give to his Polish subjects privileges not even possessed by the Russians, he asked, with the greatest simplicity, why the same benefit should not be extended to the whole of Russia! [*]

---

[*] "Why indeed should representative institutions not be accorded, at the same time, to the kingdom of Poland and to the empire of Russia?"— *Despatch of Lord John Russell to Lord Napier,* 10th *April,* 1863.

Count Rechberg, that fatal minister then at the head of foreign affairs in Vienna, also wished to show himself compassionate, and gave himself the malicious and somewhat expensive pleasure of repaying the Cabinet of St. Petersburg in Polish coin for the sympathies which it had lavished on the Italian cause. As though Austria had not already sufficiently suffered from the imaginary grievances of the Muscovites on the subject of the so-called "treachery" during the Crimean war, it meant now to afford Russia some really tangible grievances by a very palpable "connivance"* in Galicia, a province that became in effect the refuge, the armoury, and the centre for supplies for the insurgents of the kingdom.

It is but right to say that it was only after prolonged hesitation that the French Government followed in this perilous track. In the beginning of the Polish agitation, a note, published in the *Moniteur*, put the press and the public equally on their guard against "the supposition that the Emperor would encourage any hopes which he had no means of satisfying." "The generous plans of the Czar," continued the note, "are a certain pledge of his desire to carry out every amelioration possible in the state of Poland, and we can only hope that he may not be thwarted in his designs by any irritating manifestations."

The French Government persevered in this sensible

---

* "This connivance on the part of Austria is not the least remarkable feature in the history of this insurrection."—*Confidential Despatch from M. de Tengoborski to M. d'Oubril*, 4th February, 1863.

and friendly attitude towards the Czar during 1861 and 1862, in spite of the interest taken by the Parisian press in the " dramatic " incidents at Warsaw; and in spite of several animated debates which took place in the English Parliament, which referred to France, however, more than to Russia. British statesmen, indeed, had thought fit, during the two consecutive years of 1861-62, to embarrass the Cabinet of the Tuileries in no small degree in its Russian leanings, by frequent and sympathetic allusions to Poland.

Lord Palmerston especially, in a very clever speech of April 4th, 1863, took an opportunity of extolling the Poles, of celebrating their " untamable, inextinguishable, exhaustless patriotism;" and did not neglect to remind them of the cruel deceptions practised upon them " at a former period" by a French emperor.

Napoleon III. continued to withstand all unwise emotions from within, as well as all interested suggestions from without. Even on the 5th February, after the event of the fatal rising, M. Billault, the spokesman of the Corps Législatif, sternly condemned the Polish insurrection as the work of "revolutionary passions," and forcibly insisted on the danger " of useless speeches and vain protestations ;" but the noisy language of the English minister, the enigmatical attitude of Austria, and finally the military convention concluded by M. de Bismarck with Russia (February 8th, 1863), and which he loudly proclaimed, at last turned the scale After having laboured so hard during seven years in order to gain Russian *cordialité*, after having sacrificed to this object nearly all the fruits of the Crimean war, Napoleon III. shattered by one blow the whole edifice erected with such pains, and set himself to address a "great European remonstrance" to the Government of the Czar, the first terrible effect of which was naturally to swell the torrent of blood and tears already flowing in Poland. The universal cry in Warsaw thenceforth was, to "continue" the insurrection, in order to justify the interference of Europe;* so long as the sympathetic ink flowed from the pens of foreign chancellors, so long also should the blood flow from Polish veins. We all know the deplorable end of this diplomatic campaign, which lasted nine months, and only served to show how completely the Western Powers disagreed with each other.

The pride of Russia was deeply wounded by foreign interference, and she undertook against the Polish nation a work of methodical and implacable extirmination, which since then has never ceased. However frivolous and unstable the diplomatic tournament in favour of Poland may in reality have been, the Russians nevertheless believed themselves to have been for some time in imminent peril, and to have only escaped from it through the firmness of their "national" minister—through his patriotic courage and clever, dignified, and vigorous despatches.

It was certainly not in human nature to have protested against so flattering a belief; and the

---

* The Emperor Napoleon III. said himself (November 5th, 1863) that the length and duration of the Polish insurrection had "stamped it with a national character."

minister is quite excusable for not having done so. He let them have their say and cover him with the glory of having repulsed a fresh invasion, and "vanquished Europe :" *scripsit et salvavit!*

He was loaded with favours by his august master, received the enthusiastic ovations of his compatriots, and became the idol of the nation, side by side with M. Katkof and the sanguinary Mouravief. During an entire year, throughout the whole of Russia, even in its most obscure corners, no banquet was ever held without the three "blessed saviours" being eulogised in speeches, pledged in toasts, or congratulated by telegrams; and, whatever repugnance the descendant of the Rouriks and the nursling of the classical humanities may have felt at being coupled with a raging journalist and a bloodthirsty executioner, he sacrificed his feelings to the love of country and of popularity. In his benevolent anxiety to receive the homages which were being showered upon him on all sides, he forgot himself so far as to thank, with his stereotyped smile, the German nobility of the Baltic for a diploma of honorary citizenship which they had sent him; and the national party reproached him somewhat bitterly for the "culpable effusion" which he had displayed on the occasion.

Alexander Mikhaïlovitch received all the honours of the melancholy campaign of 1863. The profits were absorbed by another—by his former colleague at Frankfort, the President of the Council at Berlin, who used them to construct a secure and solid foundation for his future plans.

We are now able to contemplate, from a Prussian point of view, the situation created about the end of 1863 by the great European interference in the affairs of Poland.

England's state of beatific quiescence had been duly verified; France and Russia were irreparably embroiled; the ill-feeling against Austria had become even stronger in St. Petersburg; the Prussian minister had more than ever the right to reckon upon the grateful friendship of Prince Gortchakof; and, lastly, it was not difficult to foresee that, after his palpable repulse at Warsaw, the Cæsar of the "new right" would hasten to cast his eyes on Venice, would wish to "do something for Italy," and would show himself all the more favourable towards "a youthful Northern power" in its enterprises against the Hapsburgs, as the Napoleonic spirit of prophecy had already long ago assigned to this youthful power "the highest destinies in Germany."

It would, however, be doing too much honour to human genius to suppose that M. de Bismarck had any clear or precise idea of the benefits which would accrue to him through the Polish insurrection. Many circumstances tend rather to indicate that, especially at first, the Prussian minister was only groping in the dark, and seeking a path in a somewhat haphazard direction and by cross-roads. Another fact worthy to be noted, and which now offers some food for reflection, is, that M. de Bismarck, who had lived for several years in Russia, and made the country his especial study, seems to have entertained the most serious doubts as to the strength of that empire in 1863, and to have even carried his doubts so far as not to believe it capable of quelling the foolhardy rebellion of the unfortunate Polish youths.

He expressed his apprehensions on this point to the plenipotentiaries of England and Austria,* and actually went so far as to make some astonishing confidences on this subject to the Vice-President of the Prussian Chamber, M. Behrend.†

"This question," said, in the month of February, the minister of William I., "may be decided in two ways: either we must lend our prompt assistance to Russia, and aid it in quelling the insurrection, so as to be able to lay before the Western Powers a *fait accompli*; or, we must allow the situation to become more developed and more aggravated, wait until the Russians have been driven from the kingdom or reduced to ask for help, and then advance boldly, invest the kingdom with troops, and take possession on Prussia's account; at the

---

* "At every preceding interview M. de Bismarck has always mentioned to me the probability that the Russian army would not be sufficiently strong to stifle the insurrection." — *Despatch of Sir Andrew Buchanan, February* 21, 1863. He held the same language to the Austrian minister, Count Karolyi. On the other hand, immediately on hearing of the arrival of the Prussian envoys for the conclusion of a military convention, the Grand Duke Constantine's diplomatic Secretary wrote, on February 4, "While duly recognising the courteous intention of these gentlemen's mission, I cannot quite see its motive. There is no *pericolo* (sic!) *in mora*, and we scarcely yet require the co-operation of foreign troops. . . . . The Prussian Government is painting the devil much blacker than he is in reality."—*Confidential Despatch of M. de Tengoborski to M. D'Oubril, Russian minister at Berlin.*

† The German papers of the time published this conversation as coming from M. Behrend himself, who never contradicted them. See, among others, the *Cologne Gazette*, February 22nd, 1863.

end of three years everything down there would be Germanised." "But you mean this for a ball-room joke!" cried the stupefied Vice-President (this conversation took place at a court ball). "No," was the answer, "I am speaking seriously on serious topics. The Russians are weary of the kingdom; the Emperor Alexander told me so himself at St. Petersburg."

This plan of recovering the frontier of the Vistula, lost since the battle of Jena, often haunted the mind of M. de Bismarck during 1863. Let it, however, be well understood that this "rectification of the Prussian frontier" was only meant to be obtained with the willing acquiescence of Alexander II., though means were not neglected that might have forced him to give it.

M. de Keudell, one of the most confidential friends of the minister and the present representative of Germany at the Court of Victor Emmanuel, was then a very large landed proprietor in the kingdom of Poland, and took advantage of his intercourse with the leaders of that unhappy country to insinuate the advisability of their appealing to Berlin, and asking for a temporary occupation of the country by Prussian troops, who would protect them from Russian cruelties!

If we were to go more deeply into the history of this fatal insurrection, we might light upon other Prussian agents, more obscure perhaps, but far more compromising than M. de Keudell.

Did the President of the Berlin Council ever seriously hope to obtain such important results from the "weariness" of the Emperor Alexander, or from the friendship of Prince Gortchakof?

Whatever may have been his hopes or his after-thoughts, M. de Bismarck displayed an almost feverish anxiety in airing before the Western world his thorough agreement with the Russian Vice-Chancellor. He made him the spontaneous, almost impetuous offer of a military convention; defended him on every occasion; and never failed to assist him most faithfully in every passage of arms with the Cabinets of England, France, and Austria; bearing with pleasure the first fire of M. Drouyn de Lhuys' notes, cheerfully enduring the universal clamours of the press, and haughtily replying to all interrogations put to him by his Parliament. The great men of the "progress" party were puzzled, and on this occasion, as on many others, could not understand the politics of their "Polignac;" they considered them to be inopportune, even perilous, and demanded where in all this lay the interests of Germany? To which the "Polignac" replied one day by this veiled but significant imagery, that, "placed before the diplomatic chessboard, the uninitiated spectator thinks the game finished with every fresh move, and often fancies that the players must have lost sight of their original plans."

Certainly M. de Bismarck never lost sight of his one object, namely, the aggrandisement of Prussia; but it is certain that up to the autumn of 1863 he had not yet settled upon any plan, but was "moving his pieces forward in various directions, waiting for the inspiration of chance to direct him as to where he was to strike his first blow, whether on the banks of the Main, of the Vistula, or of the Elbe. For one moment he had thought of Cassel, and had thrown himself, with some heat, into the constitutional conflict then taking place in that country with the Elector; and by so doing had offered the somewhat strange spectacle of a minister interfering with a neighbouring State in order to force its prince to a stricter regard of parliamentary rule, while governing his own country regardless of the constitution, and by means of taxes raised in opposition to the vote of the Chamber. Without speaking of the adventurous projects that were formed in Berlin respecting the possible rectification of the frontier in the direction of the Vistula, there still existed on the banks of the Elbe the ancient but ever-renewed question of the Duchies, a question that had lain dormant since the Treaty of London, but that had been re-awakened in 1859, in consequence of the events in Italy, and that had grown to importance since the well-known despatch, so fatal for Denmark, which Lord John Russell had had the inconceivable folly of writing at Gotha, September 24th, 1862, the very day of M. de Bismarck's accession to the ministry.

The secondary States, the Diet of Frankfort, and M. de Rechberg himself, developed the strongest feelings of German patriotism on the question of Schleswig-Holstein, believing all the time in their hearts that it was a mere chimerical question, but seizing it as a weapon against Prussia and as a means of accusing her of patriotic lukewarmness.

Prussia was greatly tempted to take the secondary States, the Diet of Frankfort, and M. de Rechberg at their word, and to drag them into a war against Denmark, which would endow Prussia with the magnificent harbour of Kiel, and permit it to make a first trial of "the instrument" which William I. had been toiling to "perfect" during the last four years, if it could but have felt convinced that the war would remain local, and that the other European powers would not interfere as in 1848! The President of the Council at Berlin did not despair of obtaining his object by means of patient and wise manœuvring. He reckoned on the friendship of Prince Gortchakof, on various political accidents, and lastly, on the strange confusion, and, to speak with Montaigne, on the "noisy clatter of brains" which some of the principles of the "new right" had evoked in a certain foreign office of the Continent.

He often thought that in this serious enterprise the only declared enemy that he would have to encounter would be the worthy Lord John Russell, who, after his fatal despatch from Gotha, had thought better of it, and had constituted himself the advocate, protector, and mentor of the unfortunate Danish Government; but such an adversary did not appear very formidable in the eyes of the Knight of the Mark. At first, however, and as long as the Polish negotiations were pending, M. de Bismarck thought fit to display much prudence in dealing with the Cabinet of St. James, and to express the greatest indifference to the vexatious topic of the Duchies.

Nothing can be more instructive than to follow in the State papers and in the documents sent to the *Rigsraad*, the various confidential disclosures which M. de Bismarck indulged in almost daily, in order to convince Lord John Russell and his envoy, Sir A. Buchanan, as well as M. de Quade, the Danish minister at Berlin, that this Schleswig - Holstein question was merely a hobby ridden by Austria and the secondary States, and that Prussia, so far from sharing this German covetousness, was doing all in her power to restrain and modify it! On the 14th of October, 1863, a fortnight after the Diet of Frankfort had decreed the federal execution in Holstein, M. de Bismarck actually declared, in a minute to the envoy of Great Britain, that he would *prevent this execution* if Denmark would accept the English mediation.*

Denmark accepted, and Lord John Russell breathed again. Later on (November 6th, 1863) M. de Quade wrote from Berlin to his Government: "The Prussian Premier, whether influenced by his personal views or by the attitude assumed by England, has placed the affair in a position which *surpasses all we could ever have hoped*. I am not sure whether the question has been taken up with as much clearness and warmth (warmth for the Danish interests!) in Vienna as here." This was the opinion shared by M. de Quade and Sir Andrew Buchanan until the 6th of November, when they were roughly undeceived by a piteous

---

* Despatch of Sir Andrew Buchanan, October 17th, 1863. (Inclosure: Minute of Conversation between M. de Bismarck and Sir Andrew Buchanan.)

despatch from the English Secretary of State, dated November 9th, in the following terms: "If the information which I have received is exact, M. de Bismarck no longer offers any objection to the federal execution in Holstein; and Her Majesty's Government can but leave the responsibility to Germany of exposing Europe to a universal war." The information was but too exact, and the mortifications of poor Johnny were about to begin.

Two important events had taken place during the interval of three weeks which had elapsed since the minute of October 14th. In that interval the Cabinet of St. James had sent to Russia an acquittance in full on account of the Polish question, and the Emperor Napoleon III. had given to the world a fantastic project for a congress *which should settle all impending questions!* Delighted beyond measure at the co-operation afforded him by M. de Bismarck in the Danish difficulties during the month of October, the First Secretary of State had at last resolved to sacrifice to him the Polish question, and had even recalled, by a telegraphic despatch, a courier carrying a very threatening note to the Russian Government, and had replaced this missive by one of a very humble nature, in which he agreed to abandon any further interference on the subject of Poland (October 20th).*

---

* In seeking a decent exit from the foolish campaign in which he had engaged himself, the chief of the Foreign Office had thought fit to declare that the Emperor Alexander had forfeited his rights over Poland, "as he had not fulfilled the conditions on which he had obtained possession of the kingdom in 1815." France was to make a similar declaration; but M. Drouyn de Lhuys, becoming cautious (and with good reason), would not expedite his note until the English despatch was in the hands of Prince

On his side the Emperor of the French, fully aware of all these underhand proceedings, was profoundly displeased by the defalcation of England, and not being able to make up his mind quietly to accept the repulse, nor especially to confess it to the Legislative Body, had formed the plan (November 5th) of calling together a general congress; a plan which only served to increase the universal uneasiness felt in Europe, and inspired more particularly the diplomatist of Downing Street with the utmost consternation.

Not satisfied with replying in the bitterest terms to the invitation of the French Cabinet, Lord John Russell actually exerted himself to preserve all other foreign courts from the contagion of the French idea; he almost lost sight of the dangers menacing Denmark in his eagerness to frustrate the project of Napoleon III., a project that could scarcely be very long-lived, and that

Gortchakof. Lord John Russell, therefore, wrote his despatch; it was read to the cabinet, approved of by Lord Palmerston, and a copy given to the Minister of Foreign Affairs in France. Lord Napier had already received notice that he was to inform Prince Gortchakof of a "very important communication" which he was about to have the honour of laying before him; and the Duke de Montebello had been equally instructed by the French Government to support his English colleague in his solemn declaration. Already had the important document left for its destination, and was proceeding rapidly towards St. Petersburg, when suddenly, to the utter astonishment of the initiated, a telegraphic message stopped the bearer of the note in Germany, and another telegram informed Lord Napier that nothing more would be heard of the "important communication." The fact was, that in the interval Count Bernstorff had read to the Foreign Office a Prussian despatch, in which M. de Bismarck bade the Secretary of State be careful as to what he was about; for if the Czar was declared to have forfeited his rights to Poland by his violation of the Treaty of Vienna, the German Governments on their side might well declare that the King of Denmark had forfeited his rights to the sovereignty of the duchies of the Elbe for not having fulfilled all the engagements of the Treaty of London. Lord John Russell recalled the courier, and tore up the despatch."—*See* "*Études de Diplomatie Contemporaine,*" part i., chap. i.

would certainly have died a natural death without so much unnecessary exertion on the part of the English minister. The President of the Prussian Council thought the moment had arrived to show his hand. The last shadows of a western alliance had faded from the horizon; alone the bond between Russia and Prussia remained intact, immovable in the midst of the general confusion existing in the various cabinets. No European combination for the protection of Denmark was to be feared. M. de Bismarck now might "have no further objection" to the federal execution in Holstein, and soon an unlooked-for event, one of those splendid strokes of fortune which have so often befallen the minister of William I. in his marvellous career, occurred to prove that he was decidedly in a lucky vein.

The sudden death of Frederick VII. (November 15th, 1863) was in itself so tragic, so fatal an event for the destinies of Denmark that it reminds us of one of the most desolate sayings bequeathed to us by antiquity, that lugubrious cry of the historian: *Non esse curæ deis securitatem nostram, esse ultionem.*

This death effectually gave an entirely new shape to the German demands on the unhappy Scandinavian monarchy. Germany no longer declared herself satisfied with a federal execution in Holstein; no longer recognised the sovereignty of the new King Christian IX. over the Duchies; but demanded the instalment there of the intriguing and treacherous family of Augustenburg, for whom M. de Bismarck himself had already obtained one million and a half of rixdalers from the

Copenhagen Government on condition that they gave up all further claims to the Duchies. It seems as if it was only at this juncture that the mind of M. de Bismarck came to a final decision. It was evidently towards the Elbe that Prussia was going to begin to fill out her outlines and complete her unity!

His resolution once taken, M. de Bismarck brought all his energy, all his audacity and incomparable astuteness to bear upon the accomplishment of his design. His first attempt was a masterly one, and the great Machiavelli himself would have taken a "divine" pleasure in contemplating the address, or, as he would have said, the *virtù* with which the Knight of the Mark, in the space of a few weeks, managed to trick poor Lord John Russell, make a fool of the Emperor Napoleon III., draw Austria off on a distant, unjust, and foolish expedition, put forward the Bund and set it aside at the same time, terrorise the secondary States and turn out their *protégé*—in a word, take into his own matchless hands the holy cause of the German fatherland, and, as the apostle has it, be all things to all men!

The spectacle which Europe presented at the beginning of 1864 was certainly the most curious and the most afflicting which history has ever witnessed. Two great Powers, jealous of each other, and destined to quarrel over the remains of their victim; two great Powers, urged on and condemned at the same time by a whole league of German peoples and German princes, were to be seen attacking a State which, though feeble, was yet an ancient and glorious monarchy whose existence had at all times been declared by the various cabinets to be necessary to the balance of power in Europe; and attacking it on the most futile pretext, in the name of a cause which was once stigmatised by its present chief as " eminently iniquitous, frivolous, disastrous, and revolutionary." It was moreover, to punish King Christian IX. for his disobedience to the Bund that Prussia and Austria undertook this work of "justice;" and they began their work by a formal declaration of their own disobedience to the same Bund. They were acting as the " agents of Germany," and the whole of Germany protested against the assumption! Europe contemplated these monstrosities and remained quiescent; the same Europe which, in 1848, at the time of the first German aggression against the Scandinavian kingdom, had not failed to do its duty nobly, in spite of the revolutionary troubles which were then distracting it, and which might have served as an excuse for inaction. The Powers were then unanimous in their defence of the weak against the oppressor. The Emperor Nicholas was agreed on this point with the Republic of General Cavaignac, and even the newly fledged diplomatists of the "surprise" of February showed their appreciation of the necessity to maintain the balance of power. It was reserved to experienced statesmen, to chancellors grown old in the service, imbued with the respect due to treaties, to the representatives of strong and well-established monarchies, to witness, unmoved, the consummation of a revolutionary work which such as Bastide and Petetin had thought it their duty to forbid.*

Without doubt England will bear in the eyes of posterity the shame and disgrace of Denmark's ruin, for it was she who took in hand the cause of the Scandinavian kingdom, who counselled it, guided it, and nursed it till the very end, and who solemnly declared that in the hour of danger it should not fight alone; but nevertheless it would be incorrect to exonerate completely all the remaining European powers from blame. More than one clear-sighted and honest mind predicted that this dismemberment of a monarchy in the nineteenth century would prove as full of disastrous consequences as had done another dismemberment in the previous century, and looked forward with the greatest anxiety to the formidable confusions and catastrophes looming in the future. The more simple, or, to use M. de Bismarck's words, the "uninitiated spectators," might fancy the game finished after this first blow dealt to the rights of nations, after this first exploit of the marvellous "instrument" which the Prussian Government had devoted so many years in bringing to perfection; but the cannon of Missunda was to the Knight of the Mark only what the cannon of Toulon had been in former years to a young officer from Corsica, and the short campaign in

---

* In 1848 Denmark demanded the protection of France; M. Bastide, then Minister for Foreign Affairs under the Republic, took up its cause with warmth, and it was even suggested to send 10,000 men to assist the Danes in the defence of their country.—*Despatch of Lord Cowley, February 13th,* 1864. (See also the curious despatches of M. Petetin, the Republican Envoy at that time at Hanover.)

the Duchies revealed a new future to the eventual conqueror of Europe. He learnt therefrom that legitimate rights, pledged words, treaties sacredly sworn to, stipulated conditions, and many other old-fashioned and respectable usages, once considered inviolable, were now even more feeble and worn out than the poor fortresses erected in past ages by the Danes; and, if Moltke and Roon were quite satisfied during this war with the execution done by their needle-guns, he, on his side, was equally contented with the precious and overwhelming qualities of his own "instrument."

It is incontestable that throughout the entire expedition against the Danes, Prince Gortchakof was unceasing in his efforts in favour of the Prussian minister, and was always extending a hand, generally a stealthy one, to aid him in his frequently perilous predicaments.

His concurrence was absolute, and all the more efficacious, as it assumed the outward appearance of a neutrality busily seeking to compass pacific ends.

Thus he aided the President of the Prussian Council to infuse the idea into the muddled head of Lord John Russell that the occupation of Holstein by the federal troops would act as a ratification of the validity of the title of the King of Denmark. "M. de Bismarck tells me," wrote Sir Andrew Buchanan, November 28th, 1863, "that a federal execution will prevent all revolutionary movements in Holstein, and will be at the same time a kind of indirect recognition of King Christian IX.'s claims to the dukedom of Holstein on the part of the Diet of

Frankfort. His Excellency affirms that the alarming state of Germany requires that this step should instantly be undertaken, but he cannot or will not explain how such an execution can possibly be a recognition of King Christian's rights or avoid the appearance of an armed occupation."

Three days later, on the 1st of December, Lord Napier wrote from St. Petersburg: "The language of Prince Gortchakof leads me to suppose that he is persuaded that M. de Bismarck's views are *moderate* on this subject. The Vice-Chancellor is favourably disposed towards a federal execution if well carried out, and considers it in the light of a conservative measure. In his opinion the federal troops, acting on judicious instructions, will preserve order, and will maintain the necessary distinction between the legislative and the dynastic questions." "I deprive, therefore I recognise!" said M. de Bismarck, in that style of logic so peculiarly his own, but which at this time was shared by his friend the Prince Gortchakof, and which the pair tried to apply to Schleswig, as soon as the Minister of Downing Street had given way to them in Holstein.*

"The Russian Vice-Chancellor made the suggestion to me this morning," wrote Lord Napier again from St. Petersburg, January 11th, "that we ought to advise Denmark to consent to the occupation of Schleswig by

---

* The official journals at Berlin renewed this style of reasoning in their recent discussions on the laws of guarantee accorded to the Papal seat. The Pope, they argued, cannot be treated as a sovereign, as we cannot exercise against him the law of reprisals and seize his States.

the Austrian and Prussian forces, in return for a guarantee to be given by these two powers with regard to the German population of the duchy."

In this way we are instructed and edified by the "State papers" and documents sent to the *Rigsraad*: we cannot discover a single insinuation or suggestion issuing from Berlin which was not immediately countersigned at St. Petersburg. And yet Denmark had always been the friend and the *protégé* of the Empire of the Czars!

To Russia, more than to any other power in Europe, was it of importance to preserve the freedom of the Baltic, and not to prevent the harbour of Kiel from falling into the hands of the Germans; it was also of more importance to her than to any other to remember that the people of Courland and Livonia spoke a much purer and more harmonious German than the people of Schleswig!

Lastly, this quarrel on the Eider was in truth a quarrel of the revolution warring against legitimate sovereignty. Old Count Nesselrode, in a celebrated circular, had once declared it to be so; and what would the Emperor Nicholas have said to a Russian Vice-Chancellor allowing these privileges to the spirit of revolution? But Alexander Mikhaïlovitch will astonish history by the immensity of his gratitude to M. de Bismarck.

CHAPTER VI.

THE WAR IN GERMANY.

Second Period of Prince Gortchakof's Ministry—Reveries of Napoleon III., and sulky Attitude of Alexander Mikhaïlovitch—"Napoleonic Ideas" on the Subject of Germany—Isolation of France in 1864—Convention of September—Arrival of M. de Bismarck in Paris (October)—Tenor of his Language while there—The *Parti de l'action* in the Councils of the Empire—Encouragement carried to Berlin by M. de Bismarck—Prussian Circular of December 24th concerning the Duchies—Consultation and Decision of the Syndics of the Crown (1865)—Proposition made to Austria—Threatenings of War—First Campaign in Bohemia (July, 1865)—Convention of Gastein (August)—The Madame Lucca Incident, and Letter to M. André (de Roman)—Austrian Sympathies of M. Drouyn de Lhuys—Prussian Sympathies of the *Parti de l'action*—Chimerical Project of the Emperor Napoleon III.: he reserves for himself the *Rôle* of Umpire and Protector of General Rights—Interview at Biarritz (October)—The Word of the Sphinx—Venice and the great War for German Nationality—Daring Policy of Prussia (1866)—Germany shows itself Hostile to the Enterprise of M. de Bismarck—Violent Opposition of the Chambers and the Prussian People—The *Perruques* of Potsdam and the Scruples of William I.—Secret Negotiations with Italy, and with the European Revolutionary Party—General Govone's Mission, and Treaty with the Cabinet of Florence (April, 1866)—Fresh Indecision on the Part of William I., and peaceful Manifestations in France—The Speech of Auxerre (May 6th)—The Battle of Sadowa (July 3rd)—Terrible Awakening at the Tuileries—Prince Gortchakof rejoices and meditates.

Thus was inaugurated, in the Polish and Danish questions, the first action of that mutual combination between the two Ministers of Russia and Prussia, which was to endure for so long and exercise so considerable and so disastrous an influence over the affairs of the Continent.

With the year 1863 begins the second period of the ministry of Prince Gortchakof, "his second manner," certainly more questionable than his first. To the French "cordiality," on the whole a moderate and a healthy one, succeeds the Prussian friendship, which assumes a far too absorbing and too passionate a form. During this second period, Alexander Mikhaïlovitch no longer preserves the calm reserve and the intelligent selfishness which made his fortune during his intimacy with Napoleon III.; he adopts all the opinions, maintains all the ideas of his powerful Prussian friend, but without, unfortunately, possessing his astonishing flexibility of mind, or his marvellous art of twisting and adapting himself to the situation.

Nothing, for instance, can equal the tact with which, when occasion demands it, M. de Bismarck can forget an unpleasant past,* and particularly the wrong he may have done to others, explaining everything away under the delightful name of a "misunderstanding."

This is the gentle term he has often publicly applied to his long and outrageous quarrels with the Parliament, and even to the war with Austria in 1866 (a slight misunderstanding which cost 40,000 lives); and it is

---

* And yet the Emperor William I. was not wrong in saying one day, to M. d'Arnim, that rancour was the dominant passion in M. de Bismarck's character! (*Pro nihilo*, "Vorgeschichte des Arnimschen Processes," p. 77.)—The following is a very characteristic maxim of M. de Bismarck's, written in a lady's album: "I sometimes forget, I never forgive!" . . .

impossible to refrain from admiring the affection, the enthusiasm even, with which he has at last inspired the worthy Lord John Russell, the statesman whom, among all others, he had the most ridiculed and ill-treated during the Danish negotiations.

As to his Polish quarrels in the same year (1863) with the Western Powers, he was all the more prompt to wipe them from his memory, as those Powers showed themselves conscious of having committed a great folly. He dictated to King William one of the politest answers, filled with tender souvenirs of Compiègne, in reply to a letter from Napoleon III. concerning the congress; and towards the close of the year he was on the most intimate terms with the Cabinet of the Tuileries on the subject of the Treaty of London, a treaty which had guaranteed the integrity of the Danish monarchy, and which M. Drouyn de Lhuys now qualified as an "impotent work." As for Austria, he soon granted her plenary indulgence for her Polish mistakes in the spring, and even for her far more culpable enterprise of the month of August, on the "Day of Princes," at Frankfort; and in the month of November he had already made her his companion and accomplice in the war of the Duchies. Far other was the conduct of Prince Gortchakof: he never could forgive France and Austria for their interference in the affairs of Poland, and rejected every offer of reconciliation. He no longer remained intimate with any other cabinet but that of Berlin, and his former colleague of Frankfort became his sole confidant and ally.

The famous maxim of 1856 underwent from that time an important modification; from 1863 the Russian Chancellor began to sulk as well as to meditate, and the Achæans had to pay dearly for this ill-temper of Achilles! The sulks of Alexander Mikhaïlovitch were nearly as fatal to Europe as the reveries of Napoleon III.

A vision—a very Midsummer Night's Dream—does the Napoleonic policy with regard to Germany now appear to us; a policy that was at once chimerical and yet reasonable, clever and yet foolish, having only worthy aims and yet accumulating nothing but ruin and disaster.

A splendid dream was one day dreamed in the Tuileries: Italy was to be united, Austria raised up again, Prussia rendered more homogeneous, Germany more satisfied, Europe regenerated, and France re-assured and glorious. All this depended only on one event—an event that was a certainty; on a battle fought and won by the Kaiserliks—those brave and tried warriors—against that Prussian *landwehr* which for half a century had not smelt powder.*

* The following is a specimen of what was being instilled into the minds of the French soldiers respecting the two German powers on the very eve of Sadowa: "The Prussian army, in which service is of very short duration, is nothing but a kind of *landwehr* school. It is a magnificent organisation on paper, but a very doubtful weapon of defence, and most useless during the first period of an offensive war. Austria, whose population numbers about thirty-seven millions of inhabitants, has a large and splendid army, which is far superior in its organisation to the Prussian or Russian armies. After France, she occupies the first rank as a military power."—*Course of Artillery at the Practical School of Artillery and Engineering at Metz*, 1864. In the beginning of 1866, it is true, the military attaché of the French Embassy at Berlin, M. de Clermont Tonnerre, drew the attention of his Government to the new Prussian arms—"*armes terribles.*" But even taking them into consideration, Prussia still seemed to have but a poor chance in a very unequal contest, whose issue could be in nowise doubtful.

And it was in this frail skiff, this "nutshell," as Puck in "The Midsummer Night's Dream" would have said, that the fortunes of France and of Cæsar were embarked! The whole world believed at that time in the immense superiority of Austria's army over that of her daring rival in Germany. No one admitted the possibility of a Prussian victory, still less of a victory as decisive and as annihilating as that of Sadowa. "That was," said M. Rouher later on, during a memorable sitting of the Legislative Body, "that was an event which Austria, which France, which every soldier, which every citizen, had considered as impossible; for it was universally believed that Austria would be victorious, and that Prussia would have to pay, and pay dearly, for her imprudence." This belief, so universal at that time, will remain in history as the sole excuse for Napoleon III.—as the sole palliation for the lamentable phantasmagoria which he introduced to the world in his speech at Auxerre in the month of May, 1866, but whose origin dates back to the convention of September, and to the first visit of M. de Bismarck to France after his Danish campaign, in the autumn of 1864.[*]

"I have at least one superiority over my conqueror," said the Emperor of Austria, Francis I., with subtle dignity to M. de Talleyrand, the negotiator of the peace of Presburg after the battle of Austerlitz. "I can re-enter my capital after so great a disaster; whereas your master, with all his genius, could scarcely

---

[*] See "Préliminaires de Sadowa;" also the instructive work of General La Marmora, "Un pó più di luce," Firenze, 1873.

do as much in a similar situation." This remarkable speech defines in the most striking manner the deep, the incurable vice of all Cæsarism. Not any more than for the victor of Austerlitz was it possible for Napoleon III. to accept a defeat : he was bound to *faire grand,* condemned to success and to prestige. Immediately after his misadventures and mistakes in the affairs of Poland, in those of Denmark, and in the matter of the congress, he had to think of a retaliation, to turn his attention north and south, and to " take up a position " in the convention of September, which should appear as the preface to a new and great work. He was isolated in Europe, embittered against England, awkwardly placed with regard to Russia, more than cold towards Austria ; and M. de Bismarck's visit to France, immediately after the convention concluded with the Turin Cabinet, caused an inward thrill of satisfaction. Evidently "something would be able to be done for Italy." Without ill-feeling, and utterly unprejudiced, the President of the Prussian Council came to renew the conversations begun two years ago during his short mission to Paris. He brought no fresh news ; he simply declared that his alliance with the Hapsburgs during the Danish war was a mere incident, and clearly showed his desire to retain for Prussia the countries recently taken possession of on the Elbe in the name of the German Confederation.

Beyond this, he did nothing but revert to the old theme of the inevitable and impending duel between Berlin and Vienna ; on the advantages that Italy might derive from it; on the benefit it would be to France if Prussia were better outlined and more securely situated, in which case she would naturally become the unfailing ally of France in every question of progress and of civilisation. Such confidences, coming from a minister who had just given proof of his importance in the Danish campaign, were received in a very different spirit than had been accorded to those in which he had indulged in 1862.

Without, as yet, giving him credit for any great depth of character, his hearers were agreed to recognise in him all the qualities of a useful man, a man of the future, whom it would be well for Italy to cultivate, whom France, on her side, would do well to watch, to urge forward, and to prompt. The leaders of Imperial democracy—first among them Prince Napoleon—were especially delighted with the prospects opened out before them. A distinguished member of this group, a diplomatist of renown, and whose very name inclined him towards the Italian cause, was drawn from his retreat, and placed at the head of the mission to Berlin, now promoted to the rank of an embassy. Another member of the *parti de l'action*, then equally at liberty, a former ambassador to Rome, was also recalled to the councils of the Empire, and, side by side with M. Rouher, was intended to form a "make-weight" to the somewhat antiquated ideas of M. Drouyn de Lhuys. Lastly, beyond the Alps, at Turin, a general well known for his Prusso mania had taken in hand the direction of political affairs on September 23rd. Each of these three personages—M. Benedetti, M. de La Valette, and General La Marmora—will have his part to fulfil in the great drama of 1866.

At this time, however (in the autumn of 1864), no plans were formed or even discussed. Nothing took place of more importance than a few confidences, a few private and desultory conversations, scarcely to be termed an exchange of ideas; but the impression which the Prussian minister carried away with him from this rapid trip to France was sufficiently favourable to induce him to issue that circular of December 24th, 1864, which was the first step in his subsequent undertaking against Austria. In this circular, M. de Bismarck touches for the first time on the question of the Duchies, which he well knew was a question of war. Six months before this, in the peremptory declaration made at the conference in London, Austria and Prussia had demanded "the re-union of the duchies of Schleswig and Holstein into a single state under the sovereignty of the hereditary prince of Augustenburg," and the Berlin Cabinet was then careful to add that this prince "was regarded in Germany as having the *greatest right* to the succession, and that his recognition by the Bund was in consequence a certainty; and that, moreover, he was assured of the certain votes of the great majority of the populations of the two provinces."

But very different to the above were the opinions held by the Prussian minister towards the close of the same year, shortly after his return from Paris. In a circular despatch addressed to the German Courts, the President of the German Council now declared (December 24th, 1864) that his mind was assailed by the most serious doubts touching the titles of the Duke of Augustenburg; that several important aspirants, such as the Princes of Oldenburg and of Hesse, had arisen during the interval;* that, amidst so many and such confused claims, he was puzzled; that his conscience was by no means certain of the right path; and that he felt it was necessary to pause and consult the jurists.

We know the splendid decision pronounced by these "jurists"—the syndics of the Crown—and we also know what conclusions were drawn from it by this "conscientious" minister.

"There were judges at Berlin," and they proved it by rejecting every one of the claimants, and declaring all their pretensions to be null and void; Hesse, Oldenburg, Brandenburg, Sonderburg-Augustenburg, were one and all without any just claim to the Schleswig-Holstein duchies; alone, the King of Denmark held any recognised right! But as the King of Denmark

---

* It is of some interest to notice, in passing, the circumstances under which these new candidates arose. Summoned by the conference in London to declare his pretensions, M. de Bismarck could not do otherwise than follow Austria's lead, and declare himself (May 28th, 1864) in favour of the Duke of Augustenburg. On the 2nd of June, when the conference met again (the telegraph had had time to work), the Russian Plenipotentiary declared most unexpectedly that the Emperor, his august master, "desiring to facilitate the impending arrangements in every way that lay in his power," had given up his eventual rights, as chief of the House of Holstein-Gortorp, to his relative, the Grand Duke of Oldenburg! On the 18th of June another relative of the Emperor Alexander II., Prince Frederick William of Hesse, came in his turn to lay his rights to the succession before the conference in London. This is an example of the numerous and discreet services which Prince Gortchakof rendered to his Prussian friend during the sad campaign of the Duchies.

had been forced by the war to abandon the provinces of the Elbe to the sovereigns of Austria and Prussia, M. de Bismarck concluded that these two sovereigns were at liberty to dispose of their "property" as it might seem fittest to them, and without any interference on the part of the Bund; and he demanded of the Emperor Francis Joseph that he should give up his share in the conquest for a compensation paid down in hard cash. This impudent demand was contained in a haughty and menacing despatch dated from Carlsbad, July 11th, 1865; from the very spot where the old King William was enjoying the hospitality of the Austrians during the watering season. For a short time everyone was on the alert. M. de Bismarck did not attempt to conceal the negotiations into which he had just entered with Italy; he said to M. de Gramont "that so far from dreading a war, he desired it above everything;" and shortly afterwards he even declared to M. de Pfordten, President of the Bavarian Council, "that Austria could not sustain a campaign—that it would require but a single blow, a single battle fought in Silesia, to bring the Hapsburgs to their senses."

In reality he was only feeling his way and reconnoitring. At this time he did not feel sufficiently sure of the Emperor Napoleon III. to risk any very great stake; and he also required time in which to persuade the pious Hohenzollern to pronounce the "God wills it" of a fratricidal war. He was forced to content himself with the convention of Gastein (August 14th, 1865), which was only a provisional arrangement, a first breach made in the rights of the Bund, and which operated as an indirect confirmation of the conclusions which he had drawn from the judgment pronounced by the famous syndics of the Crown. The same day on which M. de Bismarck signed this equivocal transaction at Gastein, he wrote as follows to his wife: " For some days I have not had a moment's leisure in which to write to you. Count Blome is here again, and we are doing our best to maintain peace, and stop up all the cracks in the edifice. The day before yesterday I devoted an entire day to hunting. I think I told you that on the first occasion I returned empty-handed from my expedition; this time I at any rate brought down a doe, but that was all I saw during the three mortal hours which I passed in prey to all sorts of insects, and while the eternal noise of the cascade overhead forced me to exclaim: *Petit ruisseau, laisse là ton murmure.** After all it was a splendid shot across the precipice; the animal fell from a height of several church-steeples dead into the torrent at my feet." It was also not a bad shot which brought down and totally disabled that cherished candidate of the Bund, the unhappy Augustenburg, and filled the Prussian game-bag with the little duchy of Lauenburg! The noise of this diplomatic hunting feat re-echoed loudly throughout Germany and France, and even Lord John Russell experienced a shock. The Secretary of State felt himself bound to join M. Drouyn de Lhuys in a very eloquent protestation against the conclusions de-

---

* A line of a German song.

termined upon at Gastein; and the British ironclads, which had kept out of the Baltic during the Danish campaign, now paid a visit of ceremony to the French fleet at Cherbourg; but that was the sum total of the demonstrations made by the two Western Powers, and M. de Bismarck was left to enjoy his triumphs in peace, and to wear the count's coronet which he had gained during the successful campaign of 1865.

May we be allowed to depart from the gravity of history and relate another incident which occurred at Gastein: a little sketch of life and manners which drew a great deal of attention upon him at the time, and even led to private explanations between the President of the Council and a devoted friend? And why should we not, if the letter of M. de Bismarck to M. André (de Roman) on the subject of Mademoiselle Pauline Lucca is one of the most curious pages of his private correspondence, if it illumines with a picturesque light the vast and denuded brow that William I. had just graced with a count's coronet! It appears that, in the midst of his political negotiations and his doe-hunts, M. de Bismarck had found time to have his photograph taken in a romantic attitude with Mademoiselle Lucca, the *prima donna* of the Royal Opera at Berlin. The photographs were a source of considerable scandal on the banks of the Spree; the heads of the "Cross party" were more especially shocked at the watering-place licence in which the former Levite of the Tabernacle, the fervent disciple of MM. Stahl and Gerlach, was indulging. M. André (de Roman) was kind enough to take upon himself the character of a modern Nathan, and, in an epistolary and confidential sermon, he sorrowfully spoke of the operatic Bathsheba, adding a few touching words on the duellistic reparation which the Prussian minister had wished to impose quite recently on the good Doctor Virchow, the wise and peaceful discoverer of *trichinæ*. M. André did not consider this to be the conduct of a true Christian; nor did he conceal the fact that his former friends were groaning in spirit at the non-appearance of their Eli at divine service, and were even very uneasy as to the state of his soul. To this tremendous lecture M. de Bismarck replied by the following confidential letter, which a fortunate indiscretion has since made public—a most characteristic letter, reminding us of those peculiarities of Cromwell, which have been more than once alluded to in these pages :—

"Dear André,*—Although my time is very limited I cannot deny myself the satisfaction of replying to a summons addressed to me by an honest heart, and in the name of Jesus Christ. I profoundly deplore that I should have caused any scandal among Christians holding the faith, but I am convinced that it is sometimes unavoidable in my position. I do not speak of the sections politically opposed to me, and who nevertheless reckon many Christians among them — people who are far in advance of me on the heavenly road,

---

* We have tried to preserve the edifying style of obscurity which characterises the original.

whom I have yet to oppose in matters which in their opinion, as in mine, are purely terrestrial. I will only deal with that which you yourself assert. You say, 'that nothing which is done or left undone in elevated spheres remains hidden.' Where is there a man in such a position who willingly or unwillingly does not cause a scandal of some sort or another? Again, your expression, 'does not remain hidden,' is not correct. Would to God that, outside of all the sins of which the world knows me guilty, I had not others for which I can only hope for pardon through my faith in the blood of Christ!"

"As a statesman, I think that I am too careful—I am even cowardly at times; and that because it is not so easy to discern, amid the entanglements placed before me, that light which springs from a perfect confidence in God. He who reproaches me for being a statesman devoid of conscience does me a wrong; he ought to begin by exposing his own conscience to a few trials in the same arena. As for the Virchow affair, I am long past that age in which one asks advice of flesh and blood; if I expose my life for a cause, I do it in the faith which I have fortified by long and painful conflict, and by fervent and humble prayers to God; that faith, no word of man can shake it; not even the word of a friend in the Lord, and a servant of his Church.

"It is not true that I never go to church. For the last seven months I have been either ill or absent from Berlin; who, then, has been able to take notice of my negligence? I confess most readily that I may have sometimes omitted to go, not so much from want of time as out of regard to my health, more especially during the winter; and I am quite ready to offer more circumstantial evidence to anyone who considers he possesses the vocation of being my judge in this matter. As for you, I know you will believe me without any further investigation. As for the Lucca photographs, you would perhaps be less severe in your judgment if you knew to what a mere accident they owe their origin. Besides, Madame Lucca, although a public singer, is a lady who has never been reproached, any more than myself, with any improper *liaisons*. Nevertheless, I should certainly have been careful to keep myself out of the range of the lens turned upon us, had I for a moment foreseen all the scandal my friends would have discovered in so simple an occurrence. You see, by the attention I give to the details of your letter, that I consider it to be well meaning, and that I do not think of placing myself above the judgment of those who share the same faith with myself; but I expect from your friendship, and from your Christian enlightenment, that you will recommend to others to be more indulgent and more charitable in their judgments in the future; believe me, we all stand in need of indulgence. I am among the crowd of sinners to whom the glory of God is wanting, but, with them, I do not despair that in His mercy He will not take away from me the staff of humble faith with which I seek my way amid the doubts and dangers of my position; this faith, however, does not make me deaf to the reproaches of my friends, nor impatient of their scornful, harsh judgments."

Let us lay aside the hair-shirt and knotted rope, and only see the diplomatist in his tunic and helmet—" the iron count " (*der eiserne graf*), as his fellow-countrymen soon called him. It is time for us to consider the feelings of France towards him at the time when, after having quitted the rocky valley of Gastein, he was preparing himself for a visit to the gentle sands of Biarritz, to salute the sphinx, to question, to divine, and—to cast it down !

In France, in the councils of the empire, the debates were every day becoming more and more lively between the ancients and moderns—between the zealous adherents of the "new right," and the partisans of a more circumspect and traditional policy, in proportion as the Austro-Prussian conflict became more accentuated and aggravated.

The more ardent among them would have insisted on a defensive and offensive alliance with Prussia. They pointed to the irresistible movement that was drawing Germany on to a complete union, and to the great advantages which France would reap if she encouraged instead of opposing this movement, and so drew to her, in the bonds of an eternal gratitude, the Piedmont of Germany as she had drawn to her that of the Peninsula.

As the passionate friends of Italy, and the still more passionate enemies of Austria, whom they considered the bulwark of reactionary feeling, of legitimacy, and of the temporal power, they saw in the kingdom of Frederick the Great the incontestable representative of civilisation, and trembled at the thought of its being exposed to certain defeat in an unequal combat with the Kaiserliks. According to their opinion, it only required the co-operation of France, Prussia, and Italy to ensure the cause of progress, and to settle Europe on a new and immovable basis. Then again, why should not Belgium become the legitimate reward of the French efforts in favour of Germany, just as Savoy had done after the formation of the kingdom of Italy? And why reject such a combination, by means of which each of the three nations principally representing modern ideas on the Continent might complete their respective unity?

Very different on these topics was the opinion of the "ancients," of the statesmen of the old school, of a complete political group, whose most authoritative and clear-sighted representative in the cabinet was M. Drouyn de Lhuys.

Setting aside at once all weak delusions regarding Belgium as being an inevitable source of war with England, they affirmed that it would be impossible to find any compensation for France to equal the damage she would sustain by the union of Germany. Without overlooking the German aspirations towards a Federal reform, and towards a more united and more homogeneous constitution, they asked themselves wherein the necessity lay for France to hasten such a work, and whether in every case it would not be more desirable that such a transformation should be accomplished by the more enlightened and peaceful classes, by the Diet, even by Austria—at all times a respecter of acquired right and of the lesser princes—rather than by a power whose ruling principles were of the military, bureaucratic, and centralisation order. And was not this also the prevailing opinion on the opposite shores of the Rhine, the opinion of dynasties as well as of parliaments, of princes as well as of the people? and had not the pretensions of Prussia to appropriate to herself all profit derived from the conquest of Denmark caused universal dissatisfaction?

Only the Italian and French press continued to speak of the "Piedmontese Mission" of the Hohenzollerns; on the banks of the Main and the Elbe everyone else scouted the idea of this so-called mission; and even the discredited *National-Verein*, while continuing to cherish hopes of a "Germany united by means of a Prussian needle," nevertheless repudiated M. de Bismarck, and declared him to be unworthy of undertaking such a holy cause.

As to the danger of Prussia being defeated in the contest, and so rendering the House of Hapsburg all-powerful in Germany, there was a very simple way to avoid such an eventuality, by refusing all assistance to the Berlin Government in the enterprise she was contemplating. However bold M. de Bismarck might be, he still was not thought capable of defying Austria and her allies of the Bund, in the face of a formal veto pronounced by the French Government, which would at the same time deprive him of any hope of assistance from Italy.*

The line of conduct to be pursued under such circumstances seemed, therefore, to be clearly marked out and easy to follow. Without interfering directly in the affairs of Germany, without hurting German susceptibilities, an impassable barrier might be raised in opposition to Prussian ambition. All that was to be done was to maintain the *statu quo*. Such a policy would certainly receive the warmest support from England, and would encourage Austria and the secondary States in their resistance. No doubt this would set aside the Venetian question, but the peace of Europe and the grandeur of France were worth more than " the pearl of the Adriatic ;" and, besides, it was not forbidden to hope that the city of the lagoons might profit by the progress of time and the increasing good understanding between France and Austria. Remaining silent in the midst of these contradictory debates, preferring to soar above the passions and agitations of his surroundings in all the sereneness of a calm and meditative mind, the Emperor Napoleon III. was slowly bringing a project

---

* " Whatever may be the opinions held at the present time, if France had opposed these proceedings (the treaty of Italy with Prussia), we could not have encountered the risk of finding ourselves face to face with an Austro-French alliance. Prussia was as anxious as ourselves, perhaps even more so, about the attitude which France might assume in the case of a war against Austria, undertaken by the combined forces of Italy and Prussia."—*La Marmora*, " Un pò più di luce," p. 80. Three days before the signature of the secret treaty with Italy, M. de Bismarck said to General Govone, " All this, understand, if France is agreeable, for if she objects, nothing can be done."—*Despatch of General Govone to General La Marmora, April 5th*, 1866, *ibid.*, p. 139.

to perfection which in his eyes would answer the difficulties on both sides of the disputed question; and which, moreover, would carry out the maxim which he was instilling at that time into the mind of his Minister for Foreign Affairs—*inertia sapientia!* Italy was naturally more dear to him than to M. Drouyn de Lhuys; to him it was a passion, a relic of his youth; and even the Empress Eugenie had become an eager partisan for the liberation of Venice since the accession of M. de La Valette to the Ministry, and also since the day on which M. de Nigra had composed certain couplets full of grace and allusions to a gondola which she had caused to be constructed for the lake at Fontainebleau. No less fatal and inveterate was Louis Napoleon's love for the land of Blücher and Scharnhorst: "the great destiny" of the monarchy of Brandenburg was one of the articles of his cosmopolitan faith. "*The geographical situation of Prussia is badly defined!*" were still his words in the following year in a too-much-forgotten document.*

He certainly had no intention of destroying the Empire of the Hapsburgs, nor of extending that of the Hohenzollern from the Sund to the Adriatic, as might be imagined by the politicians possessed of but one idea, and the "know-nothings" of the principle of nationality. Keenly appreciative of the use of logic in political affairs, and in that (in that alone,

* Letter of the Emperor to M. Drouyn de Lhuys, June 11th, 1866. It is from this letter, which was solemnly laid before the Legislative Body, that the following quotations are taken.

perhaps) displaying a really French disposition, the former prisoner of Ham would willingly have attempted the construction of a new Prussia, essentially Protestant, side by side with a new Austria, traditionally Catholic, in the heart of Germany; leaving the secondary States in a kind of intermediary position, and differing both in their religion and in their politics. A Prussia, enlarged and amplified on the Elbe and the Baltic, and thus rendered stronger and more "homogeneous to the north," seemed to him to be a useful and almost necessary combination with regard to Russia; and it was only just that in return for the new and vast Protestant territories which she was about to acquire, the monarchy of Frederick II. should give up Silesia, a Catholic country, and the ancient patrimony of the Hapsburgs; and that she should also give up the Catholic provinces of the Rhine, as being situated outside of her natural sphere.

"Thus Austria would still maintain her powerful position in Germany," and more especially her power as a great Catholic state; and the acquisition of Silesia would amply compensate the Emperor Francis Joseph for the Venetian province which he would then give up to King Victor Emmanuel. As for the secondary States, several of the smaller and more useless principalities should be abolished and annexed to them, perhaps even the Rhine provinces which were to be taken from Prussia might be added to them as a new member of the Bund; and, at any rate, "a more complete union, a more powerful organisation, and a more important position," would be assured them, such as the leaders of the Wurtzburg party, MM. de Beust, de Pfordten, and de Dalwigk, were incessantly demanding.

Yet, strange to say, in the midst of these vast projects which embraced the Continent, and were intended to satisfy " the legitimate wants " of Italy, of Prussia, of Austria, and of the German Confederation, the only question which remained obscure and was never fully realised in the mind of the French sovereign was that of the compensation which he might demand, in return for this universal setting to rights, on behalf of his own country. "I dare not touch on the Belgian question : it would be," he very honestly said, "an act of robbery."* "Nor did he delude himself as to the possibility of annexing any important German territory; he more frequently stopped at the simple rectification of his frontiers on the banks of the Sarre, and towards the Palatinate, and at a neutralisation of the line of German fortresses on the Rhine.

Reduced even to such modest proportions, his aim did not appear to him to be less worthy of being ardently pursued, seeing how great a moral satisfaction France would derive from the accomplishment of her work in Italy, and in a rational settlement of German affairs.

Moreover, that which flattered his naturally generous and vaguely humane instincts, was the hope

---

* He made use of this expression more than once, and in tones of conviction, in the councils of his ministers before 1866. It was only at a later period, after Sadowa, that he gave way for a moment to the *parti de l'action* in its views respecting Belgium, and gave his consent to the concealed negotiations of the month of August, 1866. See further on, chapter vii.

of reaping considerable benefits for his country—for the whole universe, indeed — without drawing his sword or shedding a drop of blood, "by moral strength alone," by the ascendency of the name of France. He was resolved to maintain an attitude of "attentive neutrality," and only to quit it in the extreme case of one of the belligerents becoming too completely victorious, and attempting to menace "the equilibrium, or alter the map of Europe to its own advantage." He proclaimed this loudly and on several occasions, priding himself on such a "disinterested" policy—a policy of a very strange nature, nevertheless, and one that, according to the very judicious speech of Prince Napoleon, declared itself beforehand as *hostile to the victor*! "You have changed the address of your letter," said the conqueror of Austerlitz, with subtle raillery, to the Prussian envoy, when he brought him the felicitations of his sovereign. The nephew of Napoleon I. placed himself in a position that would render any change of address impossible, and would render the yet unknown victor antagonistic to him. It is true that he thought he already knew him, that, in unison with the rest of the world, he assigned that post to the Emperor of Austria, and that he thought it wise to adopt some preventive measures towards him.

Even should the army of William I. show itself to be far superior to the general opinion which the world held of it—and more clear-sighted on this point than his surroundings, he fully admitted the possibility of such an eventuality—he only foresaw in this case a long and fatiguing contest which would exhaust both combatants, and would permit him all the more easily to intervene as military judge and protector of the right of nations. He always hoped to be able, at his own time and convenience, to pronounce a word of peace, of equity, and of equilibrium, convinced that his word would be listened to.

The important point now was that Prussia should declare war, and in order to encourage her to do so, her alliance with Italy must be insured. It was also needful to avoid entering into any unseasonable debates with the Berlin Cabinet on the subject of compensations and combinations to come; the slightest insistence on these topics might ruffle the patriotic sentiments of William I., cool his warlike ardour, and crush in its shell a whole world of great events, *novus rerum ordo!* Better to ask for nothing, promise nothing, and compromise nothing. What object, indeed, was there in demanding the promissory notes of a bankrupt, in taking sureties from one to whom destiny seemed to assure so little, and whom, in all probability, he would soon have to protect and defend against the too severe conditions which his Austrian conqueror would most probably impose upon him?

However complicated and specious the strategy imagined by the French Emperor may have been, there is not the slightest doubt that M. de Bismarck saw through it from the very beginning—that he divined it, foresaw it in some way, even before it was completely fixed in the mind of its author. We have a most striking proof of the truth of this.

In the month of August, 1865, at the time the first conferences hostile to Austria took place between Prussia and Italy, conferences brusquely interrupted by the armistice at Gastein, M. de Nigra wrote to General La Marmora, inspired, evidently, by the observations of his Prussian colleague in Paris, Count Goltz: "The Berlin Cabinet has no wish that, war being once declared, France should start up, like the Neptune of Virgil, to dictate peace, lay down conditions, or convoke a congress in Paris."*

Thus all is foreseen in these few lines written anterior to Biarritz, even to the congress which a Napoleon III. naturally would not be able to abstain from proposing, and which he actually did propose in the month of May, 1866. "The difficulty consists, therefore," pursued M. de Nigra, in his despatch, "in obtaining from France a promise of absolute neutrality. Will, and can, the Emperor Napoleon give such a promise? and *will he give it in writing, as Prussia desires?*"

M. de Bismarck was certainly not able to obtain this promise of absolute neutrality while at Biarritz (October, 1865), and still less was there mention made there of any engagement in writing; but he learnt there from august lips that Italy was right in "seeking to complete her unity," and that she would no doubt seize the first favourable opportunity of doing so; that France was resolved to respect Germany, and not to interfere with her "national aspirations." Unless the map of Europe were to be altered to her detri-

---

* Despatch of M. de Nigra, August 8th, 1865.—*La Marmora*, p. 45.

ment, France would remain neutral, and her neutrality would not fail to be favourable to any combination by which the Italian cause would benefit.

It is curious to note a reminiscence of the Biarritz interview in a remark made six months later by M. de Bismarck to General Govone, to the effect "that without considering any profit he might derive from it, and only considering it from the standpoint of his principles, the Emperor would more readily approve of a war of German nationality than of the war for the duchies of the Elbe!"

That which, during his sojourn in Biarritz, must especially have impressed the sagacious Prussian, was the hold which the Italian cause had on the mind of Napoleon; there was the very key of the position, the answer of the sphinx; and the certainty of this compensated the Prussian minister for many other disturbing doubts, and made him overlook many reticences on the part of his taciturn Majesty.*

In a certain sense, he was able even to congratulate himself on the reticence observed towards him, on the care which was taken to avoid entering into any detailed discussion; it kept him free, on his side, from any precise engagement, from any premature offers; it permitted him to confine himself to generalities, to take fantastic flights through space and time. He spoke of Belgium and a part of Switzerland as being the necessary and legitimate complements to

* It was on his return from Biarritz that M. de Bismarck made use of the following significant language to M. de Nigra: "If Italy did not exist, we should have had to invent her."—*La Marmora*, p. 59.

French unity; of the joint action of France and Germany in the cause of progress and humanity; of a future combination between Paris, Berlin, and Florence, and even London and Washington, that should regulate the destinies of Europe—nay, those of the whole world; that would give back to Russia her true vocation in Asia, and to Austria her mission of civilisation on the Danube. How many times on those Biscayan sands, now so historical, Napoleon III. was to be seen pacing slowly to and fro, leaning on the arm of Prosper Mérimée, while at a respectful distance M. de Bismarck followed alongside, gesticulating, perorating, and generally receiving as his answer a look half dim, half incredulous; and how painfully our thoughts revert now to that singular group—to the romantic Cæsar, the Cæsarian romancer, and the terrible realist, who, then so obsequious to his imperial host, was four years later sternly to assign him to the prison of Wilhelmshöhe!

From time to time Napoleon III. would, by a furtive pressure on the arm of the author of "Colomba," indicate his amusement at the fertile imagination of this diplomatist, this representative of a more than problematic Power, and smile to hear him lightly speak of the parcelling out of Europe and the distribution of kingdoms. "He is mad!" was his whispered commentary on one occasion to his companion; but before condemning an opinion so bitterly expiated in later years, we should do well to read an extract from a despatch written in the following year by General Govone: "In mentioning M. de

Bismarck to me, M. Benedetti told me that he was a mad kind of diplomatist;"* and M. Benedetti was careful to add that he had known his man for a long time, and had closely followed his political career during the last fifteen years. And, indeed, was it not necessary to be somewhat of a madman to possess that little grain of folly which Molière attributes to all great men, and which Boerhaave maintains to be present in every great mind,† to have been capable of launching the monarchy of Brandenburg on such an eminently perilous adventure as that of 1866 ? The minister of William I. admitted the fact, when in Paris, that perhaps he was about to encounter a second Olmütz; and his biographers cite a still more characteristic saying of his : "That death on the scaffold, under certain circumstances, was neither the worst nor the most dishonourable exit from life." From a diplomatic point of view his only assurance lay in the deep love of Napoleon III. for the Italian cause; and after, as before Biarritz, "the Neptune of Virgil" was always rising up before him, with a threatening expression, and about to pronounce his *quos ego*. War once declared, France might always dictate terms of peace, lay down conditions, and convoke a congress.

The great object was, therefore, not to give Napoleon's benevolent neutrality time to undergo these inevitable changes ; a blow must be struck, and struck quickly and well—a blow that should dictate

* Despatch of General Govone, April 6th, 1866.—*La Marmora*, p. 139.
† "Est aliquid delirii in omni magno ingenio."—*Boerhaave*.

peace in Vienna and respect in Paris. And this blow must be dealt by the hand of victory. Now, besides that in all earthly matters are found indifferently fortune and misfortune, and that "Almighty God is capricious," according to a singular expression of M. de Bismarck, uttered on a most solemn occasion;* up to what point could he reckon on an army, formed during the last few years, and that never, any more than its chiefs, had gone through a great war? It is a most extraordinary circumstance, and one fruitful of much astonishment to coming generations, that of the two eminent men who took upon themselves the frightful responsibility of the coming war, neither had ever held any command of importance, nor had made their names illustrious on any field of battle.

Previous to 1864, the only campaign in which General von Moltke had ever taken part was that in Syria, between the Turks and the Egyptians. In 1864 he had carried arms against his native land in that invasion of Denmark which was certainly not calculated to produce Turennes or Bonapartes. General von Roon had joined a "party of observation" in 1832, to watch the French besieging Antwerp, and since then had only distinguished himself by his books on military geography.

"From all that we have heard from the officers," writes General Govone from Berlin, April 2nd, 1866, "we think that the army is not enthusiastic about the war against Austria; on the contrary, there is a con-

---

* At the very moment of the commencement of hostilities. Despatch of M. de Barral, June 15th, 1866.—*La Marmora*, p. 332.

siderable amount of Austrian sympathy in its ranks. I have no doubt that war once declared the army will rouse itself and do its duty bravely, but at present its mood is neither a stimulant nor a support to the policy M. de Bismarck is so anxious to make popular." *

As to public opinion in Germany—as to the national sentiments of the fair-haired sons of Arminius —the policy of M. de Bismarck, far from finding in them a stimulant and a support, found only repugnance and condemnation.

It required all the Napoleonic *idéologie* to see in the contest that was about to begin " a great war for German nationality;" it required all the blindness of the official and democratic press in France to compare the work of M. de Bismarck in Prussia with that of M. de Cavour in the Peninsula.

German nationality was not being either oppressed or menaced in any quarter; none of the States of the Bund were oppressed by foreign dominion; the reigning houses of Hanover, Saxony, Wurtemberg, Bavaria, &c., were indigenous, antique, and glorious dynasties, popular and liberal; the greater number of these States were in the enjoyment of a constitutional and parliamentary system unknown in Berlin; the towns of Frankfort, Hamburg, Lübeck, and Bremen were even republics! Now that success has obscured not only the public conscience, but even the very memory of the present generation, and that some pitiful historic philosophy is always at hand to justify

* Despatch of General Govone, April 2nd, 1866.—*La Marmora*, p. 131.

the present by falsifying the past, every one is ready to recognise the "providential" and irresistible movement which drew Germany on towards a Prussian union, and even to join M. de Bismarck in calling the campaign of 1866 "a simple misunderstanding." The truth is, that the campaign of 1866 was nothing less than a civil war, a fratricidal contest, the thought of which was repudiated by the Prussian people, and whose author they cursed on the very eve of Sadowa.

On the eve of Sadowa the principal cities of the kingdom—Cologne, Magdeburg, Stettin, Minden, &c.—sent addresses to the sovereign in favour of peace and condemnatory of "the fatal policy of the Cabinet;" and the powerful corporation of Kant's city of Königsberg actually decided to discontinue the illuminations on the king's birthday.

Immediately after his arrival in Berlin, General Govone wrote as follows: "Not only the upper, but also the middle classes, are averse to the war. This aversion is palpable in the popular journals; and I cannot detect any hatred of Austria. Moreover, although the Chamber does not enjoy any great popularity or prestige, its debates continue to increase the number of M. de Bismarck's enemies." Two months later, when hostilities were about to begin, he wrote: "Unfortunately, the public spirit of Prussia does not rouse itself in any marked fashion, even in the face of a situation so decisive, so full of vital importance for the country.*

* Despatches of General Govone, April 2nd and May 22nd, 1866.—*La Marmora*, pp. 131, 245.

It is true that none of these obstacles were of a nature to shake the Prussian Prime Minister in his resolution, nor to turn him from the path which he had marked out for himself. His real difficulties he met at the court itself; they were really caused by the *perruques* of Potsdam, more especially by his sovereign; and in more than one circumstance he might well have exclaimed with a certain cardinal, "that the cabinet of the king and his *petit-coucher* gave him more trouble than the whole of Europe."

In spite of William I.'s belief in his "mission from on high," and in spite of his strong desire to retain, at any price, his good harbour of Kiel, he could not regard a contest with the venerated House of Hapsburg in any other light than that of a last expedient, which ought not to be brought to bear until every amicable effort had been exhausted. In this doubtful position his views were very similar to those of Napoleon, and he infinitely preferred the petty war for the Duchies to "the great war for German nationality;" but that which was, above all, repugnant to his soul, was the idea of a compact with Italy; of a genuine offensive and defensive alliance, instead of a "generical" treaty, bearing the vague title of an "alliance of friendship," and only destined, as he was at first made to believe, to make Austria reflect and bring about a composition. He, the loyal Hohenzollern, to fight with a Hapsburg, and partly on account of a foreigner !—he, the Lord's anointed, the old warrior of the Holy Alliance, to become the

o

brother-in-arms of a Victor Emmanuel, that representative of revolution, that usurper, who had overthrown so many legitimate princes, besieged and dethroned his own nephew, and placed by his side, in the royal carriages, Garibaldi in his red shirt! These faintings of the spirit and remorseful feelings were really sincere, and it took all M. de Bismarck's marvellous art to cure these syncopes of the "mission," and to operate successfully on these tumours of the conscience.

"There is my doctor!" said the old Prussian monarch, one day, to a Russian princess who was congratulating him on his health; and he pointed to his minister.*

The difficulties of *drawing on the king*, of triumphing over his *prejudices*, over his *antique ideas*, and his *legitimate scruples*, made up the list of M. de Bismarck's daily toil, and were incessantly on his lips during the confidential interviews of the spring of 1866, as we are able to gather from the invaluable reports which General Govone has fortunately preserved for futurity.

When we study these reports, as well as others which General La Marmora has given to the public, we seem to have unfolded before us a comedy in some hundred acts, all very little to the honour of human nature; and we are forced to ask ourselves who are the better masters in brazen duplicity—the grandsons of Machiavelli or the heirs of the Teutonic order? It is, however, amusing to watch—to employ the in-

* George Hesekiel, iii., p. 271.

genious expression of the Italian negotiator—the way in which the southern viper essays to bite the northern charlatan, and the charlatan essays to tread down the viper.*

The most curious and the most instructive part of these documents is, perhaps, that which shows us what an enormous number of novelties M. de Bismarck was able to teach his royal master in the short space of a few months, and also what a vast number of things he was able to make him forget. One of the most remarkable cases of this forgetfulness was most decidedly when the word of honour of a certain august personage was given in June, 1866, to the Emperor Francis Joseph, *that there had been no treaty signed with Italy*,† though at that very moment a treaty offensive and defensive, duly drawn up and signed on the 8th of April by the respective plenipotentiaries, ratified by the king of Italy in Florence on the 14th, and subsequently ratified on the 20th by the king of Prussia at Berlin—had been in existence for more than two months.

Besides uniting himself to official Italy, the minister of William I. was equally careful to win the friendship of that subterranean Italy which lurked and plotted beneath the throne of the youthful monarchy; and General La Marmora complains several times in his

* "... E la vipera avra morsicato il ciarlatano." Despatch of General Govone, March 15th, 1866.—*La Marmora*, p. 88.

† It was Queen Augusta who stated this in a letter to the Emperor of Austria, saying that she had received the word of honour of her royal husband to that effect. See the curious despatch of M. de Nigra, June 12th, 1866, as well as General La Marmora's telegram of the same day.—*La Marmora*, pp. 305, 310.

interesting work "of the intimate and cordial relations existing between Count Usedom, the Prussian minister at Florence, and several members of the *parti de l'action*, whose ill-judged advice he too often followed."

In the meantime, the Prussian consul at Bucharest held in his hands (February, 1866) the threads of a conspiracy that was to end in the overthrow of Prince Couza, and bring considerable gain to the Government of Berlin. " Liberalism is child's play, and easily checked; but Revolution is a power which one must know how to employ," was the saying of the knight of the Mark when in Paris, and he lost no time in proving the truth of his two maxims. We know that his intercourse with Mazzini continued even long after Sadowa,* and the engagements entered into by the Magyar chiefs with Prussia in 1866 have weighed (and continue to do so) more heavily than is generally supposed on the foreign policy of the Hapsburgs.

It was in the consultations of the revolutionary party that the fantastic campaign was first thought of which M. d'Usedom sought to force on General La Marmora in his famous despatch of June 17th.† He urged him to commence a "thorough" campaign, to outflank the Quadrilateral—to skirt the shores of the Adriatic, and to penetrate Hungary, which would

---

* After the death of the great Italian agitator, the Florentine journals published his letters to M. de Bismarck during 1868-69. Foreseeing a war between France and Germany, Mazzini suggests the overthrow of Victor Emmanuel should the latter become the ally of the Emperor Napoleon III.

† It will be of importance to observe that the strategic portion of M. d'Usedom's note was almost a *literal copy* of one of Mazzini's articles published in the *Dovere* of Genoa, May 26th, 1866.

rise to a man at the very name of Garibaldi; "we should thus deal Austria a blow which would strike, not her extremities, but her heart."

As to the attempt of forming a legion composed of deserters from the Austrian army under the command of the refugee general Klapka, the Prussian Premier affirmed, in the presence of the Chambers at Berlin, in his celebrated discourse of January, 1874, that he had energetically repulsed all such offers at the beginning of the war. "It was only after the battle of Sadowa, at the moment when Napoleon III., in a telegraphic despatch, intimated the possibility of his intervention, that, in self-defence, I did not order, but merely tolerated, the formation of the Hungarian legion." Unfortunately, the dates by no means tally with the German Chancellor's declarations.

The battle of Sadowa took place on July 3rd; but it was on the 12th of June that M. de Bismarck made known to the Italian Government that he had definitely accepted the assistance of the Slavonic and Hungarian deserters,* and the fact remains that long before Sadowa, even before the beginning of the war, the Prussian Government had had recourse to means which, to use the Chancellor's own expressions, would "excite the Dalmatian and Magyar regiments of Austria to revolt and desertion."

Neither must we forget to mention that, while treating secretly with Mazzini and M. Klapka, the minister of William I. was openly denouncing the

---

* See M. d'Usedom's notes of June 12th and 17th, as well as Count Barral's despatch of June 15th.—*La Marmora*, pp. 316, 331, 345—348.

Jacobin spirit of the House of Hapsburg: "The King, our august master," so ran a Prussian despatch of January 26th, 1866, "is grievously affected by the sight of the anti-monarchical and revolutionary tendencies which are being displayed (in the duchies of the Elbe) under the protection of the Austrian eagle. If Vienna can witness unmoved the transformation of a country hitherto distinguished by its conservative sentiments into a hotbed of revolutionary agitation, we, on our side, cannot, and will not, do so."

It was thus, in the midst of similar underhand devices, of more or less regular negotiations, of preparations for war, of a continual exchange of notes, of daily contests with the Chambers and with the *perruques* of the court, that the President of the Council passed the first six months of 1866, and rarely has any statesman had to pass through a more troublous or more bewildering period. The tide of events sometimes carried him towards the shore, sometimes carried him out to sea, and flung him back farther than ever, as it seemed, from the goal of his wishes. For instance, the revolution in Roumania, and the acclamation of the Hohenzollern prince by the people of Bucharest, was a great stroke of good fortune; for this incident brusquely closed a door through which, according to the opinion of more than one politician of the time, the Venetian question might have gone its way in peace;* and it was

---

* In a despatch of March 1st, 1866, M. de Nigra informs General La Marmora that, agreeably to his instructions, he had attempted to open the question of exchanging the Danubian Principalities for Venice. He had set

French influence which had contributed to install the young Prussian prince on the banks of the Danube!

Immediately afterwards, however, M. de Bismarck was aroused from his state of security by vague rumours of conferences taking place between Austria and France respecting Venice. He took advantage of them to induce the king to sign the secret treaty of April 8th with the Florentine Government; but soon after the offer of disarmament made by the Viennese Cabinet, the debates in the *Corps Législatif* and the manifestations of public opinion in France, which were more and more favourable to the cause of peace, brought about a desperate state of stagnation, and infused fresh courage into the Austrian sympathisers at the court of William I. The Emperor Napoleon III. then rendered a signal service to the Prussian minister by setting the flagging political machine again in motion; he made his speech of Auxerre on May 6th, in which he threw a scornful defiance at the treaties of 1815. This, however, did not prevent him from utterly routing all M. de Bismarck's plans by the sudden proposition of a congress, and, under the shock of this fresh incident, which seemed to compromise everything, M. de Bismarck spoke, for the first time, of compensations for France. "I am far less German than Prussian," said he to General Govone; "I should have no difficulty in giving up to France all the territory which lies

forth the advantages which this termination to the question would have for England and France, who would thus behold the peaceful accomplishment of the two programmes of the Crimean and Italian wars. The minister adds that Napoleon III. seemed struck with the idea.— *La Marmora,* p. 119.

between the Moselle and the Rhine, but the king would have the greatest scruples on this point."*

Of course he would have demanded in return from the French Government their active co-operation in the war—a demand which would not have suited the views of Napoleon III., and which public opinion in France would have made it impossible to listen to. " The congress and the peace," wrote M. Benedetti † on May 29th, " would completely upset all the projects of M. de Bismarck, and that on the very eve, as he supposes, of their realisation. He is not one of those minds who delude themselves easily, and he feels convinced that, brought face to face with the powers assembled in conference, his ambitious policy would be checked, and perhaps annulled . . . He also fears to facilitate by his absence (in attending the congress in Paris) the success of the occult influences which have never ceased to attempt the reconciliation of the two great German sovereigns. Were he to absent himself, the king might be prevailed upon to consent to an interview with the Emperor of Austria, and it is of importance that he should keep watch in person over all the avenues to the palace. His fears in this respect are so keen that he intends to follow the king on the campaign in case war should be declared . . ."

Meanwhile, he learned that fresh negotiations had been entered into between France and Austria on the subject of Venice, and that in another direction the king was, unknown to him, making friendly offers to

---

* Despatch of General Govone, June 3rd, 1866.—*La Marmora*, p. 275.

† "My Mission in Prussia," pp. 125, 129.

the Emperor Francis Joseph of an amicable arrangement. William I. still preferred the little question of the Duchies to the great war for German nationality.

It is almost possible to question what must have been, at this time, the state of mind of the minister, who for several months past had been complaining to Count Barral, the Italian plenipotentiary at Berlin, of the treachery of his agents in London, Florence, and Paris. He, moreover, had thought his life in danger, ever since the attempt made on his person on May 7th, and was not without uneasiness concerning his sojourn in Paris during the congress which he was to attend, and which he dreaded for so many other reasons. " He no longer goes out unaccompanied," writes Count Barral, "and French detectives are to meet him on the frontier, and escort him throughout his entire stay."*

The journey never took place, as we know. Prussia, to use the expression of M. d'Usedom, was "saved from the congress," and Prince Gortchakof had no small share in the work of salvation.

Always ready with his friendship, he was the first to consider that the Austrian reservations † would leave the congress no "practical aim," thus giving the signal for a general dispersion. From that time M. de Bismarck set himself to "work the mind of his royal master," and finished by removing his very last scruple. " His Majesty" (telegraphs Count

---

* Telegrams of Count Barral, April 7th and June 1st, 1866.—*La Marmora*, pp. 141, 266.

† Telegram of M. de Launay, from St. Petersburg, June 1st, 1866.—*La Marmora*, p. 266. We can also see, in the same work, with what alacrity M. de Bismarck seized this opinion of the Russian chancellor's, and transmitted it by telegraph to the various Cabinets.

Barral, May 23rd, from Berlin) "was deeply touched by the situation, and spoke of it with great tears in his eyes." A fortnight later (June 8th), the king no longer wept, " but there was still a sadness in his voice, indicative of the feelings of a resigned man, who has come to an unavoidable but unwished-for decision. His Majesty tells me that he is fully convinced of the justice of his cause. 'I have a clear conscience,' he said, laying his hand on his heart, and apparently much moved; 'I have been for a very long time accused of being led by ambitious motives to undertake this war, but now the whole world knows who is the aggressor.'"*

"I shall return through Vienna or through Munich, or I shall charge with the last squadron—with the squadron that never comes back," said M. de Bismarck to a foreign ambassador at the moment of leaving Berlin with the staff, June 30th, 1866. Two days later he was already at Gitschin, on the field yet reeking with the fumes of a great battle. "I have just arrived," he writes to his wife; "the ground is yet covered with corpses, horses, and arms. Our victories are much greater than we at first believed. . . . Send me some French novels to read, but not more than one at a time, and may God have you in his keeping!"

This was written on the 2nd of July, 1866. The morrow was the day of Sadowa—the morrow all Germany was at the feet of this singular amateur of French romances, and the Emperor Napoleon III. was painfully awakened from his romance—from his long

---

* Telegrams of M. de Barral.—*La Marmora*, pp. 218, 294.

humanitarian dream. Like Titania, in "A Midsummer-Night's Dream," imperial France suddenly perceived that, possessed by some inconceivable hallucination, she had caressed a monster.

While so many terrible and marvellous events were taking place in the arena of the world, Russia continued to sulk and to meditate — to meditate in a perpetual adoration of Prussia. We seek in vain for any trace of her influence in events which yet so closely concerned her interests, her family alliances, her ancient traditions. "As I am on the Russian topic," said M. Benedetti, writing to his chief in the spring of 1866, "allow me to mention that I have always remarked, and not without surprise, the indifference with which the St. Petersburg Cabinet has regarded, from the very first, the pretensions of Prussia and the probability of a war between the two great German powers. Nor have I been less impressed by the *constant security* in which I have always found M. de Bismarck indulging with regard to the attitude and the intentions of the Empire of the North"... Russia remained silent in 1865 during the crisis of Gastein; in the month of May, 1866, she only accepted the invitation to the congress in order to be the first to despair of its utility and to discourage the other powers from attending it; she was absent from the deliberations of Nikolsburg and Prague, and left to France the task of exerting herself there on behalf of the south of Germany and of Saxony; she even delegated to her the honour of stipulating one poor little clause in favour of unhappy Denmark, the country of her future empress.

For one moment, it is true, M. d'Oubril, the Russian ambassador at Berlin, a diplomatist of the old school, showed himself greatly alarmed at the conquests of the Hohenzollerns. He was recalled in haste to St. Petersburg, "and came back, after an absence of a few weeks, totally reassured, and affecting an amount of satisfaction that was not dimmed for a single instant either by the reverses of the German princes allied to the House of Russia, or by the development which Prussia was giving to her military power."*

Prince Gortchakof did not sacrifice at the ancient altars of the rights of nations and of European equilibrium; he did not share in certain prejudices concerning "the union that ought to exist between all conservative interests;" and his soul was too lofty to be jealous of a good neighbour. Besides, had he not also "vanquished Europe" three years before, in the memorable Polish campaign? In vain might august personages, princesses, and grand-duchesses say, with the women in Holy Scripture, that Saul had killed his thousands, but David his tens of thousands; in vain point to their spoliated relatives and their confiscated inheritances. Alexander Mikhaïlovitch was not envious of the laurels of his former colleague of Frankfort, now become Chancellor of the Northern Confederation. He rejoiced to see Austria well punished and France thoroughly mortified; further than this, he considered that there was but little difference on the face of the globe, only that there was one more great chancellor in this century.

* Benedetti, "My Mission in Prussia," pp. 99, 254. The proposition of a congress made by Prince Gortchakof, the day after Sadowa, but abandoned by him as soon as made, we mention in a later chapter.

CHAPTER VII.

THE ECLIPSE OF EUROPE.

Illusions of M. Thiers in the Autumn of 1870—The Russian Portfolio at Versailles—Precise Date of the Understanding between Russia and Prussia antagonistic to France—The Months of July and August, 1866—Fears prevailing at the Court of the Tuileries after Sadowa—Measures proposed by M. Drouyn de Lhuys—Opposition of the Palais-Royal Party and of M. Rouher—What was to be done?—Urgent Necessity for a Congress—Napoleon III. decides upon an isolated Mediation, and sends M. Benedetti to the Prussian Headquarters—Peculiar Language used by M. de Bismarck in the Presence of M. Benedetti at Nikolsburg and Brunn—Trap laid for France—She frees Prussia from all European control, and hastens on the Preliminaries of Nickolsburg, July 26th—Saying of M. de Bismarck on the *politique de pourboire*—Secret French Despatch of August 5th, demanding the Left Side of the Rhine with Mayence — M. de Bismarck's haughty Refusal—Dilatory Negotiations—Journey of M. Benedetti to Paris, and Abandonment of the Despatch of August 5th—Difficult Situation of M. Benedetti: he pleads for a Secret Alliance with Prussia on the Subject of Belgium—Conferences concerning this Secret Treaty—Inconceivable Folly on the Part of the French Ambassador at Berlin—Final Peace with Austria, August 26th—M. de Bismarck's sudden Suspicions: he hesitates to Sign the Secret Act—Resignation of M. Drouyn de Lhuys, and Circular from the *ad interim* Minister, M. de Lavalette, September 16th—Use made by M. de Bismarck of the Two Secret Propositions of France relative to the Rhine and to Belgium—Military Conventions with the States of the South, August 17th-23rd—General Manteuffel's Mission to St. Petersburg, August—Agreement entered into between Prussia and Russia in case of a War with France—Chief Fault of the Napoleonic Policy after Sadowa—Elimination of Europe.

IN the beginning of the gloomy month of November, 1870, two illustrious persons were seated by the fire in the small parlour of the "Maison Jessé," situated in the Rue de Provence, at Versailles, two persons whose slightest act all Europe was watching with anxiety at the time.

Leaning with both arms on a work-table, on which "two bottles, with candles stuck in their necks, did duty as candelabra,"* M. de Bismarck asked permission of M. Thiers to smoke a cigar, and relaxed, after the negotiations which they had been discussing throughout the day, relative to the armistice and to the peace, into a gossiping conversation full of abuse of the war. Among other things, he mentioned the fact that the Emperor Napoleon III., on seeing him approach in the little garden, in which they met after the capitulation of Sedan, armed with a pair of pistols, had turned pale : "He thought me capable of an act of bad taste." There is no doubt that in this, the man who, ever since the attempt of Blind, had shown the greatest nervousness about his own personal safety,† attributed, and most ungenerously, to the unhappy monarch thoughts he was very far from entertaining.

---

* These details, as well as the subsequent ones, are borrowed from the account of this interview given by M. Thiers himself, a few days later, at the Bishop's Palace at Orleans, and published by M. A. Boucher in his "Récits de l'Invasion," pp. 318—325.

† We have already quoted the despatch of M. de Barral from Berlin, June 1st, 1866, three weeks after Blind's attempt : "M. de Bismarck no longer goes out alone, and French detectives will meet him on the frontier and accompany him throughout the journey." M. Jules Favre ("Histoire du Gouvernement de la Défense Nationale," vol. i., pp. 163, 164) speaks of the uneasiness displayed by the Prussian minister during the interview at the Castle of Haute Maison, at Montry : "We are very badly placed here; your franc-tireurs can take aim at me through any of those windows." We may also recall the language used, later on, in the Chambers, by the German Chancellor, on the subject of Kulmann's attempt on his life.

With anecdotes and reminiscences of this description the Prussian minister amused himself for several hours; M. Thiers, on his side, only just returned from his forty days' journeying, in which he had twice crossed Europe, and had negotiated with so many sovereigns and ministers, was not in want of piquant anecdotes and lively sketches. He found it to be necessary after a while, however, to recall to M. de Bismarck's mind the important topics which had brought him to head-quarters; but M. de Bismarck—that "savage filled with genius," as the French statesman called him later on in his confidences at the bishop's palace at Orleans—seemed desirous of prolonging the delightful gossip as much as possible. Taking the hand of M. Thiers, he cried: "Let me continue yet a little while; it is so delightful to find oneself once more in the society of a *civilised being!*" The *civilised being*, when at last permitted to plead his cause anew, found that the "Iron Count" was still there, though for a short time it had pleased him to assume the *rôle* of agreeable companion. Contact with civilisation had not at all softened the political manners of the *savage*. M. Thiers then remembered the favourable dispositions which he had met in Russia, and thought it advisable to make use of them at such a critical moment.

While at St. Petersburg, M. Thiers had already sent a very sanguine telegram to the delegates at Tours. In it he said: "I have every reason to be satisfied with the reception I have received from the emperor and from the imperial family, from Prince Gortchakof and other dignitaries, as well as from Russian society in general. The emperor and his chancellor have expressed themselves very strongly against the exorbitant demands of Prussia; they have declared that Russia will never give her consent to any unjust conditions, and that consequently the consent of the other powers will equally be wanting. The exactions of Prussia would therefore be only the exactions of brute force, and would not be founded on any sanction." *

Without entering into any details, M. Thiers spoke to the Prussian minister in general terms of the marks of solicitude shown him by "his friend, Prince Gortchakof," and concluded by saying that Russia was becoming alarmed and irritated. At these words M. de Bismarck rose and touched a bell. "Bring me the portfolio containing the Russian papers." The portfolio was brought. "Read," said he; "here are thirty letters from St. Petersburg." M. Thiers was not slow in profiting by the permission: he read, and his eyes were opened.

It must be said, however, that the illustrious historian of the Consulate and the Empire brought this cruel deception on himself. He might have spared himself this, as well as many another mis-

---

* These details are taken from a despatch of Lord Lyons, of October 6th, 1870. M. de Chaudordy had communicated M. Thiers' telegram to the British ambassador. It is curious to compare this singular telegram of M. Thiers with the opinion expressed by Prince Gortchakof in the presence of the English ambassadors, "that the conditions indicated in the circular of M. de Bismarck, September 16th, could only be modified by military events, and that nothing could at present authorise such a conjecture."—*Despatch of Sir A. Buchanan, October* 17*th.* The conditions then indicated in the Prussian circular were already *Alsace* and *Metz.*

take of his rapid journey across Europe, had he but consulted competent men, or even paid them the slightest attention. M. de Beust, for example, was eminently in a position to have given him the most edifying details as to the real state of the relations existing between Russia and Prussia. There was also M. Benedetti, who could have given him the precise date of the agreement entered into between the courts of Berlin and St. Petersburg in case of a war with France, and who could at the same time have informed him of the extraordinary circumstances under which this agreement was made. Let us call these circumstances to mind, and strive to free them from the cloak of mystery with which certain interested persons continue to envelope them; let us once more go back to the day after Sadowa, to the public and secret transactions which followed that sad event. The majority of the political combinations, which were to prove so fatal to France in the war of 1870, were woven and consolidated during that fatal epoch— during the two months of July and August, 1866.

"None of the questions which affect us will be settled without the assent of France," was the declaration made by Napoleon III., in a solemn document laid before the Corps Législatif on the 11th of June, 1866; and among these questions the "modification of the map of Europe to the exclusive benefit of any great Power," naturally held a prominent position. Now, in virtue of the victories, as vast as they were unexpected, of the 3rd July, 1866, Prussia intended altering the map to her exclusive benefit. Instead of "maintaining Austria in her great position in Germany," as the imperial letter of the 11th of June demanded, Prussia exacted the entire exclusion of the Empire of the Hapsburgs from the German Confederation; instead of granting "a more important *rôle*, a more powerful organisation" to the secondary States, she claimed jurisdiction over the whole of Germany; and contemplated into the bargain annexing large portions of the countries occupied by her troops.

In fomenting this war, which was to end in such an unexpected manner, the imperial policy had intended, above all, to secure two results: the freedom of Venice, and an equitable arrangement of affairs in Germany.

Venice had been given up—given up even before the war, and in accepting this cession, in announcing this "important event" in the *Moniteur*, after General Benedeck's great disaster, the Emperor Napoleon, according to the opinion of his Minister for Foreign Affairs, was all the more bound to protect Austria and her allies, as it was now a question of the vital interests of France herself.

The minister, in consequence, advised his august master to convoke the Corps Législatif, to send to the eastern frontier an army of observation, which Marshal Randon at that time was rapidly organising, and to declare to Prussia that France would occupy the left bank of the Rhine unless she showed herself more moderate towards the vanquished, or if she attempted any territorial acquisitions that might endanger the equilibrium of Europe.

Certainly, after the terrible experiences of 1870, we may feel some very reasonable doubts as to the propriety and wisdom of the measures proposed by M. Drouyn de Lhuys in the month of July, 1866; but still, we must bear in mind that the prestige of France was then very great and almost unshaken, that in a week Austria would be able to bring back 120,000 or 130,000 soldiers from Italy, and that General Moltke's troops were already beginning to feel the effects which every war—even a fortunate one—will produce. "Prussia is victorious," said the French ambassador at the Court of Vienna, "but she is exhausted. From the Rhine to Berlin you will scarcely meet with 15,000 men. You may make yourself master of the situation by a simple military demonstration, and in perfect security, as at this moment Prussia is incapable of entering on a war with France. Let the Emperor make a simple military demonstration, he will be astonished to find with what facility he will, without striking a blow, become the arbiter and the master of the situation."

In the private letters of M. de Bismarck to his wife during this campaign, can be found traces of the cares which at the time assailed his spirit, especially of the trouble it cost him to moderate the enthusiasm of his hot-headed friends, "good people who cannot see beyond their own noses," "*et qui nagent à leur aise sur la vague écumante de la phrase.*" The week after Sadowa, during his march to Vienna, he wrote from Hohenmauth: "Dost thou yet remember, dear heart, that nineteen years ago we passed through here on our way from Prague to Vienna? Neither then nor later on, when I travelled along this same line with the amiable Lynar, did I imagine what the future had in store for me! . . . All goes well, and we shall have a treaty of peace worth the making if we do not exaggerate our demands, and fancy that we have conquered the world. Unfortunately we are as prone to become intoxicated with success as we are to despair of it; and the ungrateful task devolves upon me of pouring water into heated wine, and of showing that we are not alone in Europe, but that we have three neighbours."

Again, in his celebrated speech of the 16th of January, 1874, to the Reichstag, the Chancellor of Germany, in speaking of those decisive days, made the important confession that, "although France herself had at that time but a limited number of troops at her disposal, nevertheless, a few of them would have sufficed to form a very important army when united to the numerous forces of the south of Germany, which, on its side, could furnish excellent materials, and whose only fault was a defective organisation. Such an army would immediately have forced us to fall back to protect Berlin, and to abandon all our successes in Austria."

Let us add to this that Germany was still violently averse to the "fratricidal" policy of Prussia, and that the proceedings and exactions* of the two generals Manteuffel and Vogel von Falkenstein had caused the greatest exasperation among the people on the banks of the Main. For one moment, one very transitory moment, it is true, the sight of French troops on the Rhine would not have wounded Germanic susceptibilities, and would even have been hailed with joy. "Sire," said at this time one of the most eminent ministers of the German Confederation to the Emperor Napoleon III., "Sire, a simple military demonstration on your part may save Europe, and Germany will be eternally grateful to you. If you allow the present opportunity to escape, before another four years have elapsed you will have to go to war with Prussia, and you will have the whole of Germany against you." But the terror which the prodigious victories of the Prussians had infused into the ruling mind of the Tuileries was too great to allow it to retain the coolness of judgment so necessary in such a momentous crisis. The needle-gun was also a novelty, whose importance, now exaggerated, now depreciated by authoritative opinions, contributed in no small degree to add to already numerous perplexities; and, finally, there arose a doubt as to the possibility of raising the number of men fixed upon by the Minister of War; the fatal Mexican expedition had swallowed up nearly all the arms and troops of France.*

The French Government was thus forced to confess

---

* This was the opinion set on foot by the *parti de l'action*, and it was even rumoured that Marshal Randon (Minister of War) had been arrested and imprisoned at Vincennes. In April, 1867, the chief political personages of the Empire, notably the members of the Privy Council, received a confidential memorandum from the former Minister of War, who had been superseded in the month of January by Marshal Niel. In this document that it had arduously desired, favoured—nay, even provoked—one of the greatest European complications, without having asked itself whether, in the event of a crisis or of the rupture of the equilibrium of Europe, it was even in a position to make a simple military demonstration.

The *parti de l'action* henceforward had an easy task to uphold Prussia as the powerful agent of civilisation and of progress, to condemn the Austrian sympathies that perennially clung to the offices of the Quai d'Orsay, and to recommend more than ever an alliance with M. de Bismarck: he was to be given *carte blanche* in Germany, and the unity of France was to be completed by the seizure of Belgium.

M. Drouyn de Lhuys did not fail to point out the weakness and folly of such suggestions, and asked with some bitterness how France, who was not even capable of organising an army of observation on the Rhine, could possibly be strong enough to attack Antwerp, to provoke England, and bear the probable hostility of all the other European Powers—Prussia, no doubt, among the rest. He did not spare his reproaches, and exposed the officious and culpable zeal that had been employed in bringing about a war whose consequences he had never ceased to dread, and inveighed more especially against the unconditional freedom of action granted to the most dan-

---

Marshal Randon endeavoured to expose the folly of all the accusations brought against him, and maintained that after Sadowa it would have been easy for him to have assembled at the shortest notice at least 100,000 men on the Rhine frontier. This confidential paper was published, at the desire of the author, in October, 1870, under the title, "De la Situation de l'Armée en l'Année 1866. Grenoble, 1870."

gerous, the most powerful side—to the very side from which sureties should have been exacted.

Where he had been at liberty to do so, he had taken every precaution that lay in his power. In the event of Austria being victorious, Venice would always have remained to Italy. "In my opinion," added the minister ingenuously, "from a French point of view, this was a bad result; but, as the emperor desired it above everything, I procured it for him."

It was now the least that could be done, he thought, to allow him to obtain from the other side some compensation for France, this time, which would justify in the eyes of the nation the indulgence shown to Prussia. For several days the debates were prolonged and lively, and agitated by conflicting influences. The Palais-Royal party was not the only one to advocate the desertion of the Austrians: up to a certain point this line of action was upheld by several statesmen whose judgments and opinions were usually most moderate.

M. Rouher was one of the first to oppose any military demonstration on the eastern frontier; he was soon, indeed, to make a speech in favour of "a necessary and remunerative alliance between France and Prussia." "Austria," according to the opinion of another important member of the Privy Council, "now only inspires that amount of interest which is next door to indifference, and which is always inspired by the strong when they have lost their strength by their own fault, by their own want of foresight and care. *Up till now everything has happened for the* *best."* * While M. Magne was thus pronouncing the *væ victis* over the House of Hapsburg—little dreaming, alas! that four years later Europe would pronounce an almost identical sentence with regard to France—an august lady, a sister of the King of Wurtemberg, and closely related to the French imperial family, was expressing herself very differently. "You are deluding yourselves strangely," said she; "your prestige has diminished more during this last fortnight than during the whole of the imperial reign! You countenance the destruction of the weak; you tolerate the unlimited insolence and brutality of your next neighbour; you accept a gift, and you have not even a good word for the giver. I regret that you should think that my interests dictate my opinions on this subject, and that you do not foresee the fatal danger of a powerful Germany and of a powerful Italy. It is the *dynasty* which is menaced, and which will have to bear the consequences.

"Do not think that the disasters which have befallen my country have made me unjust or suspicious. Venice given up, you should have succoured Austria, have advanced your troops to the Rhine, and laid down your own conditions! To permit Austria's annihilation was worse than a crime, it was a mistake."

Whether mistake or crime, the French had decided how to act before this spirited appeal of the Queen of Holland reached the Tuileries.†

---

* Confidential note of M. de Magne for the Emperor.—*Papers and Correspondence of the Imperial Family*, vol. i., p. 240.

† This letter, addressed to a former French minister at the Hague, and laid before the Emperor, was found at the Tuileries, after the 4th September.—*Papers and Correspondence of the Imperial Family*, vol. i., p. 14.

Napoleon III. was very ill at the time, suffering from the first effects of a painful malady (from which he was never afterwards to be free), and, in consequence, less than ever inclined to adopt any vigorous measures; so that on the 10th July, after a council of ministers held in the Emperor's presence, Prince Metternich had to inform Vienna that France would interfere no further in the conflict than by means of her diplomatists.

Yet, something more efficacious, more loyal at any rate, might have been attempted than such an empty and isolated mediation, filled, as it was, with perilous reticences and egotistical calculations. The whole of the European Powers might have been interrogated on such an eminently "European" question—a question which so closely affected the equilibrium of the Continent. A word from France on the subject "would certainly have been listened to," to use an expression contained in an imperial letter of June 11th; for even Prince Gortchakof himself spoke of the necessity of a general congress at this time.*

Under the first and violent shock caused by the sudden foundering of Austria and her hopes, at the spectacle of so many of his august master's relatives menaced by spoliation and ruin, the Russian Chancellor had indeed involuntarily expressed the true remedy for the situation.

However devoted he might be to his old Frankfort

* This was, however, but a passing weakness on the part of Prince Gortchakof, a suggestion carrying no weight, and whose only authentic source can be traced to an obscure sentence in a despatch of the French ambassador at Berlin.—*See Benedetti, My Mission in Prussia,* p. 226.

colleague, however fascinated by his genius, Alexander Mikhaïlovitch had still too much of the old Adam about him—too much of the *attaché* of Prince Nesselrode, in the days of Laybach and Verona—to admit, at the first onset, the possibility of such a considerable alteration in public affairs being effected without the knowledge of Europe and without his consent.

Why did not the Cabinet of the Tuileries take the Chancellor at his word ? Why did it not at least attempt to convene an assemblage of the Powers in presence of an upheaval which threatened to overthrow the balance of the States ? Why did it not see that in treating separately with M. de Bismarck, it was but playing the conqueror's own game ?

In spite of his triumphs, in spite even of his audacity, the Prussian minister could not but have been embarrassed had he been called upon to face the Areopagus of the Powers, and propose to them the almost entire abolition of the treaties of 1815, the dethroning of the ancient House of Guelph, and the exclusion of the empire of the Hapsburgs from the bosom of the German Confederation; and we shall see what subtleties he practised in order to save himself from such a necessity, and to make France his accomplice in this eclipse of Europe.

Strange fatality of the Napoleonic idea ! the dreamer of Ham had passed his whole life in proposing congresses, in calling them together at the most inopportune moments, under the most inauspicious circumstances; and yet he neglected to apply his much-esteemed and celebrated panacea on the only occasion when justice and good sense demanded it—on the only occasion when it might have proved useful or salutary !

Fortunate, surprisingly fortunate, was the minister of William I., who, according to Count d'Usedom, was thus "saved from the congress" twice over during the space of a few weeks—in the month of June, thanks to the kindness of Prince Gortchakof; in the month of July, thanks to the infatuation of France ! The passing weakness of Alexander Mikhaïlovitch was certainly not unknown at the Tuileries ; but the treaties of 1815 had been so eloquently denounced in the Auxerre speech, so much importance —Paris had been illuminated—had been attached to the cession of Venice. The reigning sovereign there still clung to his "*prestige*," still to his character of the "Neptune of Virgil," were it only in the eyes of the uninitiated; and still hoped to receive some good reward by obliging once more "the Piedmont of Germany." In consequence, M. Benedetti received orders to repair to head-quarters in Moravia, to offer the French mediation to M. de Bismarck, and to "sift him" also as to the advantages which he, with his sense of justice, could not fail to grant to so warm a mediator.

Nothing can be more singular than the language of the Prussian minister during these interviews in Moravia with the French ambassador. M. de Bismarck began by renewing his fantastic Biarritz speeches ; it was a travesty of Tilsit that he seemed to be performing at his head-quarters at Brünn. The son of Frederick William III., the conquered of Jena, was to divide the world with the nephew of Napoleon I., and divide it to the detriment of Russia and England! "He tried to prove to me," wrote M. Benedetti (July 15th), "that Austria's reverses would permit France and Prussia to recast their territorial possessions, and at once end the difficulties which were continuing to menace the peace of Europe. I reminded him of the existence of certain treaties, and that the war which he was desirous of hindering would be the very first result of such a policy. M. de Bismarck replied that I was mistaken; that were France and Prussia united by solemn engagements, and resolved to alter their frontiers, they would together be in a position to do so without having to fear any armed resistance either from England or from Russia." In other words—and these words are also in the report of M. Benedetti —the Prussian minister "wished to free himself from all European control," and thought to obtain this freedom by means of a separate understanding with France. As for the means by which this valuable understanding was to be effected, they were of the simplest description. France was to seek her fortune along the banks of the Maese and the Scheldt. "It will not be news to your Excellency," wrote M. Benedetti to his chief, a few days after Nikolsburg, "when I inform you that M. de Bismarck is of opinion that we ought to look for compensation in Belgium, and that he has offered to come to an understanding with us." He did not, however, abandon all idea of giving France something on the Rhine—not in Prussian territory, which it would be impossible to make King William give up; but "something might be found in the Palatine," that is to say, in Bavaria. He was still "far more Prussian than German," and it was possible to come to terms with Walhalla. The French Government fell completely into the trap laid, for it, and afforded Prussia, from the first, the help it required " to free itself from the control of Europe," by assisting it to complete the preliminaries of Nikolsburg, which were signed on the 26th July, and by which the exclusion of Austria from Germany was accomplished, and which created a Northern Confederation under the sceptre of the Hohenzollerns.

Once this serious assault on public right and on the equilibrium of the world was consummated, and the war virtually at an end, compensations were again talked of. In a letter from M. Drouyn de Lhuys to M. de Goltz, dated from Vichy (August 3rd), he says that the Emperor, his august master, "had not wished to complicate the difficulties of a work of European interest, by treating prematurely with Prussia on the subject of territory;" but now the time seemed to have come at which to touch upon these questions, and all the more as Prussia was preparing to annex considerable territories on the north of the Main. "The king," had already written M. de Bismarck to M. de Goltz (July 10th), "the king attaches less importance to the constitution of a political confederation in the north than he does to the annexation of territory; he would prefer to abdicate sooner than return without some important territorial acquisition." *

In addition to the possession of the duchies of the Elbe, already claimed at Nikolsburg, Prussia now wished to absorb the free towns, also Cassel, Hanover, and even Saxony; and in the Tuileries it was thought possible to measure French exigencies according to the number of human souls and square miles William the Conqueror would demand for himself.

"The great war for German nationality," so much recommended by the popular Cæsar at Biarritz, was thus turning into a "market of human animals," the reproach bitterly addressed to the Congress of Vienna, to the "accursed" treaties of 1815; and it is undeniable that in all this France played a part that was but little worthy of her. She ignored every ancient and modern right, the principles of national will as well as those of hereditary sovereignty; and all this, moreover, in the hopes of an illegitimate and petty reward which was to be derived from a great and universal calamity. In the words of the English humorist, it was taking advantage of an eruption of Vesuvius to boil an egg! M. de Bismarck made use at this time of a cruel but not altogether unmerited expression: "France's policy," said he to a former minister of the German Confederation, "France's policy is one of taking tips" (*fait une politique de pourboire*).

---

* Despatch in cipher, intercepted by the Austrians, and published in the "History of the War of 1866," by the Austrian Staff.

A letter written by M. Rouher, August 6th, 1866, and since found among the papers of the Tuileries,* reveals to us the strange delusions cherished at this time by the French Government—delusions which the Prussian ambassador in Paris encouraged to the best of his ability. "M. de Goltz considers our demands to be correct in principle," wrote the minister; "he considers that the sole desire of our country ought to be satisfied, and a *necessary and remunerative alliance* formed between France and Prussia. The difficulty is to decide the limit of our demands. The Empress would ask for much or for nothing, in order to avoid compromising our final pretensions." As for M. Rouher himself, he thought that "public opinion would have something to satisfy it if to-morrow we could say officially: " Prussia consents to our retaking the frontiers of 1814, and thus obliterating the consequences of Waterloo." But, be it well understood, the minister did not admit "that this rectification was to be an acquittal in full of all future demands."

"Doubtless fresh events must precede fresh demands, but fresh events will most certainly take place. Germany has only accomplished one of the many oscillations she will require to make before she steadies

---

* "Papers and Correspondence of the Imperial Family," vol. ii., pp. 225, 228. The editors affirm that this letter was addressed to M. de Moustier, which must be an error, as M. de Moustier was then at Constantinople. We are inclined to think that it was destined for M. Conti, who had accompanied the Emperor to Vichy. Napoleon III. was at that time very ill, and in an irritable state of mind, and had gone to Vichy on the 17th of July, where M. Drouyn de Lhuys saw him for a moment. The Chief of the State was not, however, able to prolong his visit at the watering-place, and returned to Paris on the 8th of August.

herself on her new basis. Let us be more ready in future to profit by passing events, they will not be wanting."

"The States south of the Main will, no doubt, become during the next few years an apple of discord or a subject of barter. M. de Goltz even now does not disguise his feelings of covetousness for this group of confederates." Thus, at the very time when the French Government was priding itself on "saving" the Southern States; on establishing, on the opposite banks of the Rhine, a new political combination — a combination to which the Minister afterwards gave the famous name of "*les trois tronçons*," and declared most reassuring to France, it was already contemplating the desertion of this combination, or the sale of it for "a reasonable price!"

But what folly it was to think, after Sadowa and Nikolsburg, after the downfall of Austria, after all European intervention had been set at naught, and the military weakness of France exposed on every side,* that Prussia would be accessible to arrangements which she had declined to agree to before her immense victories; in her time of perplexity, when she was in the very throes of a crisis which the whole world recognised as perilous in the extreme! As early even as the 8th of June, on the eve of the war, M. Benedetti described, in the following manner,

---

* "There has been too much said lately about the unreadiness of France." —*Confidential note of M. Magne, July 20th* (*Papers and Correspondence of the Imperial Family*, vol. i., p. 241). M. de Goltz had penetrated this secret at an early hour, and continually advised M. de Bismarck to maintain a firm attitude with regard to France.

the state of public opinion in Prussia with regard to France : " The apprehensions with which France fills Prussia are still as great as ever, and would be aroused, in a violent and unanimous manner, at the slightest indication on our part of a wish to extend our possessions towards the east. By no Prussian, from the king to the humblest of his subjects, would the bare supposition of any sacrifice on the Rhine be endured at this moment. The Crown Prince, though convinced of the political dangers by which he is surrounded, declared not long ago, with great energy, to one of my colleagues, that he would prefer war to the cession even of the small county of Glatz."*

And it is this same diplomatist who showed such a complete appreciation of the situation before the Bohemian campaign—it is this same ambassador who afterwards took upon himself to present to M. de Bismarck the demands of the Cabinet of the Tuileries, going actually so far as to submit to him, on the 5th of August, an outline of a secret treaty, abandoning to France the whole of the left bank of the Rhine, without even excepting the great stronghold of Mayence !

" In contemplating the important acquisitions which

---

* " My Mission in Prussia," pp. 171, 172. M. Drouyn de Lhuys, who had already obtained the cession of Venice from Austria, whatever might be the result of the dispute, insisted, at this time, on sureties being in a like manner taken from Prussia, "the cleverest and most dangerous of the two contending parties." M. Benedetti did not cease to oppose such a step, in the fear that, if it were suggested, Prussia would entirely abandon her designs against Austria; and the despatch of July 8th was only a fresh appeal in favour of the unconditional freedom (*laisser-aller*) to be accorded to M. de Bismarck.

the peace would ensure to Prussia, I was of opinion that some fresh territorial arrangement was necessary to our security. I provoked nothing, neither did I guarantee success; I only allowed myself to hope for it so long as our tone remained resolute and our attitude firm."

Was there too great a show of resolution, or was there a want of firmness? In M. de Bismarck's retort there certainly did not seem, however, to be any want of firmness. "Very good," was his reply to the pressing entreaties of the ambassador, "then we shall have war! But do not fail to remind his Majesty the Emperor that, under certain circumstances, such a war might be waged with revolutions, and that, in the presence of revolutionary dangers, German dynasties would prove to be built on more solid foundations than that of Napoleon."*

This was not, however, to be the Prussian minister's last word. Although fully decided not to admit any discussion on the subject of the Rhine provinces, he still did not wish completely to discourage the French ambassador, and continued a game with him that he designated later on in his circular of July 29th, 1870, by the epithet, hitherto unknown to diplomatists, of "dilatory negotiations." He spoke of his affection for Napoleon III., of the ambition he still cherished of resolving in concert with him the many important problems of the future.

---

* Benedetti, "My Mission in Prussia," pp. 177, 178; Prussian *Moniteur* (*Reicksanzeiger*), October 21st, 1871.

"Prussia requires the alliance of a great Power:" this was his supreme conviction, which he unceasingly instilled into the mind of his august master; and what alliance more desirable, from the standpoint of progress and civilisation, than that of the French empire?

Returning thus to his former confidences of Nikolsburg and of Brünn, he insinuated "that other *arrangements might be made* that would satisfy the respective interests of the two countries,"* and strengthened M. Benedetti in his resolution of returning to Paris to explain the situation.

In Paris, the battle of influences had begun with renewed vigour between the Minister for Foreign Affairs and the Prussian ambassador, M. de Goltz, who was powerfully seconded by the *parti de l'action*, and to whom the arrival (August 11th) of M. Benedetti proved of great service. M. Drouyn de Lhuys did not show the slightest surprise at the "Prussian ingratitude," as M. Benedetti had termed it in one of his last despatches," † but by a logic which we fail to understand, he was all the more satisfied to see the French demands take a definite shape.

"They could be withdrawn at a suitable time;"

---

* "My Mission in Prussia," p. 181. This assertion of M. Benedetti is fully confirmed by a note found among the papers in the Tuileries, of which mention will be made later on.

† "Prussia would be ignoring the rights of justice and would be displaying at the same time a depth of ingratitude were she to deny us the guarantees which her extension of territory obliges us to demand."—*Despatch from M. Benedetti, August 5th, 1866, found in the château of Cerçay, among the papers of M. Rouher, and published in the Prussian "Moniteur" of the 21st October*, 1871. About the same time the ingratitude of Italy also became the topic of the day. "The unjustifiable ingratitude of Italy irritates even

little suspecting to what uses the project of the treaty of August 5th would soon be put to on the banks of the Spree! He hoped, moreover, that the repulse which French views had received at Berlin would offer food for reflection to those ardent promoters of dangerous connections, and prevent certain engagements for the future, which he especially dreaded; but here also his judgment was at fault. M. de Goltz suddenly informed him that he had come to an agreement with the Emperor as to the annexations to be made by William I. in the north of Germany, and a letter of the 12th of August, addressed to the Marquis de Lavalette by the head of the State cut short all controversy with Prussia. "I gather from my conversation with Benedetti," wrote Napoleon III. to the Minister of the Interior, "that we should excite all Germany against us, and should derive but a very small benefit. It is of importance that public opinion should not err on this subject." The misfortune was, however, that the Imperial Government allowed its opinion to be at fault on a far more difficult point, and that it allowed Belgium henceforth to become the object of a negotiation as deceptive as it was fatal, from the overpowering responsibility of which it

---

the calmest mind," wrote M. Magne in his confidential note to the Emperor, July 20th. The Cabinet of Florence was indeed causing endless trouble to France by its susceptibilities and exigencies, which were, to say the least, very misplaced. After having been defeated by land and by sea, at Custozza and Lissa, and after having received as a recompense the magnificent gift of Venetia, the Italians still extended their demands to the Tyrol. For a moment the Emperor was tempted to resign the fatal gift which he had received, and to release Austria by an official act from her pledged word.—See the curious note of M. Rouher for the Emperor: *Papers and Correspondence of the Imperial Family*, vol. ii., pp. 229, 230.

vainly essayed to escape on the outbreak of the war of 1870.

That M. de Bismarck was from the very first the originator of the gloomy conspiracies against the land of the Maese and the Scheldt, that he was also the tempter of the French Government—a tempter oftentimes repulsed—cannot now be doubted, as authenticated documents have since been published of a nature to convince the most incredulous minds. It was not only in his conversations with General Govone that the Prussian Prime Minister clearly indicated Belgium and certain portions of Switzerland as being the most suitable territories "for the indemnification of France." Even prior to the spring of 1866, even before the interview of Biarritz, M. de Bismarck had essayed to sell the bear's skin (*vendre la peau de l'ours*), as Napoleon III. said to him on one occasion. General Marmora, whose knowledge was tolerably acute, adds, "that the bear lived neither in the Alps nor in the Carpathians; it was perfectly well in health (*stava benone*), and had no intention either of dying or of being locked up in a cage."*

Such suggestions were not of a kind to inspire much aversion in the hearts of the *parti de l'action* in the councils of the Empire; they were even well received; but M. Drouyn de Lhuys rejected them scornfully. Stigmatised as "projects of robbery" by the chief of the State, they had to await the hour of patriotic

---

* La Marmora, "Un pó più di luce," p. 117; Report of General Govone, June 3rd, 1866, *Ibid.*, p. 375.

anguish which M. Benedetti's arrival announced, to be taken into serious consideration.

Certainly the French ambassador at the Court of Berlin occupied during 1866 a very onerous and painful, we might almost say pathetic, position. He had devoted himself to bring about that *connubio* of Italy with Prussia, which seemed in his eyes to be of such value to the Imperial policy, to be such a signal victory over the ancient order of things, such a benefit to the *idées Napoléoniennes*, and to the "new right." In the well-grounded fear of seeing his work collapse and Prussia draw back, if there were any mention made of future compensation or of preventive engagements, he was unceasing in his endeavours to dissuade his government from any attempt of the kind, and depicted the fierce, intractable, and gloomy patriotism of the House of Hohenzollern so strongly that he was sometimes suspected at the hotel on the Quai d'Orsay of using rather strong colours, and of painting a certain devil rather blacker and more German than he was in reality.

The work had succeeded—succeeded beyond all expectation—succeeded in a manner which convinced M. Benedetti "that a territorial reformation was necessary for the security of France." This reformation he had for a moment fancied he might have obtained on the Rhine; "he did not guarantee its success, but allowed himself to hope for it."

Firmly, even haughtily rejected on this point, and "having sounded the depths of Prussian ingratitude," he yet started again with renewed hope as soon as the minister of William I. had insinuated to him "that *other arrangements* might be come to that would suit the respective interests of the two countries," and he clung to the expedient thus held up to his dazzled gaze with a feverish energy that was all the greater, as he thought he foresaw a fresh triumph of the "new right," and of the principles dear to his party. Anxious to repair the consequences of a policy, whose consummation he, more than any other, had assisted in bringing about, conscious of the impracticability of hoping that the Berlin Court would give up the smallest portion of German soil, and still convinced of the sincere desire of M. de Bismarck "to indemnify France,"* he constituted himself the interpreter to the Emperor Napoleon III., in this decisive hour, of the ideas which he had collected at the Brunn head-quarters, and warmly advocated that "necessary and remunerative alliance" with Prussia, which had for so long been extolled by the Palais-Royal, and which recently had even found favour in the ponderous mind of M. Rouher.

There was of course no intention of undertaking any immediate steps, the military state of the country, if nothing else, forbade it; it was only a question of unity of purpose, of a bond to be established to meet future eventualities—to meet the moment, for instance, more or less in the distance, but none the less inevitable,

---

* "The numerous efforts which he (M. de Bismarck) has unceasingly made to cement an agreement with us, are sufficient proofs that in his opinion it is most essential to indemnify France."—*My Mission in Prussia*, p. 192. These were the opinions of the ex-ambassador of France even in 1871.

when Prussia would seek to crown her work, would cross the Main, and extend her territories from the Baltic to the Alps ; it was with this movement in view that they must now *boldly take up their stand on the basis of nationality!* " If France boldly takes up its position on the basis of nationality," says a curious note found among the papers of the Tuileries, and which undoubtedly reflects the ideas of the *parti de l'action* at that period,* " it is important at once to establish that there is no such thing as a Belgian nationality, and to settle this essential point with Prussia."

"As the Cabinet of Berlin seems disposed to enter into the arrangements France finds it convenient to make with it, it will be necessary to negotiate a secret treaty which will be binding on both parties. Without supposing that this treaty can be a sure guarantee, it will serve a twofold object in compromising Prussia, and in being a pledge of the Emperor's political sincerity and of his intentions. . . . In order to inspire the Berlin Cabinet with the confidence which is always necessary to the maintenance of friendly relations, we must endeavour to dissipate the apprehensions which it has always entertained, and which our recent communications have served to reawaken and excite. This result cannot be obtained by words, it will require acts ; and the act of regulating the future destiny of Belgium in concert

---

* "Papers and Correspondence of the Imperial Family," vol. i., pp. 16, 17. The editors fancied they recognised the handwriting of M. Conti, chief of the Emperor's cabinet, but was it not more likely to be in that of M. Benedetti ?

with Prussia, in proving to Berlin that the Emperor is in truth seeking elsewhere than on the Rhine for the extension of France, which has become necessary since the events of which Germany has just been the theatre, will also afford us a relative certitude that the Prussian Government will not oppose our extensions in the north."

It was, therefore, charged with the mission to negotiate a secret treaty, which was to bind both parties in the sense indicated by the foregoing note, that M. Benedetti left Paris towards the middle of the month of August, 1866. The treaty was to recognise an offensive and defensive alliance between the two States, and in exchange for the Emperor's recognition of deeds already done or about to be done in Germany, was to contain a promise of Prussian diplomatic concurrence in the acquisition of Luxemburg, and its armed concurrence whenever France thought fit to annex Belgium.

As soon as he returned to his post, the French ambassador set himself resolutely to work, and conducted the negotiations unknown to his immediate chief,* referring only to the Emperor and to M. Rouher.

---

* "At the time of my departure from Paris, towards the middle of the month of August," says M. Benedetti in his book, "My Mission in Prussia," "M. Drouyn de Lhuys had tendered his resignation, and I had sufficient reasons for supposing that his place would be filled by M. de Moustier, then ambassador at Constantinople. There was therefore, at that time, no Minister for Foreign Affairs; and, under existing circumstances, I considered it more fitting to address the letter to M. Rouher, in which I gave an account of my interview with M. de Bismarck, and in which was enclosed the project of a treaty relating to Belgium. . . ." M. Drouyn de Lhuys did not send in his resignation in the month of August; rightly or wrongly he believed at this time "that he was acting in an honest and disinterested manner in remaining," and his portfolio

He begged the Prussian minister to consider the propositions of the 5th of August—those relating to the left bank of the Rhine—as meaningless, as a freak on the part of M. Drouyn de Lhuys, during the illness of his august master, and submitted a new treaty, in five articles, concerning Belgium. It matters but little whether the French ambassador brought the project with him, or whether he wrote it out in the study of the Prussian minister; perhaps "to his dictation" and at his demand. This we know, that M. Benedetti was acting in accordance with instructions received in

was only taken from him on the 1st September, 1866. Up to that time M. Drouyn de Lhuys did not cease to direct his department; the ambassador himself quotes in his book several despatches which passed between them on serious topics, dated the 21st and 25th August (pp. 204, 223), and M. Benedetti must hold very singular views on hierarchical duties if he can think it fitting to escape from the control of his actual chief on account of his coming retirement. The continuation of the passage quoted from M. Benedetti's work is no less peculiar: "M. Rouher never deposited the letters, which I wrote to him at the Foreign Office, as he never assumed the direction of affairs there. If I were to give them here I could not refer my reader to the archives, so that he might verify their correctness, as I feel bound to do with all the documents I quote." What can this matter? Once having made up his mind to disclose his doings, M. Benedetti might as well have produced his correspondence with M. Rouher on such a debatable question, and at the same time have conscientiously warned his readers that the originals were not to be found in the archives. (We know that these originals were seized by the Prussians, with a large number of other important documents, in the château of M. Rouher at Cerçay.) As we are attempting to throw "a little more light" on all these unnatural obscurities we may also remark that it is wrongly stated (but with what design is clearly to be seen) by M. de Bismarck, in his celebrated circular of July 29th, 1870 (at the outbreak of the war) that the secret treaty on Belgium was negotiated at a later date—that of the year 1867—immediately after the settlement of the Luxemburg question. This allegation cannot hold good after the slightest examination, or after a simple comparison of the different papers which have been given up to the public. The mysterious negotiation on the subject of Belgium took place in the latter part of the month of August, 1866, as declared by M. Benedetti.

Paris,* and that M. de Bismarck, on his side, did not in the least decline his overtures; he even made several observations on certain terms employed in the wording of the treaty, and insisted on several alterations being introduced into the text. The project, thus amended, was sent to Paris and returned to Berlin with the rectifications made by the Emperor and M. Rouher. On the banks of the Seine, in the meetings of the few who were in the secret, the most joyful expectations were felt; the question of the probable successor of M. Drouyn de Lhuys was discussed, and opinions were divided between M. de Lavalette and M. Benedetti; ideas were exchanged which were soon to be embodied in a document of sorrowful celebrity, and great were the rejoicings to see "the treaties of 1815 torn up, the coalition of the three Northern Powers broken, and Prussia rendered sufficiently independent and sufficiently compact to be able to break away from her traditions." †

Suddenly a piteous despatch from the French ambassador at the Court of Berlin (August 29th) filled all hearts with dismay, and fresh apprehensions arose on the subject of that "necessary and remunerative alliance" which it had been hoped to establish.

The conferences had been continued until the close of August, and M. de Bismarck had lent him-

* The Prussian *Moniteur* of October 21st, 1871, gives some extracts (gleaned from the papers seized at Corçay) from the instructions sent from Paris (August 16th) to M. Benedetti concerning the secret treaty. A passage of these instructions contains the "names of the persons to whom this negotiation was to be alone confided."

† Expressions used in the circular of M. de Lavalette, September 16th, 1866.

self most graciously to these "dilatory negotiations." Meanwhile, the Peace of Prague—the conclusive peace with Austria—had been signed (August 26th); the Southern States had unanimously adhered to the stipulations of Nikolsburg, and had solemnly recognised the Confederation of the North, as well as the territorial acquisitions of Prussia. The secret treaty concerning Belgium was in the hands of the minister of William I., and only required to be copied and signed; but at this moment M. Benedetti was suddenly met with the strangest, the most inconceivable suspicions, which did not fail to wound him deeply. M. de Bismarck began to hesitate, to express his fears "whether the Emperor Napoleon would not make use of such a negotiation in order to create ill-feeling between Prussia and England." The stupefaction of the French ambassador was extreme. "What confidence can we, on our side, give to men capable of such suspicions?" he asks in his despatch of August 29th.*

This new behaviour seemed most unjustifiable to him, and in order to avoid being tempted to express an opinion respecting it, he thought fit "to go to Carlsbad for a fortnight, where he held himself in readiness to return to Berlin on receipt of the first telegram sent him by M. de Bismarck."

Though slightly disturbed by this incident, the Court of the Tuileries still remained unshaken in its belief in the secret treaty which was being

---

* These details, as well as the following, are taken from papers seized at Cerçay, and published in the Prussian *Moniteur*, October 21st, 1871.

prepared at Berlin. M. Drouyn de Lhuys received his dismissal, and long before the arrival from Constantinople of his successor, M. de Moustier, haste was made to publish the famous' circular of September 16th, which bore the signature of the minister *pro tem.*, M. de Lavalette, and which was but another pledge in the hands of the victor of Sadowa.

The manifesto lauded the theory of agglomeration, and affirmed that "Prussia, enlarged, and freed henceforth from all bonds, secured the independence of Germany." As to the hopes which were secretly cherished, they were only alluded to in the following expressions: "France can but desire the accomplishment of territorial enlargements which would not affect her own powerful cohesion" . . . Nothing ensued, however, and M. Benedetti waited in vain, under the shade of the elms and the pine trees of Carlsbad. M. de Bismarck gave no sign of life. He left Berlin for his estates, and did not return until the month of December.

The "dilatory negotiations" had borne all their fruit by the month of August, and the French Government might have congratulated themselves had these underhand negotiations been nothing worse for them than a deception. They were to recoil upon them as a chastisement. And yet M. Benedetti had declared that he knew his man—had followed his course for fifteen years. He had most certainly followed him during the spring negotiations, which ended in the treaty between Prussia and Italy: he had then been able to observe the interesting tournament between the viper and the charlatan, and had happily characterised a situation in which the plenipotentiaries of the two countries had surpassed each other in miracles of true Punic faith. "M. de Bismarck and General Govone have all along distrusted, and continue to distrust, each other," had written M. Benedetti in his despatch of March 27th, 1866. "It is feared in Florence that Prussia, having in her possession an act which to *a certain extent places Italy at her mercy,* may divulge its contents in Vienna, and by intimidating the Austrian Cabinet, force it to give up pacifically the concessions which she covets. In Berlin it is feared that, if negotiations are continued on these foundations, Italy will disclose all to Austria before concluding anything, and will essay by these means to obtain the cession of Venice."

After such experience *in anima vili,* how could M. Benedetti leave on the Prussian Premier's table his autograph on the compromising Belgian question, an autograph *which to a certain extent put France at the mercy of Prussia?* How could he be surprised that his interlocutor "should be assailed by certain suspicions," when he himself was imbued with similar feelings? It was but very natural to credit M. de Bismarck with the desire to do to others that which he would not allow others to do to him. The French ambassador would not have been far out had he credited M. de Bismarck with this charitable, though scarcely scriptural desire; for the most amusing, or rather the saddest part of this affair—the humour of the whole *embroglio,* as Shakespeare's Bardolph has it—is that the knight of the Mark had already executed the manœuvre (scarcely a knightly one, indeed) of which he pretended to suspect the Emperor Napoleon III.; and that the trick was already done by this cunning conjurer at the very time he was pretending to be anxiously watching the hands and the pockets of the rival wizard. Two secret and highly dangerous documents had been confided to his care—the two projects of treaty on the Rhine and Belgium;* and he did not delay to disclose them to the parties who were most interested in them, and whom he was particularly desirous of attaching to himself.

The preliminaries of Nikolsburg, as may be remembered, had stipulated that the Southern States should not be included in the new confederation governed by Prussia, and that they were to form a restricted union among themselves. This was the great triumph obtained by French mediation, this advantageous combination of "*les trois tronçons*" which, it was alleged, was to be far more favourable to France than that of the Bund, that unlucky creation of 1815. It is true that very soon the persons to whom the secret of Benedetti's mission had been confided, considered this "group of con-

---

* The two projects of treaties have since been published by the Prussian journals of July 29th and of August 8th, 1870. The Prussian Government is at present in possession of two French autographs on the subject of the Belgian project: the one, left by M. Benedetti at M. de Bismarck's in the month of August, 1866; the other, also in the writing of M. Benedetti, with marginal notes by Napoleon III. and M. Rouher. This last document was seized at Cerçay. For their description, and for other details, see the Prussian *Moniteur* of October 21st, 1871, and the article in the *Gazette of Northern Germany* on the subject of the "*La Marmora*" incident.

federate states" as a mere object of barter, to be turned to the best possible account; meanwhile, however, the south was still being "saved," and M. Drouyn de Lhuys exerted himself honestly during the month of August, 1866, in assisting the unhappy plenipotentiaries of Bavaria, Wurtemberg, Hesse, &c., who were seeking to conclude peace at Berlin.

M. de Bismarck had scared them at first by his fiscal and territorial demands; they had invoked and obtained the help of the Emperor of the French; and the Court of the Tuileries flattered itself that it had brought the minister of William I. to a more reasonable frame of mind. As late as August the 24th, M. Drouyn de Lhuys wrote to his agent in Bavaria : " I am glad to think that our last proceeding has not been without some influence on the results of a negotiation which is ending in a more satisfactory manner than the Cabinet of Munich at first was able to hope;" and even M. Benedetti assumed in this matter the charming *rôle* of a moderator.*

The truth of the matter is that, if M. de Bismarck ended by moderating his views, and even became very friendly towards the Southern States, he was influenced by a totally different motive to the desire of being agreeable to the Cabinet of the Tuileries. He simply laid before the assembled confederates the projected treaty of the 5th August, and proved to them that the French Government, while pretending to protect them, was seeking an understanding with

---

* Private letter from M. Benedetti to the Duke de Gramont, August 22nd, 1866.—*My Mission in Prussia*, p. 193.

Prussia at their expense, and was demanding portions of Hesse and the Palatine. Instead of demanding from them those sacrifices which they dreaded, the minister of William I. offered to protect them from their "hereditary foe." There could be no hesitation; the Southern States gave way, and Prussia concluded with them (August 17th and 23rd) secret offensive and defensive treaties.

The contractors mutually agreed to protect the integrity of their respective territories, and, moreover, the Southern States agreed, in case of war, to put all their military forces at the disposal of the King of Prussia.*

"The object of barter," on which M. Rouher had counted, was now no longer available; the boundary of the Main had been overstepped before it had even been traced out on the official map of Europe, and from the month of August, 1866, M. de Bismarck was able to rely upon the armed co-operation of the whole of Germany.

The military conventions with the Southern States were rigorously kept secret for a considerable time; it was only in the following spring that M. de Bismarck thought fit to publish them to the world, in his sarcastic reply to a speech of M. Rouher on "*les trois tronçons.*" Up till then M. Benedetti, like the rest, had remained in total ignorance of their existence, though he had displayed more penetration with respect to another very important event,

---

* Albert Sorel, "Diplomatic History of the Franco-German War," pp. 29, 30.

which was contemporary with the conventions in the South, and had recognised from the very first the ominous importance of General Manteuffel's mission to St. Petersburg, in the month of August, 1866. It must not be overlooked that at the bottom of the "new policy," which the Tuileries hoped to inaugurate during this month by an *entente cordiale* with the Court of Berlin, lay a Russian problem. Would the House of Brandenburg, " now being sufficiently compact to break loose from former traditions, and freed henceforth from all bonds," decide to shake off the traditional ties which bound her to Russia, and which had never, as yet, been loosened ? Here was the true and vital question of the future. "Prussia must be allied to a great power," was the eternal dictum, at this time, of William I.'s minister ; and, as Austria was crushed and England for years past had condemned herself to single blessedness, there remained but France and Russia, between whom the fortunate hero of Sadowa stood like Mozart's Don Juan, hesitating between Donna Anna and Donna Elvira. Surprised in the dark, taken advantage of in a moment of deplorable misunderstanding, the proud and passionate Donna Anna assumed airs of scornful courage, and uttered vows of *venganza*; but oftener, alas! cast looks yet full of ardour, looks which betrayed her secret flame, which told, only too well, that she was ready to forgive, so long as some reparation were made, so long as a marriage, even a clandestine one, might be hoped for.

Russia was the Donna Elvira—the first, the rightful

love, somewhat put out by recent neglect, injured even in her family dignity, but still loving, still fascinated, and awaiting but a kind word to throw herself into the arms of the truant. We can scarcely tarry to allude to Zerlina, to Italy, that lively and obliging waiting-maid, also in love, poor thing, with the irresistible Don Juan, and though often very cavalierly treated, yet happy and contented by a passing caress and the "protection" of such a grand personage.

This being the situation during this decisive month, the French ambassador felt a violent shock on hearing of the sudden departure for St. Petersburg of M. de Manteuffel, the diplomatist-general, less general than diplomatist, the prime confidant of the king, and at all times the man selected for secret missions.

"I asked M. de Bismarck, immediately," wrote M. Benedetti to Paris, "what conclusions I was to draw from this mission, so suddenly confided to a general whose troops were still in campaign. M. de Bismarck, after pretending that he thought he had already made me acquainted with the project, assured me that he had informed M. de Goltz of the occurrence, in order that he might report it to the French Cabinet."

After all it was, perhaps, only natural that the king should desire to lay before his imperial nephew the extenuating circumstances of a painful situation, in which he had been forced to lay violent hands on the crowns and goods of many relatives of the House of Romanof; but the French ambassador was especially struck by the fact that the journey of M. de Manteuffel had been decided upon on the very day following that on which he had submitted his treaty. "I asked the President of the Council," he continued in the same despatch, "if this general officer had been informed of our negotiation, and he replied that he could not assure me that the king had not made him acquainted with its substance. I must add, as I have already told you in my telegram, that I gave M. de Bismarck a copy of our project on Sunday morning, and that General Manteuffel, who had but just established his head-quarters at Frankfort, was summoned on the following night to Berlin."

Towards the end of August, when M. de Bismarck was giving the first tokens of his disinclination to sign the secret treaty concerning Belgium, M. Benedetti again mentioned, in a letter to M. Rouher, the confidential mission to St. Petersburg which M. de Manteuffel was continuing to fulfil: "Prussia has obtained assurances elsewhere, which will dispense her from coming to an arrangement with us," he wrote; "if she declines our alliance it is because she has already formed, or is on the eve of forming, another." *

General Manteuffel remained for several weeks in St. Petersburg; remained there long enough to dissipate a certain melancholy caused by the recent misfortunes of the Houses of Hanover, Cassel, Nassau, &c., allied by ties of blood to the imperial family of Russia; long enough to communicate the secret of

* Papers seized at Cerçay.—*Prussian* "*Moniteur*" *of October* 21*st*, 1871.

the autograph projects by which it had been perfidiously attempted to turn the Hohenzollern from his loyal and unshaken affection for his northern relative. Thanks to all these proceedings and attentions, the harmony existing between the two courts became greater than ever; the past was easily explained away, the future was arranged, and the French ambassador at the Court of Berlin was not mistaken in his supposition as to the "bear," whose skin the diplomatist-general was disposing of on the banks of the Neva. To use the language of the Marquis La Marmora, it was a bear of the Balkan, who had not felt well for some time past, and whom the Emperor Nicholas had declared to be *very sick* twenty years before.

It will be seen presently that Alexander Mikhaïlovitch did not fail to take his aim at the poor animal during the universal *battue* which took place in 1870, and that he barely succeeded in securing a tuft of hair with which to decorate his cap. But this does not detract from the perspicacity displayed by the unfortunate negotiator of the secret Belgian treaty on this occasion. M. Benedetti soon perceived the overwhelming truth, which M. Thiers was only to discover at the bottom of the Russian portfolio that M. de Bismarck abandoned to his gaze on that eventful evening at Versailles, with a freedom that was not altogether free from malice. In striving, after the frightful disaster of the Bohemian campaign, to obtain compensations from Prussia—now on the Rhine, now on the Maese—the Emperor Napoleon III. had only facilitated during these months of July and August,

1866, the two great political combinations which were later on, in 1870, of such prodigious utility to M. de Bismarck—namely, the armed co-operation of the Southern States, and the moral assistance of Russia in the event of a war with France. The chief fault, however, of the Napoleonic policy after Sadowa lies in having assisted Prussia in her desire to emancipate herself from the control of Europe, and in having sanctioned from the outset such an immense shock to the equilibrium of the world without first laying the cause before an Areopagus of the different Powers. This neglect of what was due to the great Christian family of nations was revenged, but too soon and too cruelly, alas! and Prince Gortchakof only followed recent and fatal example in allowing France and Germany, in 1870, to fight out their quarrel alone, and in preventing any combined interference on the part of the other European Powers.

"I see no Europe!" was the exclamation of M. de Beust in a now celebrated despatch of 1870, and there was no attempt to give the lie to his melancholy assertion. A few only sadly remarked that the eclipse had now lasted for several years, and that it dated from the time of the preliminaries of Nikolsburg and from the Treaty of Prague.

CHAPTER VIII.

THE EAST AND THE WEST.

Profound Disappointment of M. Benedetti—The Luxemburg Affair (Spring of 1867)—Insurrection of Crete—Important Advances made by France and Austria to Russia on the Eastern Question—Remarkable Despatch from M. Beust, January 1st, 1867: the Question of the Black Sea, a Question of *Amour propre*—French Project of Uniting Crete to the Kingdom of Greece—Reception given by Prince Gortchakof to the Offers of MM. Beust and de Moustier—He seeks to compromise the two Powers, but maintains his close Allegiance to Prussia—*In magnis voluisse*—Chimerical Hopes entertained by the Slavophile Party of Moscow and of St. Petersburg: the West for Germany and the East for Russia—Programme of M. Halkof—The Congress of Moscow (Spring, 1867)—Plots of the Pan-Slavistic Party in the Provinces of the Danube and the Balkan (1867-68)—Prince Gortchakof pleads for the Revolutionary Party in Roumania and Greece—Ultimatum of the Porte to the Hellenic Government, and Conference in Paris on the Subject of the Turko-Greek Disputes (January, 1869)—Subsiding of the Slavonic Agitation during the year 1869—Last Will of Fuad-Pacha: His Fears for the Future of the Ottoman Empire.

"An alliance has been formed elsewhere" was the melancholy conviction of the French ambassador at the Court of Berlin during the closing days of the month of August, on seeing Prussia break off so suddenly the "dilatory negotiations" on the subject of Belgium; and it is but just to acknowledge that from that time he formed a correct opinion as to the situation, and never failed to keep his government constantly alive to the fact of the close and intimate friendship which ensued between the two Courts of Berlin and St. Petersburg in consequence of the mission of M. de Manteuffel. If for awhile he still persisted in seeking a compensation for his country (compensation of a very modest description, it is true, and suited to the altered fortunes of France)—if, especially during the early months of 1867, he flattered himself that he might obtain permission from M. de Bismarck's benevolence to purchase Luxemburg from the King of Holland—if he even went so far one day, on the occasion of a hurried trip to Paris, as to declare in a private conversation that the fortress of Alzette " was already in his pocket"—he had nevertheless entirely abandoned all hope of ever being able to return to the fair dreams of Brunn head-quarters, or to realise that " necessary and remunerative alliance with Prussia," which had been the decoy at one time of so many sanguine temperaments on the banks of the Seine. He only thought that surely the victor of Sadowa would not begrudge France the paltry satisfaction of the Luxemburg; that he would even be pleased to "indemnify" the Emperor Napoleon III. at so low a price; that, to quote the poet, " the lion would only yawn at so trifling a morsel." The lion roared, however, and shook his mane in fury, and signified that an end had come to all *politique de pourboire*; which but confirmed the opinion already formed by M. de Benedetti that an alliance had been formed elsewhere, and that for the future Prussia felt she had nothing to fear. He judged rightly that M. de Bismarck must be very sure of the support, in every emergency, of his former colleague at Frankfort, to dare to refuse France even this modest windfall, and to display to such an extent "the depth of his ingratitude." Simultaneously with the Luxemburg affair, the events of Crete proved in their turn to the Cabinets of Vienna and of the Tuileries how intimately Prince Gortchakof was united with M. de Bismarck, and how determined he was to sacrifice even the most brilliant prospects to his friendship with Prussia.

Any one perusing the curious exchange of notes which the troubles in Crete gave rise to, will at once perceive that, from the month of November, 1866, to the month of March, 1867, the two governments of Austria and France were attempting to sound the dispositions of the Court of St. Petersburg, and were making most significant advances. The Candian insurrection, it will be remembered, occurred in the autumn of 1866, and caused fresh surprise and emotion in Europe, which had scarcely yet recovered from the shock of Sadowa. The proportions of the insurrection, exaggerated by newsmongers more or less interested, after having excited the lively sympathies of Russia, ended by seriously occupying the various chancellors; and seemed for a moment destined to re-awaken the whole Eastern question. Certain cabinets, however, did not seem to be dismayed at this possibility. Instead of conforming to the usual diplomatic usages with regard to Ottoman affairs; instead of essaying to hush up the matter, and to diminish as much as possible its proportions and influence, M. de Moustier thought that "means ought to be found to pacify the East," and attempted to "call together a sort of *medical consultation* in order to ascertain the remedy to apply to the evil."* Still more astonishing was the language held by the Viennese Government, by the Power that hitherto and in all times had been contented to support Turkey *per fas et nefas,* without demanding anything either for the immediate subjects of the Sultan or for the tributary provinces. Breaking resolutely with these customs of the past, M. de Beust, who had just assumed the guidance of affairs in Austria, wrote on the 10th November, 1866, to his ambassador in Paris that, "however much Austria might wish to see the Sultan retain his throne, she could not refuse to sympathise with and assist, up to a certain point, the Christian population in Turkey, who had often just cause of complaint, and who were bound to several of the races under Austria's sway by the bonds of blood and of religion." Questioned a few days later (28th November) as to his views, by the Russian envoy at the Viennese Court, the Austrian minister did not hesitate in replying that he was disposed to encourage among the Christians of the East "a wider development of their privileges, and to promote the establishment of a system of self-government, to be limited only by a tie of vassalage."

* Despatch from Count Mülinen to Baron de Beust, December 30th, 1866.

Lastly, in a remarkable despatch addressed to Prince Metternich, and bearing the date of January 1st, 1867, M. de Beust went so far as to propose "a revision of the Treaty of Paris of March 30th, 1856, and of the subsequent acts," and announced beforehand his desire to assign in the impending arrangement a very great *rôle* to Russia. He found no difficulty in demonstrating that "the remedies, which had been applied during the course of the last few years to the maintenance of the *statu quo* in the East, had proved themselves powerless to master the difficulties which were increasing every day."

"The Eastern question, taken as a whole," continued the despatch, "presents a very different aspect to that it did in 1856, and the stipulations of that period, exceeded as they have been on more than one important point by events which have since then arisen, no longer suffice to the necessities of the present situation." In a word, M. de Beust aimed at nothing less than a collective interference of the Powers in the affairs of Turkey, without disguising from himself that it would become necessary "to take into consideration the natural part which a community of religious institutions assigns to Russia in the East," and that it would also be necessary to release the Empire of the Czar from the onerous conditions imposed upon it in the Black Sea," in order to obtain the sincere co-operation of this power in the questions of the Levant.

The project was certainly a bold one, and did not fail to surprise the public mind of France. Was it not in truth an obliteration of the last ten years? a yielding-up of the fruits of the Crimean war? It was repugnant to own that the treaty of 1856 no longer existed, alas! since the day when the French Government, by its gratuitous indulgences towards Russia, burst the bonds that united the three great Western Powers, which alone could have assured its efficacious working. Since that time the treaty had been crumbling away piecemeal, and the greater number of its stipulations had been violated.

The Conference of Paris, which was nominally charged with the guardianship of the treaty, had contented itself (as it was stated in the Austrian despatch) "with sanctioning, after the fact, deeds accomplished without its sanction, and which were in opposition to the conventions placed under its care." Moreover, immediately after the battle of Sadowa, Prince Gortchakof had profited by the very first occasion to write, as it were, the epitaph of the Treaty of Paris.

"Our august master," writes the Russian Chancellor, in a document stamped with a refined irony, and bearing the date of August 20th, 1866, "our august master does not intend to insist upon the general fulfilment of treaties *whose only value depended on the agreement existing between the great Powers to see them respected*, and which have received, *from a want of that collective agreement*, such frequent and serious attacks as to have become *invalidated*." It was precisely this "collective agreement" that M. de Beust wished to revive and dignify by his proposal to revise the treaty of 1856.

According to his opinion, the Treaty of Paris had not fulfilled its object, which was to secure the integrity and vitality of the Ottoman Empire. On the one hand the Western Powers had imposed on the shores of the Euxine restrictions on Russia of its sovereign rights, that no great empire could submit to for long, and from which it would sooner or later seek to free itself. On the other hand, with regard to the Levantine populations, it had been considered sufficient to register a firman promising reforms, and to leave Turkey to herself, instead of reserving to Europe the means of bringing a gentle and permanent pressure to bear on the Ottoman Government in order to induce it to fulfil its duties towards the *raïas*, and to become, by wise and honest administration, independent and strong.

The Treaty of Paris, in the opinion of the Austrian minister, had only given back to Russia that which the Crimean war should for ever have deprived it of —namely, the monopoly of influence over the *raïas*; a monopoly it continued to exercise as in the past, after a more concealed fashion, perhaps, but the more dangerous owing to the absence of competition. M. de Beust wished to re-establish this competition, or rather wished to establish a general agreement "to put the Christian populations of the Sultan under obligations to the whole of Europe, by endowing them, under guarantees from all the courts, with independent institutions in accordance with their various religions and races."* And he was all the more inclined to sacrifice to this vast conception the article concerning the Black Sea contained in the Treaty of Paris, from the fact that Austria had opposed it from the first, only consenting to it in the end in order to satisfy the Western Powers and to put a stop to the Crimean war; and also that succeeding events had since exposed its complete uselessness.

It was under the influence of the disaster of Sinope that France and England had thought fit to restrain the Czar's naval power in the Euxine; they imagined that by doing so Constantinople would be sheltered from any sudden attack from Russia; but in this respect, as in so many others, the Eastern aspect had materially altered. Russia no longer meditated any sudden attack; she was advancing more slowly, but more surely, towards her aim.† The pacification of the Caucasus, the incurable weakness of the Porte, the daily increase of dissatisfaction among the *raïas*—who were as impatient of the Turkish yoke as they were devoted to the Czar, their sole protector—were of more value to her than the presence of her ships in the Black Sea. Besides, had Constantinople ever really been delivered from all danger in that direction? asked the Austrian minister. " Supposing Russia were to construct ships of war

---

* Despatch of M. de Beust to the Baron de Prokesch at Constantinople, January 22nd, 1876.

† "That which alarms me most, is the important change wrought in the Russian position by the pacification of the Caucasus. It is clear to me that in the future Russia will direct her most serious operations against our provinces in Asia Minor." This was the opinion of Faud Pacha in his political will addressed to the Sultan. (See note on page 282.)

in the Sea of Azof, would war be declared in order to prevent her from doing so?" Finally, the Cabinet of Vienna summed up in the following characteristic words: "*Amour propre* ought to be set aside in the presence of such immense interests as are now at stake." And, in fact, one cannot give this truth a too important place; the clause on the subject of the Euxine had been for a long time past but a question of *amour propre* between the Western Powers and Russia; and M. de Beust showed himself to be clear and far-sighted in his despatch of January 1st, 1867.*

After Sadowa he sought to reconstitute Europe—to rediscover her, if we may use the expression—and he knew what price would have to be paid for doing so. In a different direction France was exerting herself to meet the views of the St. Petersburg Cabinet by concentrating her principal efforts on the vital question of the hour—namely, the Candian insurrection, which

* No doubt the project set forth by the Austrian minister was simply that of making Turkey a ward of Europe; but was not this also the plan formed nine years later by the firmest upholder of the integrity of the Ottoman Empire, he who was sometimes called the originator of the Crimean war? It is interesting to compare the despatch of M. de Beust, of January 1st, 1867, with the manifesto published by Lord Stratford de Redcliffe (formerly Turkish ambassador), on the last day of the year 1875, relating to the Eastern question, in which we read the following remarks: " Objections may be raised to necessary measures, but their necessity makes them a part of the lesser evil, and, in consequence, they must be accepted with it. The measures in question are a joint organised supervision within, and a pressure agreed upon by convention from without. The difficulties which this double arrangement would have to encounter are far from insurmountable, and its inconveniences would be compensated by its results. These measures, reduced to a system, would no doubt be equivalent to a guardianship; but the Turkish Empire has for some time past been virtually in that position, a position which, had it been firmly imposed upon it as a right, would have saved the Porte from its present embarrassments."—*Letter from Lord Stratford de Redcliffe to* "*The Times*," *December* 31st, 1875.

was meeting with so much sympathy in Russia. M. de Moustier proposed to Prince Gortchakof that they should come to "an agreement as to the eventualities which were arising in the East," and, after having already spoken of a "medical consultation," went so far as to pronounce the words "heroic remedies," in a despatch to the French ambassador at Constantinople (December 7th, 1866).

By this medical allegory the Parisians understood the joining of the island of Crete to Greece, " the only possible escape," as Prince Gortchakof had affirmed on November 16th, 1866, "open to the Powers from the course of expedients and palliatives which up to the present time had but served to increase the difficulties." The marriage of the young King of Greece with the Grand Duchess Olga was at this time decided, and the Court of the Tuileries would have been delighted to "dower" the Russian princess with the island of Crete, and would not even have objected to increasing the dowry by the addition of Epirus and Thessaly. This was going very far, farther even than Russia desired, for that empire had no wish "to see Greece assume the proportions of a powerful State."*

It is certain, however, that from the friendship formed between France and Russia was arising the project of a combined demand, to be addressed to the Turkish Government, requesting the realisation of internal reforms and the cession of Crete, to be disguised under the proposal of a plébiscite, a demand

---

* Words used by the Emperor Nicholas to Sir Hamilton Seymour. For the rumours concerning Thessaly and Epirus, see, more especially, the despatch of Fuad Pacha to his ambassadors in Paris and London, February 27th, 1867.

which was actually preferred in the month of March, 1867, and in which Austria, Prussia, and Italy joined. No doubt the situation was as yet very disjointed and vague, but it was gradually assuming more decided characteristics; and it was to be regretted that France and Austria had not been able to come to some previous agreement as to the nature of the offers they intended to make to Russia. Nevertheless, their offers were very real and very valuable, and it only depended on the successor of Count Nesselrode to combine and adjust them, and turn them to the profit and glory of his august master. England was not in a position to offer any serious resistance to the united wishes of France, Russia, and Austria concerning the Levantine question—indeed, she was already resigned to their will; and, certainly, the fruit which Prince Gortchakof saw ripening in the spring of 1867, if it had not the attraction of being forbidden, was still far better flavoured and more wholesome than that which he picked up four years later from among the ashes of Sedan.

It is true that the French and Austrian Governments had no intention of making a gratuitous present. It was understood that, in exchange for these important cessions in the East, they were to obtain the support of the Russian Cabinet in the menacing complications of the West; and many existing circumstances seemed to plead in favour of such a combination. After all, if we deduct the vengeance wreaked on the " ungrateful " House of Hapsburg, Russia had derived but very little profit from the achievements of

s

M. de Bismarck. Without mentioning several relations of the imperial family whom the Hohenzollerns had dethroned and despoiled with a firmness softened only by a few tears, there had generally prevailed in all the proceedings and principles inaugurated on the banks of the Main and the Elbe a strong revolutionary tone, which could hardly be pleasant to a court still protected by the shadow of Nicholas. And still more serious was the fact that the battle of Sadowa had given a violent shock to, and had even threatened completely to overthrow, the venerable traditions of Russian policy with regard to Germany.

Since the days of Peter the Great, but more especially since those of Catherine II., Russia had always sought to acquire a preponderating influence among the various German courts; and the Czars had on more than one occasion carried things with a high hand in German quarrels.

"The Romanof enjoys the right of a first-born among his brethren, our sovereigns of the Bund," once said a celebrated journalist beyond the Rhine, somewhat bitterly; and the attitude of the secondary States during the Crimean war certainly did not contradict the truth of his assertion. It was, therefore, the labours of several reigns, and a policy, until then immovable, that Russia saw placed in jeopardy by the unforeseen results of the Bohemian campaign. The north of Germany had already escaped from Russian influence, and only those who were very simple-minded could delude themselves as to the destiny reserved for the south at no distant period.

"As early as the month of September, 1866, the Cabinet of Berlin had, in a circular which was designedly published, claimed for the Confederation of the North and the States of the South alone, to the exclusion of all the other powers, without excepting Austria, the right of uniting themselves as closely as they might think fit; giving thus an interpretation to Article IV. of the Treaty of Prague which it did not allow of. In his speeches delivered at the opening of the Prussian Chambers and the Northern Parliament, the king himself had, in addressing them to Germany—to the brother nations, to the land which extends from the Alps to the Baltic—made use of allusions which, to use the expression of the official journals, "had stirred the heart of every patriot."*

On his side, M. de Bismarck had said in a speech in the same Parliament (making use of the gambling similes which have become so familiar to us in his language, and so characteristic of his nature): "Our stake has become greater since our victories; we now have more to lose, and the game is far from being completely won." Indeed it was evident that unless some combined and resolute step were taken by Europe, the entire absorption of Germany by Prussia remained only a question of time; and if we consider the matter rightly, such an absorption would affect Russia more than France.

France only beheld the closer union of kingdoms and principalities which had always been hostile or opposed to her; but Russia, on the contrary, lost a

---

* Benedetti, "My Mission in Prussia," p. 249.

whole league of States whose fidelity and devotedness had never failed, which had served as a kind of barrier between her and those western dominions that were seldom in harmony with her. Their place was to be filled by a formidable power, which had proved itself enterprising and invading from the very beginning, and which was destined sooner or later, by the necessities of history, or the fatality of race, to represent the Germanic idea and oppose it to the Slavonic.

At any other epoch of the Northern Empire—in the good old times of Count Nesselrode, for instance, when, instead of a policy of spite and propaganda, the policy practised on the banks of the Neva was conservative, and in favour of European equilibrium—the conduct of a Russian chancellor under such circumstances would not have admitted of a doubt; a coalition between Russia, France, and Austria would have been formed immediately after Sadowa for the safety of Europe, and it is not saying too much when we affirm that in the spring of 1867 Alexander Mikhaïlovitch held in his hands the destinies of the world.

Thus, placed in a position to make his choice, Prince Gortchakof was careful not to decline the Austrian and French advances on the Eastern question; on the contrary, he hastened to sonorously welcome them, soaring at times into a lyrical style but little in vogue in the language of diplomacy.

He was charmed with the new Austrian minister, and let loose floods of a somewhat forced enthusiasm. "M. de Beust," he wrote to the Russian ambassador in London, "is inaugurating a new era in the political history of Austria—an era whose views will be liberal and lofty; he is the first statesman of that country and of our period who has courageously attempted to quit the field of paltry rivalry."

As for France, he was careful to note that the initiative had come from her, "and in begging the Emperor Napoleon III. to remember the interviews which the Emperor Alexander had had with him at Stuttgart" (in 1860) he seemed as though he wished to invest the present conferences with an unusual character of importance and generality. "His Imperial Majesty," continued the Russian Chancellor in his despatch of November 16th, 1866, to M. de Budberg, "has received with satisfaction the proposals which M. de Moustier has made to us with the view to an understanding between ourselves and the French Cabinet on the eventualities now arising in the East. The general principles which his Excellency the French Minister for Foreign Affairs has expressed, the assurances which he has given us, have a peculiar value in the eyes of our august master, since they emanate directly from the thoughts of the Emperor Napoleon, and that it is by his Majesty's express orders that M. de Moustier has touched upon these questions." The raptures of Alexander Mikhaïlovitch became greater and greater; he even ended by talking Latin, and crushing the unhappy Turkish envoy with a classic quotation.

"This," he wrote in the month of February, 1867, "is what I said to Comnenos-Bey: The island of Crete is lost to you. After six months of such desperate fighting, reconciliation is no longer to be thought of. Admitting even that you were able to re-establish for a time the authority of the Sultan, you could only do so over a heap of ruins and corpses."

"Tacitus has told us long ago how full of danger is that reign of silence which succeeds to devastation : '*solitudinem faciunt, pacem appellant.*'"

Unfortunately it soon became palpable that while congratulating Austria and France on their Oriental evolutions, and making them compromise themselves as much as possible in that direction,* the Russian Chancellor was extremely careful to maintain his intimate friendship with his former colleague of Frankfort, and not to run counter to any of his views with regard to the Eastern question. Although very eager for the plébiscite in Crete, he displayed the utmost indifference to an analogous case on the Eider, a far more legitimate obligation, one guaranteed by solemn treaties,† and one of the most vital importance to the noble and unfortunate country of the future Czarina. He maintained a no less significant silence on the subject of the publication made in the month of March, 1867, by M. de Bismarck, of the conventions with the States of the South, conventions

---

* "I have no objection to see your carriage standing before my door on the condition that you really enter my house," was the witty remark to M. de Budberg of one of M. de Moustier's predecessors a few years before, at the Hotel on the Quai d'Orsay, under similar circumstances, when Russia was publishing the advances of the Cabinet of the Tuileries, but taking care, at the same time, to avoid entering into any positive engagement with it.

† The preliminaries of Nikolsburg, as well as the Treaty of Prague, had stipulated for the return to the King of Denmark of the districts north of Schleswig, after a popular vote to that effect. We know that up to the present day Prussia has evaded the fulfilment of this engagement.

which made the military forces of Germany subject to Prussia, and abolished "the international and independent position" which the preliminaries of Nikolsburg had guaranteed to Bavaria and Wurtemberg.*

Alexander Mikhaïlovitch held Wurtemberg as cheaply as Denmark; the throne of Queen Olga was as little to him as the cradle of the Princess Dagmar.

In the meanwhile occurred the incident of Luxemburg, and the French Government were able to measure the amount of good feeling with which they had been able to inspire the Russian Cabinet by their "heroic remedies" with regard to Turkey. The Russian Chancellor was certainly correct, and very sincere in his desire for peace; he did not, however, show that consideration for the position in which France was placed which even England thought proper to display on this occasion, but seemed to be indifferent to everything so long as he was able to avoid giving offence to his illustrious friend at Berlin.

While praising M. de Beust for his "courageous attempt to break with paltry rivalries," the Russian Government did not fail to encourage, at the same time and in a most provoking and dangerous manner, the violent Slavonic opposition then rife in the Empire of the Hapsburgs by means of its famous

* M. de Beust writes with resigned subtlety on the subject of these military conventions: "An alliance established between two states, one of which is strong, the other weak—an alliance which depends on no particular stipulations, but which is to be permanently maintained in every and any war—is not of a kind to inspire much belief in the international and independent existence of the feebler state."—*Despatch to Count Wimpffen at Berlin, March 28th, 1867.*

Congress of Moscow, of which mention will be made later on. Other deceptions, less known to the world, but not less bitter, were probably added to the list of all these misunderstandings; for Austria, as well as France, lost no time in operating their retreat from the shifting ground of the East, and in effecting a junction with England to maintain steadfastly for the future the rights of the Sultan. The " medical consultation" was at an end, and the traditional "sick man" was none the worse; but from that time the terrible eventualities of the future were clearly visible.

"There exists an understanding between St. Petersburg and Berlin," was the reiterated warning of M. de Benedetti in the following year (January 5th, 1868); and he still designated the mission of General Manteuffel as the starting-point of this understanding that caused him so much anxiety. " Is it not, indeed, from this time," he asked, " that the policies of the two courts have assumed a more decided shape— Russia in the East and in the Slavonic provinces of Austria, Prussia in Germany—without the slightest cloud ever arising between them? Constantly of one mind on every question, they each pursue their separate ways, and work out their plans with a confidence that bears witness to the mutual guarantees which must have been exchanged between them." And the ambassador added that this conviction was beginning to be felt by many: notably by Lord Loftus, his English colleague, who for a long time had remained incredulous. "His views have visibly altered, and he is now no less persuaded than are the other members of the diplomatic body that arrangements for the future have been made between the government of King William and that of the Emperor Alexander. I, for my part, have seen it clearly demonstrated in the firm and unvarying resolution which the Cabinet of Berlin has displayed in bringing about the union of Germany, a union which is the mere prelude to a unity solely profitable to Prussia, without allowing itself to be turned aside for one moment in its designs by any fear of a future war with France. I have seen it in the care which M. de Bismarck takes to avoid explaining himself on the Eastern question. When he is interrogated, he replies that he never reads the correspondence of the king's envoys at Constantinople, and your Excellency will not have forgotten the consideration he always displays for the views of Prince Gortchakof."

M. Benedetti also noticed the fresh impulse which had been given, since the preceding summer, to the "Pan-Slavonic propaganda;" he pointed out, with great truthfulness, the vast designs and wide-spreading hopes of the St. Petersburg Cabinet in its connivances with Berlin; and in general gave a higher and more just description of Russian politics at that period than is given by certain ill-advised panygerists of our days, who, in order to prove that Prince Gortchakof has fulfilled his part as completely as possible and with as much success as could be desired, cannot find a better way of doing so than by diminishing and narrowing it.

It is the fault of most conventional praise to be

either forced in tone or in a wrong key. Incense has both perfume and ashes, said the ancients; and there is something equivocal in praising the Russian Chancellor for his "triumph" on the Euxine. To affirm that Prince Gortchakof had only favoured the audacious designs of Prussia, in order to liberate Russia from its bonds in the Black Sea—that he first gave up the world to M. de Bismarck, in the solitary hope of being able some day to repudiate the treaty of 1856—is, indeed, to do small honour to his genius and his patriotism. Certainly the eminent statesman, whose prophetic "foresight" the grandsons of Washington celebrated at St. Petersburg in the year of Sadowa, praying that the Eternal God—"who had arrested the sun's course for Joshua"—might stay the hand of death for Alexander Mikhaïlovitch, "so that the eyes of two worlds might long rest upon him"*—the consummate diplomatist who, in the spring of 1867, treated so lightly the considerable advances made to him by the Cabinets of the Tuileries and Vienna—this minister, certainly, would not have failed to set aside, with a disdainful smile, the paltry supposition that in the evident and approaching European convulsion, all that was to be assigned to Russia, its only victory or conquest, was to be the abolition of a certain painful article contained in a treaty which events had already for some time past pronounced "invalid." It was not for such a "dish of lentils," to use M. de Bismarck's

---

* Speech of Mr. Fox, Under-Secretary of State, at a banquet given by the English Club at St. Petersburg to the Mission Extraordinary of the United States in 1866.

language, that he intended selling the birthright of the Romanofs; it was not for such a contemptible price that he intended giving up the West. He aimed higher, and reckoned on the lion's share in the coming slaughter. Fortune may have betrayed his hopes, confounded his calculations, and forced him to bend to many unforeseen necessities; but, if it is puerile to wish to create virtues out of all these painful necessities with which to endow him, or to attempt to compose an aureole for his brow with the lightning of the thunderbolts of 1870, history, in its impartiality, should give Prince Gortchakof fair credit for his intentions, which were equal to the occasion, and, without seeking to hide the repulse he received, should grant him the full benefit due to one that *in magnis voluisse.*

Mighty projects had indeed been cherished on the banks of the Moskva and the Neva during the whole of the feverish and agitated period which separated Sadowa from Sedan. The most enchanting prospects were there entertained; the world was to be divided between Slavonia and Germania; and the "national" minister in truth but responded to the ardent wishes of his country in making the Prussian alliance the pivot on which his policy turned, an alliance he considered to be the one condition, the certain pledge, of a whole future of glory and prosperity for Russia. We must turn our thoughts back to the shock which was universally felt after the prodigious and unexpected victories of Prussia in 1866, to the numerous and fantastic plans which suddenly arose for the reconstruction of empires and races—we must remember the endless flight of Minervas, fully armed, which the blow from the hammer of the Germanic Vulcan caused to spring from so many cracked brains that believed themselves to be Olympian—the general *re-melting* which poor historical philosophy underwent in an hour—we must remember all this in order justly to appreciate the current of strange and imperious ideas by which the people of Peter the Great and Catherine II. were then carried away by. "An irresistible power was impelling all nations to form great agglomerations, and to abolish all minor States; and this tendency is perhaps inspired by a sort of providential foreknowledge of the destinies of the world." These were the expressions contained in an official document of incontrovertible authority, a diplomatic manifesto which announced *urbi et orbi* the lofty thoughts of the Imperial Government of France.*

How can we then feel any astonishment that the children of the Rouriks reasoned in a similar manner, that they should have openly asked themselves whether the battle of Königgratz (Sadowa) had not given up Central Europe to the Hohenzollerns, and Eastern Europe to the Romanofs? After a short period of hesitation and fear, Muscovite patriots resolved in consequence to take no offence at the ambition of King William I., but they immediately proclaimed that Russia had also a mission to fulfil, that she too had an "idea" to realise, and that the sun of national

* M. de Lavalette's Circular, September 16th, 1866.

unities and great agglomerations must shine equally on all the world.

There was, then, in the ancient capital of the Czars, a celebrated newspaper which, although it has since fallen off, and only now occupies the rank of an ordinary although still important journal, had at that time a preponderating, tyrannical influence, which was felt from the Dvina to the Oural mountains. At one time it was nicknamed "the first power of the empire after the emperor." Ever since the fatal insurrection in Poland the *Moscow Gazette* had been the representative of the people's feelings and passions in Holy Russia, the office from whence issued the word of command to public opinion in the vast empire of the North, and even sometimes formal instructions for the ministers at the head of affairs at St. Petersburg. Once again the all-powerful organ of M. Katkof became the mouthpiece of the nation, and imperiously dictated the programme of its future policy. Shortly after the treaty of Prague the Moscow journal had already decided "as an incontestable fact that the march of events had created interests which invited the two powers of Russia and Prussia to draw more closely together than they had ever done in the past;" it also affirmed that M. de Bismarck had made advances with this object in view— "advances which were all the more acceptable, as Prussia has no interest to bias her in the East; so that the Berlin Cabinet, in concert with that of Russia, may take up any position on this question which may be most convenient to it." This theme was taken up from time to time and developed under various forms and in various articles, until a leading article of February 17th, 1867, stamped it as a great principle of speculative humanitarianism : " A new era is dawning," so ran the article, " and for us Russians it is one of great importance. This era is ours : it calls to life a new world, which until now has slumbered in the shade awaiting its destinies—the Greco-Slavonic world."

" After centuries passed in resignation and servitude, this world is about to begin a period of renovation ; that which has for so long lain forgotten now returns to the light, and prepares for action. Existing generations will witness great changes, great deeds, and great formations. On the peninsula of the Balkan, and from under the rotten stratum of Ottoman tyranny, are already rising three nationalities, strong and full of life—the Hellenic, the Slavonic, the Roumanian. Closely allied to each other by the similarity of their faith and their historic destinies, these three groups are equally bound to Russia by all the ties of their religious and national life. Once let these three groups of nations be reconstructed, and Russia will stand revealed in a new light. She will no longer be alone in the world ; instead of the sombre Asiatic power she has until now appeared, she will become a great and indispensable moral force in Europe ; a Greco-Slavonic civilisation completing that Germanic-Latin civilisation which by itself would be incomplete, and would remain imperfect and inert in its sterile solitude." Descending shortly afterwards from these somewhat abstract heights to the more practical plains of ways and means, the fiery apostle of the new era wrote, on April 7th: "If France assists the revival of the Latin races with its arms and its political influence, if Prussia acts in a similar manner towards Germany, why should not Russia—as the only independent Slavonic power—support the Slavonic races, and prevent foreign powers from placing obstacles in the way of their political development? Russia ought to employ all her forces to effect among her southern neighbours a similar transformation to that which has taken place in central and western Europe; she ought, without the slightest hesitation, to adopt towards the Slaves the same course of action which France has adopted towards the Latin nations, and Prussia towards the Germans. The task is a noble one, for it is free from egotism; it is beneficent, for it will achieve the triumph of the principle of nationalities, and will give a solid basis to the modern equilibrium of Europe; it is worthy of Russia and of her greatness, it is immense, and we have the firm conviction that Russia will fulfil it."

It was under the stimulus of such theories, hopes, and passions, that the strange ethnological exhibition of Moscow* was opened. It soon became the pretext for a great popular demonstration — a demonstration too inoffensive in appearance to cause any diplomatic inconvenience, yet thoroughly calculated to produce its effect on simple and inflammable

---

* See a paper in the *Revue des Deux Mondes*, September 1st, 1867: " The Congress of Moscow and the Pan-Slavonic Propaganda."

minds, to fascinate unhappy and disinherited nations, far richer in imagination than in cultivation.

Certainly true science was likely to derive but little benefit from this projected assemblage of all the Slavonic "types," with their costumes, their arms, and their domestic utensils, in the riding-school at Moscow; but the enterprise was, nevertheless, considered worthy of the most august protection. The Emperor and Empress offered considerable sums to defray the expenses of the undertaking; the Grand Duke Vladimir accepted the post of honorary president; the highest dignitaries of the church and the state undertook its direction. The warmest appeals were addressed to the Slaves of Austria and Turkey, to their various historical, geographical, or other scientific societies, urging them to contribute, by numerous deputations, to the magnificence of the exhibition; and a whole cloud of emissaries overspread the countries of the Danube and the Balkan in quest of adherents, samples, and "types."

Committees were formed all over the empire to organise a suitable reception for the "Slavonic guests," who would not fail to attend this "national jubilee;" and soon a congress was suggested in which the wants and interests of so many "brother nations" would be considered, and where the hopes and sufferings of their great common country, their ideal fatherland, would be discussed. This, we must recollect, was the very moment when the Cretan insurrection was at its height; when, excited by Greece and exaggerated by journals more or less well informed, it served to keep the Christian populations of Turkey in a state of ferment and expectation; the very moment, also, when the Czechs of Bohemia, drawing after them nearly all the Slaves of Austria, were protesting against the Cis-Leithan constitution, and refusing to take their seats in the representative chambers of the empire.

The Kremlin, therefore, became the *Mons Sacer* of the agitators from both banks of the Leitha; the Congress of Moscow assumed all the appearance of a counter-parliament opposed to the Reichsrath in Vienna; and the language of the organs most in favour with the Cabinet of St. Petersburg was certainly not of a kind to calm the susceptibilities of interested governments, nor to dissuade their subjects from exasperating demonstrations.

Speaking of the pious pilgrims from Turkey and Austria who were preparing to visit Moscow, that "holy Mecca of the Slaves," the *Russian Correspondance*, the pre-eminently ministerial journal,[*] expressed itself as follows in the month of April, 1867: "It cannot reasonably be expected of us that we should deny our past. We shall, therefore, allow our guests to consider that they are visiting a sister nation from whom they have everything to expect and nothing to fear. We will listen to their grievances, and the recital of their woes will only serve to draw them closer to us. If they choose to compare

---

[*] It emanated directly from the Ministry of the Interior, and was written in French for the "enlightenment" of foreign opinion on the acts and intentions of the Russian Government.

their political state with our own, we shall certainly not be so foolish as to persuade them that they enjoy conditions which are the most favourable to Slavonic development. These conditions we believe, on the contrary, to be very bad ones. We have already said so a hundred times, and we are ready to repeat it."

No doubt these underhand proceedings of Russia in the countries of the Danube and the Balkan were not altogether of recent date: they were even of remote origin, and dated as far back as the reign of the great Catherine.

In an underhand and secret manner the Pan-Slavonic mission had been encouraged and protected for more than a century; but it was for the first time, during the summer of 1867, that the Russian Government had openly assumed the responsibility of such a propaganda, and had unfurled the banners of St. Cyril and St. Methodius. In an empire where everything is overlooked, regulated, and ordered from above; where nothing is done spontaneously; where everything is arranged and willed beforehand; "Slavonic strangers," subjects of two friendly neighbouring powers, were admitted, encouraged to relate their grievances, to bring complaints against their respective governments, to demand assistance and deliverance in the name of a new right, in the name of a newborn principle of great agglomerations and national unities. Russia was not foolish enough to send away these strange "deputies," or to preach reason and resignation to them. On the contrary, they were soothed with hopes "of a better fate soon to be realised;" they were conducted throughout all the towns of the empire in the midst of the most enthusiastic manifestations got up by the officers of the army and the archimandrites; were overwhelmed with expressions of sympathy, with ovations and demonstrations in which the army, the magistracy, and all the more important officials joined. Generals, admirals, and ministers presided at banquets, where the disaster of Sadowa was celebrated as a providential and fortunate event by subjects of Francis Joseph; where appeals were addressed to the Czar "to avenge the ancient wrongs of the White Mountain and of Kossovo, and to plant the Russian banner on the Dardanelles and on the basilica of St. Sophia. The shock given by such demonstrations to a whole race, to a whole religious world, was great and prolonged; and certainly contemporary annals have rarely known a period so at variance with the dictates of international right, and with the usual practices of diplomacy, than that which began with the Congress of Moscow and ended in the Conference at Paris on the subject of Greece.

It was, indeed, a peculiar epoch, with its presidents of council such as Ratazzi, Bratiano, Koumandouros; with its generalissimos such as Garibaldi, Petropoulaki, and "Philip the Bulgarian;" with its expeditions of Mentana, of Sistow, of the Arcadion and of Enosis; with, in a word, its German, Italian, Czechian, Croatian, Roumanian, Servian, Bulgarian, Greek, and Pan-Slavonic agitations. Without entering any further into the tedious history of these complicated and as yet unexplained events, it will suffice, in order to appreciate their general character and to grasp their inner workings, to read with all the attention it deserves, the report, which we have already mentioned, of the French ambassador at the Court of Berlin, dated January 5th, 1868. "M. de Bismarck," writes M. Benedetti, "requires a disturbed Italy, an Italy permanently estranged from France, in order to force us to maintain a considerable number of regiments in the States of the Church; and in order to bring about, whenever it may suit him, with the help of the revolutionary party, a violent rupture between the government of the Emperor and that of Victor Emmanuel—to neutralise, in one word, our freedom of action on the Rhine. . . . I should not be surprised either if M. de Bismarck were the instigator of the fresh impulse given since last summer to the Pan-Slavonic propaganda—it has, to him, the advantage of annoying Austria by means of Russia. Russia would certainly be less enterprising, and Prussia would certainly not advise her to reawaken the Eastern question, for the simple reason that Prussia herself could derive no benefit from it, if M. de Bismarck did not consider it the price he must pay for the liberty which he demands in Germany. The doubtfulness of the situation only draws Russia and Prussia more closely together, and makes one cause of the German ambitions of the one and the Eastern ambitions of the other."

A permanent committee to watch over the interests of Slave unity was formed shortly after the Congress of Moscow, under the auspices of a grand-duke, and its action did not fail to be felt among the Ruthenes, the Czechs, and the Croatians of Austria; but it was principally in the provinces tributary or subject to the Ottoman Empire that the agitation became as chronic as it was perilous. The unhappy Turk was assailed on all sides—one day the Vladika of Montenegro would demand such or such a port on the Adriatic; another day the Prince of Servia would exact the evacuation of some fortress, and would enforce his demand by an unusual display of arms. Numerous exportations of weapons from Russia entered the Danubian provinces under the false designation of materials for the construction of railroads;* while Greek ships of war unceasingly attempted to provoke to fresh vigour the Cretan insurrection, which was now dying out, and which had never been of great importance.

It was the period of "committees of help" and of "liberating bands," now invading the Papal States with cries of "*Roma o morte!*" now making incursions into Thessaly to revenge the "outraged shades of Phocion and of Philopœmen," or even crossing the Danube, in the direction of Roumania, five times in the space of one year, in order to awaken in the Balkan "the Lion of the Golden Mane!"

"My brethren, it is now for us to prove to the diplomatists of Europe that there still exist some

---

* See on this subject the English, French, and Austrian parliamentary documents of 1868, and notably the reports of the Austrian agents at Iassy and Bucharest.

descendants of the terrible Krum; the Lion of the Golden Mane and the trumpet of war summon you." This was the tenor of a proclamation dated from "the Balkan," and signed "Provisional Government." *

"It is a fact," wrote the Baron d'Eder, the Austrian agent in the Principalities, to M. de Beust, Feb. 6th, 1868, "it is a fact that at Bucharest, as in various other towns on the banks of the Danube, there exist Bulgarian committees, whose aim is to provoke disturbances in Bulgaria, to support them, and to give them greater proportions than those of last year. It was quite recently the opinion here, that on the return of fine weather the most serious complications would take place in Western Europe, which would permit Russia to declare war against Turkey, and, in the event of these occurrences taking place, preparations were made to energetically assist the Bulgarian rising.

"Although the government of the Principalities is in the hands of the radical party, always hostile to Russia, it inclines for some time past towards that power, and looks to her for the realisation of its hopes and efforts.

"The journals of the opposition party (Conservative) fight against the Russian tendencies of the Government; they accuse it of acting in concert with Prussia, and of raising up difficulties for Austria in the event of a war between France and Prussia. The Government journals reply by asserting that the national party is, on principle, the enemy of no power, and

---

* Enclosed in a despatch from the Consul of Knappitch to Baron de Prokesch at Constantinople. Ibraïla, August 24th, 1868.

that there can be no reason for opposing Russia, while that power is defending the cause of right and the cause of oppressed nationalities."

It would assuredly be most unjust to lay upon the Russian Government the responsibility of all the disorderly agitations which took place at this time in the Greco-Roumanian and Slavonic world, but it is nevertheless certain that it never attempted to stop or even to disown them. In reading the various parliamentary documents, the red, green, yellow, and blue books of 1867-69, we are struck by meeting, at every step, numerous and energetic representations, addressed by the Cabinets of London, Paris, and Vienna to Roumania and to Greece on the subject of their military preparations, on their clandestine despatch of arms and of invading bands, while the Cabinets of St. Petersburg and Berlin seem to have carefully abstained from ever mentioning any of these topics.

By a curious change in earthly matters, which must have astonished the Nesselrodes and Kamptz in their celestial abode, the voices of the Western Powers—those of England, France, and Austria— were now denouncing the underhand and revolutionary proceedings of the European demagogues, while Prussia was silent and Russia denied the fact or pleaded "extenuating circumstances."

Prince Gortchakof found excuses for the Athenian Government in the Hellenic constitution. "This constitution," said he, "gives every Greek the liberty to quit his native country and engage in conflicts such as took place recently in Crete."* This was certainly an odd spectacle, to see the minister of an autocrat explaining to such an old whig as Lord Clarendon the inexorable conditions of a legal and parliamentary system. The Porte, it will be recollected, could not understand a legality so detrimental to its interests; and, at last, losing patience, addressed an *ultimatum* to the Athenian Government. The result was a conference convoked in Paris in order " to find the means for smoothing away the differences which had arisen between Turkey and Greece."

Some good souls fancied that the Russian Chancellor would feel somewhat embarrassed when confronted with such an Areopagus, and even thought him capable of putting obstacles in its way; but they little knew the resources of a man as subtle as he was learned, and who actually took the opportunity of giving vent to his famous jest on Saturn.

"I am told," he wrote to Baron Brunnow in London, January 13th, 1869, " that some persons are accusing Russia of wishing to prevent the conference. Yet it is known that the conference springs from the Emperor's brain. The fable of Saturn will not apply to this last mistake of the Imperial Cabinet."

Alexander Mikhaïlovitch had not exhausted his temerity; he became bitter, almost aggressive; spoke of "excitement stirred up abroad," of "a drifting policy artfully prepared beforehand," and of "the suspicion attached to every step taken by Russia;"

---

* Despatch of Sir Andrew Buchanan to Lord Clarendon, December 19th, 1868.

and even went the length of accusing the Western Powers of devising a great conspiracy to disturb the peace of the Levant. "We cannot avoid remarking," he wrote to Baron Brunnow, in a despatch of January 17th, 1868, "that this discordant note is not the only one that has disturbed the echoes of the East. We have already beheld Servia become the focus of an agitation which has spread from the press to diplomacy. Prince Michael Obrenovitch was suspected: and it needed his tragic death to disarm the hostilities undertaken against him. The next thing was that accusations were raised against the government of the United Principalities, the Bulgarian bands formed a motive for recriminations, and that government was reproached with having tolerated—even accused of having encouraged, them. Scarcely has this complication been cleared up, when a fresh crisis springs up in the relations between Turkey and Greece: a more serious crisis and more dangerous for the general peace."

Decidedly, in default of the "Fable of Saturn," that of the "Wolf and the Lamb" could certainly be applied to the proceedings of the Imperial Cabinet of St. Petersburg.

The conference of Paris succeeded, nevertheless, in its efforts; the Turco-Grecian difficulties were smoothed over; and in the spring of 1869 the northerly blasts of the propaganda raged less fiercely in the valleys of the Danube and the passes of the Balkans. A sort of calm ensued; but the combustible materials still remained accumulated, ready to take light at the first spark. The radicals of Roumania were not the only ones to foresee that Russia would assume an offensive position in the East as soon as any serious complications took place in Western Europe. It was the universal belief, and one which the sons of the Rouriks were the first to adopt.

The close of the year 1869 was marked by an incident which did not fail to impress all thoughtful minds with a sense of its importance.

St. Petersburg was celebrating the centenary of the institution of the order of St. George, the greatest military order in Russia, and whose first class is only conferred on the hero of a brilliant victory.

The Emperor Alexander II. sent this distinction to William I., to the victor of Sadowa, and the combatant of 1814. "Accept it," so ran the telegraphic message, "as a renewed proof of the friendship which unites us; friendship founded on the memory of the great epoch when our united armies fought together for a holy and a mutual cause." The King of Prussia replied, immediately also by telegram: "Profoundly touched, and *with tears in my eyes*, I thank you for the honour you have done me, and which I was far from expecting. But that which overjoys me most are the expressions you have made use of in conferring it on me. I indeed read in them a fresh proof of your friendship and of your remembrance of the days when our united armies fought side by side for the same holy cause."*

In the beginning of the same year, while the conference was sitting in Paris, a faithful servant of the

---

* *Official Journal of the Russian Empire*, December 12th, 1869.

Sultan—one of the last of great Turkish statesmen—passed away at Nice. Before his death, Fuad Pacha wrote with his dying hand an address to his august master, which he designated as his last political testament. The document was to remain secret, and, indeed, has but recently been published.*

" When this writing is laid before your majesty, I shall no longer be of this world. You may," so runs the document, "therefore listen to me without suspicion, and become persuaded of the painful truth that the great Ottoman Empire is in danger." And after having passed in review the different states of the Continent, and pointed out the approaching inevitable conflict between France and Prussia, Fuad Pacha concludes with these words: "An internal war in Europe, *and a Bismarck in Russia*, and the face of the globe would be changed."

* This remarkable document, which bears the date of January 3rd, 1869, may be found in an interesting pamphlet of Mr. T. Lewis Farley, " The Decline of Turkey," pp. 27—36. London, 1875.

CHAPTER IX.

THE FRENCH WAR.

Surprising Foresight of M. Benedetti after 1867—He continually draws Attention to the complete Understanding between Russia and Prussia—Curious Illusions at the Tuileries on the Subject of General Fleury's Mission—The Interview at Ems between the Emperor Alexander and William I. (June, 1870)—M. Benedetti's Estimate of M. de Bismarck's Sincerity towards the Cabinet of St. Petersburg: Russia, in reality, only a Card in his Game—M. de Bismarck's successive Accomplices: M. de Rechberg, Napoleon III., and Prince Gortchakof—The Candidature of the Hohenzollern Prince for the Spanish Throne—The Russian Chancellor's significant Opinion of this Candidature — Declaration of War (July 15th)—Russia taken by Surprise—Russia prevents Austria from allying herself with France—The First Disaster—Public Feeling in Russia, and the Opportunity for a Congress—Prince Gortchakof and the League of Neutral Powers—Austria's vain Efforts to bring about Concerted Action between the Great Powers—The Russian Chancellor will only hear of "Isolated Action"—Nature of this Action—The Peace of Versailles, and the Telegram of William I. to the Emperor Alexander II. (February 26th, 1871)—Curious Similarity between the Catastrophe of 1866 and that of 1870—The Triumph of Prince Gortchakof in the Black Sea Question—What he might have accomplished—*Il gran rifiuto.*

To the Deity alone, perhaps, has it been given to look back upon his completed labour and "see that it was good." Mankind seldom tastes such a pure enjoyment, and the *parti de l'action* in the councils of the Second Empire certainly did not become acquainted with it after those momentous events of 1866 it had so powerfully helped to bring about. Amongst those whose eyes were opened was the ambassador of

France at the Court of Berlin. The completion of Italian unity but little consoled him for the dangerous blow which the disaster of Sadowa had struck at his own country. His disenchantment was great. But nothing better whets and sharpens a naturally sagacious mind than to have been grossly and painfully deceived; and if Pascal has spoken of a second ignorance which dawns upon the man who has deeply drank of knowledge, there is also a second experience, and something like a second sight, awaiting a certain stamp of politician after a passing defeat.

It would be impossible to speak too highly of the remarkable keenness of observation and judgment displayed by M. Benedetti during the last four years of his mission at Berlin. A remarkably unfortunate and imprudent diplomatist and negotiator in the fatal year 1866, he afterwards became a most active and reliable fountain of information; thenceforward the welfare of France occupied in his inmost thoughts the place too long usurped by his zeal for Italy.

From 1867, in fact, the ambassador found a patriotic delight in instructing his government as to the real condition of Europe, and in recommending it to adopt, one way or the other, a decisive resolution; either to calmly resign itself to the inevitable, or to prepare itself beforehand for a struggle near at hand and full of extreme perils. He strove to persuade it that Prussia was ceaselessly labouring at the assimilation of the whole of Germany, regardless of the risk of provoking a quarrel with France; being, indeed, but too often inclined to consider such a quarrel as the surest and most direct road to its end. In the event of such a conflict he entertained no hopes at all of the *particularists* of the south. " When a national war," he said, " once breaks out, the most headstrong among them will be powerless in presence of the masses of their countrymen, who will look upon the struggle, no matter how it arises, as a French war of aggression against their country; and if success should happen to be on their side, there will be no limit to their exactions."

He also took care to point out the " extraordinarily active propagandism " M. de Bismarck was carrying on beyond the Main ; " with the exception of a few journals in the pay of the governments (of Bavaria and Saxony) or belonging to the extreme Radical party, he is backed up by the entire press of all the Southern States." He wrote to Paris that King William's minister continued his intrigues with the revolutionary party in Italy; that he was in the habit of receiving Garibaldi's agents ; and that even the members of the regular government of King Victor Emmanuel, the obliged personal friend of Napoleon III., had, at the time the Mentana complications occurred, sounded Prussia, to discover " under what conditions it would come to their aid."*

He, too, was the first to call attention to the hidden intrigues with Prim about the Hohenzollern

---

* See, on this subject, the interesting despatch of November 10th, 1867. Mazzini's correspondence with M. de Bismarck during 1868 and 1869, suggesting the idea of dethroning Victor Emmanuel if he allied himself with Napoleon III., was not made public till later—quite recently—after the death of the celebrated Italian agitator.

candidature to the Spanish throne. And it has been already shown that he had at once recognised the alarming character and the real purport of General Manteuffel's mission to Russia.

"Difficult as it may be for a great power like France to determine beforehand its line of conduct in the actual condition of affairs," wrote M. Benedetti to his government in the beginning of 1868, "and ample as may be the allowance it is right to make for the unexpected, the concentration of Germany under a strong military government—a government that in many respects possesses nothing of a parliamentary *régime* but the external form—touches too nearly our national security to permit us to avoid the immediate resolution of the following question: Is the unification of Germany in reality a danger to the independence or position of France in Europe, and is war the only means to parry this danger? If the Emperor's government believes that France has nothing to fear from such a radical alteration in the relations of the central states of the Continent, it seems to me desirable, in the interests of peace and public prosperity, to assume an attitude entirely in unison with this belief. If a contrary conviction is entertained, it is our duty to thoroughly prepare for war; to ascertain beforehand of what use Austria might be to us; and to take steps to bring to a speedy settlement, one after the other, the Eastern and the Italian questions. We should certainly require the whole of our resources to triumph on the Rhine.

It is particularly in his estimate of the close relations between the Courts of Berlin and St. Petersburg that M. Benedetti showed the exactness and precision of his foresight. He was keen enough to detèct from the first their mutual understanding, and to firmly believe in it to the very last. In September, 1869, Napoleon III. selected as his envoy at the Russian Court one of his most trusted confidants—a zealous co-operator in the events of the 2nd of December, and one of his *grands écuyers*—a general officer as conspicuous for his intelligence as for his bravery.

This was to show clearly enough Napoleon's desire to cultivate the nearest and most direct understanding with the Emperor Alexander; and, in fact, in spite of the telegrams exchanged on the Fête of St. George, the French Cabinet was, at the beginning of 1870, full of hopes: it believed that "*l'affaire marchait toute seule.*"* The French ambassador at St. Petersburg, General Fleury, certainly a clever man, was speedily taken in by the bear hunts, the sleigh excursions, and the many other tokens of august kindness prepared for his benefit: favours which he modestly set down to the account of his master's policy, instead of attributing them, as with much better reason he might have done, to his own many agreeable qualities.

The ambassador's belief was shared by his suite, particularly by his aides-de-camp; who, in their confidential letters home, were continually alluding to the "great results" brought about by their chief, and to his increasing favour in the eyes of the Emperor of all

---

* Confidential letter from M. de Verdrière, St. Petersburg, February 3rd, 1870.—*Papers and Correspondence of the Imperial Family*, vol. i., p. 129.

the Russias, in terms that savoured more of military frankness than of diplomatic insight.* M. Benedetti, however, paid little attention to these hymns of triumph, and still retained his old convictions. Indeed, as late as June 30th, 1870, on the very eve of the declaration of war, he reiterated them in a luminous despatch, from which we shall have to quote more than one significant passage. Speaking of the interview between the Emperor Alexander and the King of Prussia at Ems, which occurred during the first four days in June, he thinks it probable that M. de Bismarck, as usual, showed himself on the one hand favourable to the Emperor's Eastern policy, while on the other he endeavoured to awaken the Czar's susceptibilities in connection with the questions of Austria and Galicia.

"While the minister," says M. Benedetti, "was probably occupied in· reassuring the Emperor on the first point, and in endeavouring to alarm him on the second, the King, doubtless, was employing his gracious charm of manner, which he has always known to turn to such good account, in winning the sympathies of his august nephew; and I have no doubt both King and minister succeeded in their task. But, whatever may have been the means they had recourse to, their purpose was certainly to strengthen the Emperor in holding the views they managed to instil

---

* "The Emperor of Russia has taken a very great fancy to the General. He is continually inviting him to bear-hunts, and often asks him to ride with him in his own sleigh that only holds two. This last is considered a supreme favour, and I think it looks well for our policy." Confidential letter from M. de Verdrière, January 25th, 1870. *Papers and Correspondence of the Imperial Family*, vol. i., p. 127.

into him; and it is certain that they more or less achieved it."

M. Benedetti, however, by no means admitted that any formal arrangement existed between the two cabinets—by no means thought that the Prussian minister had in reality and all sincerity abandoned the solution of the Eastern question to his former colleague at Frankfort—and it is in these nice gradations of appreciation that the French ambassador at Berlin showed his uncommon perspicacity. It was, of course, easy to believe that M. de Bismarck, to suit the needs of the moment, would play the indifferent in Eastern affairs; pretend that "he never took the trouble to read his Constantinople despatches," and even appear to believe the pretension of Russia " to introduce a measure of unity into the intellectual development of the Slaves"* a perfectly legitimate aspiration. But the care he was at the same time taking to keep up the most intimate relations with his Hungarian allies of 1866 ought to have opened the eyes of Russian zealots to the emptiness of their dreams of a partition of the world between the Teutons and the sons of Rourik.

"The Hungarians consider the Russians as their future protectors against Vienna," wrote Baron de Werther in a confidential despatch of June, 1867, on his return from the coronation at Buda, with the object of reassuring the Berlin Cabinet as to the recent enthusiasm of the Magyars, just reconciled to

* An expression used in the *North German Gazette* (Bismarck's principal organ) of July 20th, 1867, in speaking of the Moscow Congress.

their King. But it is not only against Vienna, it is much more against Moscow and St. Petersburg, against all Slave preponderance on the banks of the Danube, that the children of Arpad will demand in the future the aid of the Hohenzollern.

"Prussia has no interests in the East," was a favourite assertion of M. de Bismarck between 1867 and 1871; and M. Katkof's organ lost no opportunity of repeating this much-discussed expression. From the day, however, that Prussia became identified with the whole of Germany, or rather assimilated it, she perforce inherited all German interests and German influences on the shores of the Danube and at the foot of the Balkans. Thenceforward her share in Eastern policy became a large one, far larger than that either of France or England.

M. Benedetti well realised all this, and from time to time shrewdly drew attention to it in the despatches he wrote during the closing years of his stay at Berlin. Speaking, in his report of January 5th, 1868, of the obliging manner in which the Chancellor of the Northern Confederation had always agreed with Prince Gortchakof's views, he added: "He (M. de Bismarck) is doubtless convinced that there are other powers who have the greatest interest in shielding the Ottoman Empire from Russian greed, and he leaves the task to them; but he knows that *in the Eastern question no definite solution can be arrived at without the permission or adhesion of Germany, if only Germany be united and powerful.* He thinks, therefore, that just at present there is not the slightest objection to whetting the appetite of Russian ambition, if he can obtain in return an obliging abstention from all his own undertakings in Germany." "In Eastern affairs," wrote the French ambassador a little later, "M. de Bismarck wishes to take up a position that commits him to nothing, and that will allow him, as circumstances turn out, either to lend a hand to Russia or to extend it to the Western Powers. This position he can only retain by refusing to take any step that would compromise him with either the friends or the foes of Turkey."

These views were soon fully justified by the attitude taken up by Prussia during the conference at Paris on Greek affairs (January, 1869). It became evident that the Berlin Cabinet was not quite inoculated with the ardour of Alexander Mikhaïlovitch; it did not, like him, recognise the personification of persecuted innocence in young Roumania or in the Servian *Omladina*; and it was especially careful to avoid the assumption of a huge conspiracy between England, France, and Austria against the tranquillity of the Levant. In truth, the Prussian minister was by no means anxious for the decease of the Porte, still less for the collapse of Hungary, the vanguard of the " German mission " in the East;* and his sympathies with an " ideal unity " of the Slaves grew colder as the hour of real German unity approached.

" A struggle in the East would force him to follow Russia's lead," wrote M. Benedetti, on January

---

* *Drang nach osten.*

27th, 1870, " and he will do his best to prevent one ; he showed that this was his policy last year, on the occasion of the controversy between Turkey and Greece. He looks on Russia as a card in his game, to be played in case of complications on the Rhine ; *and he will be particularly careful not to change rôles* and become a card in the game of the St. Petersburg Cabinet."

A few months later, immediately before the outbreak of the war with France (June 30th, 1870), M. Benedetti, while thinking that the tie betwixt Russia and Prussia had necessarily been strengthened by the interview at Ems, concluded a despatch with the following observations : " It must not, however, be thought that M. de Bismarck has determined to closely identify his policy with that of Russia. In my opinion he has not entered into, and is not disposed to enter into, any agreement, which, by compromising Prussia in any future Eastern complications, might throw England into the arms of France, and cast obstacles in his own path on the Rhine. The courteous attention paid by the Chancellor of the Northern Confederation to Russian views, will never go so far as to limit his own liberty of action ; he promises more than he intends to perform ; or, in other words, he cultivates the friendship of the St. Petersburg Cabinet with the intention of profiting by its good offices in case of a struggle in the West, but with a full determination never to pre-engage German resources or German forces in an Eastern crisis. On this account I have always felt sure that no formal agreement has been entered into between the two courts, and it is tolerably certain that nothing of the kind was suggested at Ems."

Everything, in fact, seems to show that at Ems no treaty was signed, no conditions were formally discussed; an apparent common point of view and harmony of intention rendered unnecessary the fatiguing discussion of details. It would, moreover, have been very difficult, in any but the very gravest questions, to draw up regular stipulations applicable to coming events of which neither the exact date, the immediate effects, nor the ulterior consequences were known. It was probably considered sufficiently satisfactory that the two sovereigns were actuated by no opposing interests; were, on the contrary, penetrated with sympathetic ideas; and that an understanding existed that when the hour struck each was to fight for his own hand, and God for them both.

The Russians, it should also be remembered, are not, in their views on the Eastern question, entirely free from illusion. The rest of Europe is inclined to credit them with a more methodical programme than they really possess. Their feelings on the subject are deep and tenacious; but their projects are numerous, vague, and wanting in concentration. This powerful nation seems in this respect more under the sway of a fatalistic fascination than under the guidance of a systematic scheme of conquest. It pursues its besetting phantom without gaining upon it. It is worth notice that Russia has never found itself so far from its aims as when she has attempted to hasten the catastrophe. In 1829, when her armies were almost in sight of Constantinople, she was forced to withdraw; in 1854 the fruits of her campaign in Hungary, and the pre-eminence accruing to her from her immunity from the revolutionary wave of 1848, were entirely swept away; while, on the other hand, her prospects were never really so brilliant as on the day the signature of the Treaty of Paris seemed to exclude her for ever from the Black Sea; for, though she lost Sebastopol, she gained the Caucasus and a new world on the shores of the Amoor and of the Syr-Daria.

It was natural, therefore, when she foresaw the tremendous struggle preparing after 1867 in the centre of Europe, that she should determine rather to wait the outcome of the coming storm, than attempt to regulate it and direct its course. A war between the two most powerful States of the Continent—a war that promised to be a long and a disastrous one, and that might end by exhausting both combatants and dragging other powers into the struggle—would certainly afford Russia, so it was thought on the banks of the Neva, plenty of opportunities of pronouncing its own fiat, and of snatching its own plunder. Such a course of conduct, forsooth, seemed to naturally suggest itself to a chancellor who had already reaped so many advantages by biding his time; it appeared the logical outcome of a policy, the infinity of whose aspirations was only measured by the unknown possibilities of the future. In such cases an infinite ambition frequently runs on all-fours with an indefinite purpose, and a vague emptiness often causes an impression of profound depth.

With cruel irony the founder of German unity has generally chosen for his accomplice in one enterprise the dupe destined to be the victim in his next one. His great superiority has partly consisted in the facts that his aim has always been a clear one, his object always well defined, limited, and perfectly attainable; while his associates of the moment generally allowed themselves to be entangled in the perilous web under the impulsion of abstract principles, vague desires, and confused combinations.

At the time of the invasion of the Duchies—his first attempt to shift the equilibrium of Europe—it was certainly scarcely necessary to ask M. de Bismarck for his real intentions. There was his prey lying openly before him; the roadstead of Kiel displayed its ample splendours to all who had eyes to see. Yet M. de Rechberg still amuses himself with discovering and explaining the motives of his co-operation in that iniquitous scheme. "It was necessary to put a curb on the passions of the democracy, to give a tangible check to the spirit of revolution." Such are the pompous and sonorous phrases, borrowed from antediluvian diplomacy, with which the former Austrian minister attempted to veil, in presence of the Austro-Hungarian delegates, his piteous and fatal policy of 1863.

At Biarritz the president of the Prussian Council demanded in plain terms the Main as a boundary for his country, while the dreamer of Ham was vaguely recommending a great campaign for the consolidation of German unity, and letting his procrastinating glance stray now on the right bank of the Rhine and Mayence, now on the old boundaries of 1814; and now and again, with a perhaps more resolute gaze, fixing his visionary eyes upon the winged lion of St. Mark.

From 1867 to 1870 the Chancellor of the Northern Confederation steadily occupied himself with preparing the unification of Germany and the conquest of Alsace and Lorraine, content to leave to his old colleague of Frankfort the idle task of "awaking the echoes of the East," and of asking from them the password of Russian destiny.

In each and all of these prophetic circumstances we see the same great man of action playing at his pleasure with the different fantasies of the deluded ideologists; we see the same Fortinbras of Shakespeare —the strong in arm, indeed, of Germany—riding roughshod to his ends, where doctrinary Hamlets, melancholy or epigrammatic, were only able to blindly wander into chimerical and puerile machinations— dreamers who, face to face with crimes that cried to heaven, could only feebly utter, "The times are out of joint!"

"Prussia's increase of power can never cause Russia any anxiety,"* said Prince Gortchakof, in

---

* From one of Sir A. Buchanan's despatches, dated July 9th, 1870. For a detailed account of the diplomacy of 1870 and 1871, see the instructive work of M. Albert Sorel, "Diplomatic History of the Franco-German War." Paris, Plon, 1875. We can only find two faults with this book, written with careful truth and impartial ability; its author betrays a decided weakness for the "Tours Diplomacy," and scarcely allows sufficient breadth to Prince Gortchakof's original designs, in his understanding with Prussia, since 1867.

answer to the representations made to him at the commencement of the Hohenzollern proposal as to the peril in store for Russia from the aggrandisement of Prussia, and the growth of its influence in Europe. And the Prince reminded the alarmists that when, in spite of Russia and with the support of France, Prince Charles of Hohenzollern became, in 1866, sovereign of Roumania, the Russian Cabinet had, after merely remonstrating, accepted the position; he could not see, therefore, why on this occasion Prussia should be made more responsible for the election of another member of its reigning family to the throne of Spain.

Thus spoke the Czar's Minister at the outbreak of the struggle, on July 8th, 1870; before Prince Antoine's renunciation, before the French Cabinet had madly lashed itself into a state of excitement, and while Europe was still inclined to approve the legitimate susceptibilities of France. And when the French Government, giddy and blinded, soon, by its violent language in the Corps Législatif, by its exactions at Ems, and by its fatal declaration of war on July 15th, lost all it had gained in its marked diplomatic victory, it was impossible not to clearly understand the real sentiments of the Cabinet of St. Petersburg. "If General Fleury will permit me to say so," sarcastically wrote M. de Beust to Prince Metternich on July 20, "Russia's alliance with Prussia is so determined upon, that, in case of certain contingencies, the intervention of the Russian forces may be considered not only probable but certain." In fact, immediately after the declaration of war, on July 15th, the Russian Government clearly and distinctly informed the Viennese Cabinet that it would not permit Austria to make common cause with France; and General Fleury, indeed, may have considered himself fortunate that he was able to prevent the express mention of this injurious clause in the declaration of neutrality issued by the Emperor Alexander on the 23rd of July.*

"Russia has done us an immense amount of injury," exclaimed the Duke de Gramont, referring to this interdiction laid upon Austria.† A similar warning was sent to Copenhagen, and forced Denmark to remain neutral, in spite of the enthusiasm of that unfortunate nation for an alliance with France; an alliance in which a project of disembarkation in the north was a principal item. General Trochu, who was to take part in it, was of opinion that such an undertaking would prove of immense strategical importance.

The United States minister at St. Petersburg agreed with one of the official newspapers of that capital, "that Russia has done more to ensure neutrality than any other nation; its threats have prevented Austria from moving, and the influence of its Emperor and of the Czarovitch have succeeded in hindering Denmark from espousing the cause of France." ‡

England, it is just to add, in all this powerfully assisted the Russian policy. She was more than ever

---

* From Sir A. Buchanan's despatches, July 20th and 23rd.—*Valfrey's History of the Diplomacy of the Government of National Defence*, vol. i., p. 18.

† "La France et la Prusse," p. 348.

‡ Despatch from Mr. Schuyler to Mr. Fisk, dated St. Petersburg, August 23rd. "Pour la Vérité," by General Trochu, p. 90.

indifferently disposed towards France, in consequence of M. de Bismarck's recent terrible revelations of the "dilatory negotiations" of August, 1866, about Belgium.

It is evident that the torch was kindled a little too soon to exactly suit Prince Gortchakof. The military preparations of Russia were by no means finished. Its moral influence, even, over the Slave world had received a check since the conference on Greece. M. de Bismarck had not precisely fixed the hour to suit his colleague of the Neva; as was remarked by M. Benedetti, he had been particularly careful not to invert the *rôles*, and to act only at his own convenience, to only seize his own opportunity. Alexander Mikhaïlovitch, however, none the less strove to carry out his part to the best of his ability.

A very sagacious observer, the United States minister already mentioned, wrote about this time to his government: "The general opinion here seems to be that if Russia had been ready it would have declared war, and striven to obtain from the confusion certain advantages. . . . The government is doing its utmost to prepare for all contingencies. The cartridge factories are at work night and day; an order for a hundred Gatling cannon has just been sent to America." Thus the Russians hastened to arm themselves, and to hinder and intimidate all the possible allies of France, thinking that by so doing they were equalising the chances between the two belligerents.* They flattered themselves that a war, which Napoleon III. himself had declared would be "long and painful," would be sure to afford them more than one favourable opportunity.

But the dreadful disasters that overwhelmed France at the very beginning of the campaign, put a sudden stop to these vain imaginings, and broke up the dream of a new Greco-Slave world, which, since 1867, had ever and again haunted the dwellers on the banks of the Moskva and the Neva. The remarkable political and matter-of-fact aptitudes of the Russian nation enabled it at once to understand that all chances of an Eastern crusade were gone for the moment, that the destinies of the world were, for the time, being fought out at the foot of the Vosges mountains, and that it only remained for it to turn its attention to that which was pressing and possible.

It is a curious phenomenon that the Balkan peninsula was never so peaceful, so undisturbed by the "supreme idea," as during these years 1870-71; during that "intestine struggle in Europe" which the dying Fuad Pacha had declared would bode so much ill to the Ottoman Empire. Towards the close of August, before the catastrophe of Sedan, public opinion in Russia could think of nothing but the unpopular clause in the Treaty of Paris concerning the Black Sea.

---

* Prince Gortchakof was far from believing, at first, that the Prussians would be victorious. He told M. Thiers many interesting stories on this subject—*M. Thiers' Depositions before the Committee of Inquiry*, p. 12. In an interview, indeed, with a politician whom he knew to have intimate relations with Napoleon III., he is said to have remarked: "Tell the Emperor of the French to be moderate."—*Valfrey*, vol. i., p. 79.

"Russia," said an influential St. Petersburg journal,* "has not prevented the compulsory unification of Germany, neither, in its turn, *does it contemplate the compulsory unification of the Slaves*; but it has the right to ask that its position in the Black Sea and on the shores of the Danube be improved; we trust that these legitimate demands will be taken into consideration at the European congress which will probably follow the present war."

A European congress! This in fact would have been the only logical and moderately reassuring upshot of the important events that were disturbing the world's equilibrum; and it is only doing justice to the general Russian feeling of the moment to say that it was in accordance with the real necessities of the situation, and that it only looked forward to its country playing a part as honourable as it was legitimate. The Russians wished to satisfy their *amour-propre*, but they were far from desiring to sacrifice to it France and the general interests of the Continent. The lesser question was, in their eyes, but the corollary of the greater. Even at Constantinople, where the behaviour of the Russian Cabinet was looked forward to with anxiety, no different expectation was, in reality, entertained. As early as September 2nd, Mr. Joy Morris, the American minister to the Sublime Porte, wrote to his government that the general opinion on the Bosphorus was that Russia would take advantage of the crisis to insist upon the revision of the treaty of 1856. "It would be strange if she did not suc-

* *The Golos*; quoted in Mr. Schuyler's despatch of August 27th.

ceed in her endeavours," added Mr. Morris, " since it will fall to her to obtain honourable conditions of peace for France, and to exercise a predominant influence upon the terms of the settlement."

Unfortunately, and for the first time during his long and popular tenure of office, " the national minister" divorced himself from the general feeling of his countrymen, and, instead of behaving " like a patriotic European," to use M. de Talleyrand's favourite expression, he sought first and foremost to show his friendship for his old Frankfort colleague. He did not neglect the question of the Black Sea—he owed this little piece of consolation to his country to make up for his huge miscalculations—but he determined to separate two questions which Russia wished to see remain united; and it desired that they should so remain from political rather than from generous motives—from an instinctive perception of the vital interests of the future, rather than from a wish to satisfy the keen but passing inclinations of the moment. The Russian Chancellor deemed the fittest way to serve Russian interests on the Euxine was to damage those of Europe in Alsace and Lorraine, and did his utmost that France and Germany should be left undisturbed to fight their quarrel out. In accordance with this policy, he, immediately after the first French disaster, jumped at the ingeniously treacherous idea of *the league of neutral powers,* an idea of Italian origin, afterwards naturalised as an English one by Lord Granville, and turned, in the hands of the Russian Chancellor, as was cleverly remarked at the time, into a splendid means of "organising the impotence of Europe." M. de Beust had vainly endeavoured, while adopting the foundation of the English proposal of August 19th, to alter its character, and to make it the basis of a concerted intervention. He suggested not separate efforts, but one made in common to mediate on behalf of France, instead of the abortive scheme which only "leagued" the powers together in order to prevent them from making any collective proposal. "The combination suggested at this moment by the Austrian minister," says a judicious historian, "was incessantly proposed by him during the rest of the war; if it had been adopted it would probably have altered the course of events. It may be said, indeed, that this explains why Europe refused to adopt it." *

This is the reason why Prince Gortchakof, in particular, opposed it from first to last. For one passing moment England felt a slight compunction of conscience, and showed some desire to intervene. This supervened on M. de Bismarck's circular announcing to Europe Germany's terms of peace—Alsace and Lorraine. The Prussian ambassador communicated this circular to the Russian Government, and Prince Gortchakof abstained from any comment. Sir A. Buchanan informed him that the Court of St. James was, to a certain extent, inclined to follow the initiative of St. Petersburg. The Chancellor re-

* Sorel's "Diplomatic History of the Franco-German War," vol. i., p. 254. From a despatch of M. de Beust, dated September 29th, and intended for London, we may also quote the following: "Do not let us be afraid to say it, what is now helping to turn the struggle into a horrible war of extermination, is, on one side, illusions and unfounded hopes; on the other, the indifference to, and selfish contempt of, the conflict manifested by Europe."

plied that as Prussia had not asked his advice he had not given it.*

Lord Granville had the courage—a very unusual courage in him—to return to the subject; and Sir A. Buchanan read to the Russian Chancellor a memorandum timidly asking "whether it might not be possible for England and Russia to come to an understanding upon the terms of peace, and to make, in concert with the other neutral powers, an appeal to the King of Prussia's humanity, recommending at the same time moderation to the French Government."

Prince Gortchakof drily and scornfully received these overtures. "Prussia," said he, "has declared its terms of peace; a French victory alone can alter them, and a French victory is not likely to happen. Confidential conversations, therefore, between England and Russia are useless. Concerted representation would assume a more or less threatening character; isolated action on the part of each neutral power is to be preferred."†

Isolated action! And this was all that could be got out of Alexander Mikhaïlovitch, who contented himself with allowing the august nephew to personally address a few letters to his royal uncle—beautifully expressed letters, talking of peace and justice, humanity and moderation — which the conqueror of Sedan always affectionately answered with a swelling heart and tearful eyes, dwelling upon his duties towards

---

* Sorel's " Diplomatic History of the Franco-German War," vol. i., p. 402.

† Sir A. Buchanan's Report, October 1st.

x

his allies, his troops, his people, and his frontiers."*

This "euphemistic policy," as the historian has well termed it, was persisted in on the banks of the Neva during the whole of the war. General Fleury, as well as M. Thiers and M. de Gabriac, were treated to it, and the whole upshot of this "isolated action" of Prince Gortchakof was to utterly abandon France to the tender mercies of her conqueror, alone in her exhaustion—*usque ad finem.*

It is well known in what terms this end was announced at St. Petersburg.

"It is with a feeling I cannot express, and in returning thanks to the Almighty," telegraphed from Versailles the Emperor of Germany to the Emperor of Russia, on February 26th, 1870, "that I inform you that the preliminaries of peace have just been signed. Never will Prussia forget that to you it is due that the war did not assume larger proportions. May God bless you for it. Your grateful friend for life."

"Long and painful," indeed, was this war, as the unhappy Emperor had predicted; long enough, at any rate, to let Europe measure the depth of its degradation, and to "give its blushes time to reach their highest," as the poet happily says. If anything could be more humiliating than this degradation, it would

---

* Even the simple proposal of armistice, which could have had no influence upon the final terms of peace, Prince Gortchakof avoided making in concert. M. d'Oubril, his envoy at Berlin, was left at the last moment without instructions on this point. "It is singular enough," wrote Lord Loftus, on October 26th, "that Russia, after repeatedly proving its desire for peace, should thus hold itself aloof, and prefer isolated to concerted action."

be the recollection of the exact similarity between the two catastrophes that had happened within the short space of four years. Fate, in producing its second tragedy so soon after its first, had such a contempt for our generation that it did not even think it worth while to alter the plot or to make any outlay of imagination. The work of 1870 was a mere copy of that of 1866.

"You can take the East," said M. de Bismarck at St. Petersburg, through his mouthpiece, General Manteuffel; as on the beach at Biarritz he had told the Emperor Napoleon to take Belgium, making always the same kind of offer of what was not his to give, the same gracious gift of dragon-defended fruit.

The dreamers of Moscow believed in a new era, in "a new Greco-Slave-Roumanian world," as, in like manner, Napoleon III. had dreamt of a new Europe, reparcelled out in accordance with the principle of nationalities. "Prussia's increase of power can never cause Russia any anxiety," had declared Prince Gortchakof at the commencement of the Hohenzollern incident, just as the zealots of the "new law" had said at the outbreak of the Bohemian campaign that France need feel no alarm. In both of these terrible years France and Russia alike counted upon the chances that would occur in a protracted and even struggle; they had even in each case respectively set to work to hypothetically equalise the chances of the two combatants, and the surprise and confusion were not greater at St. Petersburg after Reichshoffen and

x 2

Sedan, than they had been in Paris after Nahod and Sadowa.

Russia was behindhand in her military preparations in 1870 as France was in 1866, and the outbreak of both these calamities, that desolated and upset the Continent, was followed by nothing but paltry and selfish thoughts. All collective intervention was purposely checked; Prussia was helped to entirely free herself from the control of Europe; in a word, a policy of justice, of preservation, and of mutual equilibrium was sacrificed to one as erroneous as it was sordid—to a line of conduct the famous humorist of Varzin once designated as "a *pourboire* policy."

The Russian Chancellor, it is true, was more fortunate after Sedan than was Napoleon after Sadowa. He did manage to get his Luxemburg; he succeeded in procuring the abrogation of the second article of the Treaty of Paris, "an abrogation of a theoretical principle without any present application," as he himself did not forget to repeat in a despatch.*

It is within the recollection of all what estimate was placed by the different cabinets of Europe upon this victory—really only a nominal one, and of very little consequence, when compared with that Alexander Mikhaïlovitch had allowed his old colleague to obtain.

Prince Gortchakof gained his point, but not by legitimate means, not with the brilliant and just

---

* Despatch from Prince Gortchakof to Baron Brunnow at London, November 20th, 1870.

triumph hoped for in Russia, dreaded in Constantinople. He did not obtain the revision of the treaty of 1856, in "endeavouring to obtain honourable conditions of peace for France, and in exercising a predominant influence upon the terms of settlement."* He purposely made choice of the psychological moment of France's weakness, of Europe's dismay, and of the fatal blow that had befallen its public rights, to deal it in his turn a last humiliating stroke—a *telum imbelli*, but not *sine ictu*.

With his own permission alone he freed himself from an engagement entered into with the Powers, as he had freed his friend at Berlin from the control of Europe. "Russia's act," said Lord Granville in his remarkable despatch of November 10th to Sir A. Buchanan, "annihilates all treaties. The object of a treaty is to bind the contracting parties one to the other; according to the latest Russian doctrine, each party obeys its own authority alone, and feels bound only to itself."

In the beginning of 1868, a large intellect—soon to be restored by his country's disasters to the political life shut out from him by the Second Empire, inveighed with passionate eloquence against "the ever-increasing neglect of that elementary principle of international justice which public honour and public good sense term the faith of treaties."† "We see every day," said he, "springing up under our eyes a luxuriant jurisprudence, whose rapid growth does not surprise

* Despatch of Mr. Joy Morris, previously quoted.
† See "Diplomacy and Principles of the French Revolution," by Prince Albert de Broglie, in the *Revue des Deux Mondes* of February 1st, 1868.

those who know what strength false principles now borrow of, now lend to, the passions they encourage. A few years ago this one-sided breach of unanimously accepted treaties was not possible without incurring risks that made want of faith, if not more legitimate, at least of less frequent occurrence and of a less evil example. It was still admitted that before a State could pretend to repudiate a regularly signed treaty, it must show that within its limits had occurred one of those general upheavals of institutions, persons, and things, termed a revolution. A revolution was the political writ by which a nation informed all whom it concerned that it was going into moral liquidation, and no longer intended to pay its debts. This, it seems to me, was already a large privilege; but the latest fashion of the new international code thinks it insufficient. The formality of a revolution is a troublesome and a costly one. A change of ministry, or, better still, a parliamentary vote, is less inconvenient. For the future this is all that is required to be able, one twelvemonth, to tread under foot an agreement which God, public honour, and public conscience have been called upon to witness in the previous one."

But, indeed, since this cry of alarm was uttered by an honest conscience, we have lived to see this new-fashioned code of rights called into play without the excuse of a revolution, a change of cabinet, or even a parliamentary vote; to hear its legitimacy proclaimed by the minister of a regular, absolute monarchy—by a Russian Chancellor. The Italians, it is true, were in a similar hurry to take advantage of France's misfortune to break a solemn engagement they had contracted with her. It cannot be denied that in 1870 they set Prince Gortchakof an example in this new-fangled style of public honour. But it was scarcely from a government born but yesterday that Count Nesselrode's successors should have stooped to take a lesson. Once, indeed, Alexander Mikhaïlovitch reproached Italy for "siding with the revolution for the sake of receiving its inheritance."* Since then he, too, has sided with the revolution—with one of the most audacious, most violent revolutions that have ever upset a throne and overwhelmed a kingdom. He has not received its inheritance, it is true (for the revolution, alas! is still alive), but he has accepted an *ante-mortem* legacy—a deed of gift, a trifling present out of all proportion to the services he rendered, but one that bears the stamp of treacherous gain, and that is an injury and an insult to the rights of nations.

The triumph of Alexander Mikhaïlovitch would have been of a somewhat noble, more enduring kind, if, in the month of October, 1870, "the national minister," inspired by the legitimate ambition of the Russian nation, had brought about a European understanding to make peace betwixt France and Prussia, and to settle the tremendous troubles of the Continent.

"We have always thought," wrote M. de Beust as early as the 10th September to St. Petersburg, "that

* Letter to Prince Gagarine at Turin, dated October 10th, 1860.

Russia should take the initiative." And, in truth, her importance abroad, her security at home, her intimate relations with the conqueror, properly assigned it to her. There is no room for doubt but that Austria, Italy, and England would immediately have ranged themselves under her banner. No need was there of any threatening intervention, no occasion even for the armed neutrality suggested by Mr. Disraeli.* The will of all the Continental powers firmly expressed in unison would have amply sufficed. In this manner the losses of France might have been lessened, and Germany might have been restricted to a less formidable position, more in harmony with the aspirations and the liberal tendencies of our century. The great vassals themselves of the new Emperor would have hastened to proffer their co-operation, and a general disarming would have restored to fruitful and recuperative labour a hardly-tried generation, unable, as matters now stand, to gain even repose from its idleness.

Who can doubt that after such services Russia would not have failed to obtain from a grateful Europe the abrogation of the obnoxious clause in the treaty of 1856? France, for one, would certainly never have dreamt of standing in the way; Austria would not have desired to retain a clause which she had opposed from the first, and which, four years previously, she had solemnly declared to be merely "a question of pride," whose sacrifice was demanded by the most weighty interests. As for England, it is

* Speech in the House of Commons, August 1st.

well known that of late it has been possible to make her agree to a great deal, or rather, that for some time past she accepts everything.*

What influence, what vigour, such a benefit, obtained for humanity by an absolute monarchical government, would have lent to the cause of order and conservatism! What a legacy of life it would have been to the monarchical principle! What prestige it would have shed upon the Russian nation! What imperishable renown it would have linked to the name of Alexander II.! The call of fate was plainly audible, the path it pointed out was easy. Count Nesselrode's successors were deaf to the one, and refused to see the other. It was but an offence of omission, perhaps; but of a kind never forgiven by that great doer of justice, Alighieri, when committed against his ideal of *justitia et pax*. Such was the sin he stigmatised with the name of *il gran rifiuto*.

* Lord Granville, in his bitter despatch of November 10th, 1870, hastened to acknowledge that England would not have refused to examine, in concert with the co-signatory powers, what modifications might have been made in the treaty of 1856, "if Russia had only gone to work in another way."

CHAPTER X.

A TEN YEARS' PARTNERSHIP.

The Emperor William's Journey to Russia in the Spring of 1873—Twelve Days of Fête at St. Petersburg—The Two Chancellors on the Banks of the Neva—Russian Opinion on the Ten Years' Partnership—For and Against—M. de Bismarck's Reassuring Words—Serious Apprehensions for the Future.

ON January 9th, 1873, Napoleon III. mournfully expired in exile at Chislehurst, and shortly afterwards William I. entered the seventy-sixth year of a life certainly not lacking in Fortune's most extraordinary favours. Germany celebrated the birthday of her new Emperor with a delight all the more exuberant and sincere, that he had marked the anniversary by ratifying a last convention with the Versailles government, which assured the payment in advance of the fifth milliard of ransom, and the speedy return of the army of occupation beyond the Vosges mountains. Having thus finally settled accounts with his hereditary enemy, the conqueror of Sedan resolved in his turn to pay a debt of gratitude. He determined to personally convey to the Emperor Alexander II. his grateful thanks for the loyal assistance he had rendered him through a long period of trial and of struggle. Long announced, and often deferred, the journey to St. Petersburg at last took place in the spring; and M. de Bismarck was careful that both the date of the visit, and the visit itself, should remind the world of the intimate association of interests that had grown up between Russia and Prussia, and that had proved so fatal to the West. "The common aim," said the official organ of the German ministry,* "which brought about the alliance between Prussia and Russia in 1863, at the time of the Polish insurrection, was the starting-point of the present policy of the two powers; a policy that the great events of the last four years have confirmed and strengthened. From the attitude assumed by Russia in the Schleswig-Holstein question, down to the important proofs of sympathy given to Germany by the Emperor Alexander during the last war, everything that has occurred has helped to cement this alliance."

Obeying that species of historical glamour, sometimes clever enough to partially deceive dispassionate examination, which the sovereign will casts over the public acts, and often indeed infuses into the public monuments of Russia, it is the fashion in official circles at St. Petersburg to consider the campaign of 1870 as the continuation of the work of 1814, as the final episode of "that momentous period in which the united armies of Russia and Prussia fought for a

---

* *Provincial Correspondence* of May 1st, 1873.

sacred cause common to both of them."* Within the Kremlin, in the splendid hall devoted by the Emperor Nicholas to his country's military triumphs, a hall that may be termed the Arc de l'Étoile of Holy Russia, the stranger is surprised to see graven in golden letters on its marbles the names of Moltke, of Roon, and of the other German leaders who distinguished themselves in the last war with France.† In fact, the conqueror of Sedan, as he crossed the wide plains of Muscovy, might have fancied that he was still surrounded by his own admiring subjects. From the frontier to the Gulf of Finland the journey was one long succession of triumphs and ovations.

At every station the imperial train stopped at, was seen in waiting a guard of honour, was heard the strains of the German national hymn. The Czar met his illustrious guest at the Gatchina, and on April 27th the two sovereigns made their public entry into Peter the Great's capital. The skies were dark and cold, and the sun refused to illumine "the city of damp streets and arid hearts," as it has been called by one of its own poets. But human industry had done its best to supplement nature and to conceal the rigours of the climate. "Every hothouse in the

---

* Telegram sent by the Czar to King William I. on December 9th, 1869. Only the other day, at the last of the St. George's banquets, the Emperor Alexander II. observed: "I am glad to be able to declare that the close alliance between our three empires and our three armies, founded by our illustrious predecessors, for the defence of the same cause, exists intact at the present moment."—*Official Journal of the Russian Empire*, December 12th, 1875.

† "A Visit to Moscow," by Count Tarnowski, in the *Cracovia Review*, November, 1875.

capital, including those in the Imperial gardens," says an eye-witness,* " were laid waste for the purpose of building up round the doors and windows a delusive spring, which, in our tardy north, never comes before summer."

Rich carpetry, displayed for miles along the sides of the houses, occasionally tempted the visitors to mistake the cold capital of the North for the smiling city of the Lagoons. "The Izmaïlovsky Prospect, the Voznessensky Prospect, the vast Morskaïa, formed one continuous avenue of Russian, German, and Prussian flags. On hundreds of balconies the busts of both monarchs were displayed, crowned with laurel and surrounded with verdure and flowers. The façade of the large Préobrajensky riding-school was surmounted with a cluster of flags, grouped round a colossal cross of that military order of St. George of which his Majesty the Emperor William is the oldest knight and the only grand cordon." The crowd pressed hotly round the guests from Berlin. The talkative Bismarck and the silent Moltke were particularly objects of curiosity.

For twelve days there was an endless succession of reviews, parades, illuminations, balls, routs, banquets, concerts, and gala performances. Amongst the latter were specially chronicled the two magnificent ballets of "Le Roi Candaule" and "Don Quixote." Nor was the populace without its share in the rejoicings; particularly on the evening of the

* From the *St. Petersburg Gesellschaft*. The rest of the description is taken from the *St. Petersburg Journal* and the *Invalide Russe* of the date.

29th of April, when a gigantic *fête* was given in the Palace Square. The two sovereigns witnessed the mammoth concert from the palace balcony.

As they stepped on to the balcony the huge square was suddenly lighted up by five electric lights, with such intense brilliancy that the features of every face in the immense crowd were easily distinguishable, and the orchestra struck up the national Prussian hymn. Fifteen hundred and fifty performers took part in this, besides 600 trumpeters and 350 drummers. The Prussian air was followed by the March of King Frederick William III., and then by a whole series of military marches—the Steinmetz March, the "Wacht am Rhein," the March of the Guards of 1808, to the tune of which the Russian regiments had re-entered St. Petersburg after the Eylau campaign; and the March of Paris, which had once resounded in the ears of the allied armies as they triumphantly entered the capital of France.

The military prayer, "How great is the Lord in Zion," produced a tremendous effect. It is a little difficult to understand how Weber's plaintive air "The Praise of Tears" (*Lob der Thränen*) wandered into the midst of these strains consecrated to Mars and Vulcan; unless as a discreet homage to the well-known sensibility of the veteran Hohenzollern, authentic evidences of which will be found by history in hundreds of his speeches, letters, and telegrams. Indeed, he did not leave St. Petersburg without displaying this characteristic sensitiveness. As the two sovereigns were bidding each other adieu in the imperial saloons of the Gatchina terminus, William of Germany was obliged to hurriedly break away, to prevent himself from yielding to his emotion. With bent head and twitching features he left the saloon with hasty footsteps, and buried himself in his railway carriage, *without once looking back.*

If, however, during this Prussian visit to the banks of the Neva the honours were all for the Czar's uncle, the eager and almost feverish curiosity of the public was a good deal more occupied with the celebrated minister whose white cuirassier's uniform lent an extra emphasis to his conspicuous stature— with the famous German Chancellor, who in one brief lustrum had known how to found an empire on the ruins of two other ones. St. Petersburg had not yet had time to forget the free-spoken diplomatist, who, from 1859 to 1862 had astonished and amused Russian society by his abuse of his own Court, by his ridicule of the "*perruques* of Potsdam" and the "Philistines of the Spree;" and who sometimes quoted—always taking care, however, to be the first to laugh—M. Prudhomme's famous saying, "If I were the government!"

Now he was, indeed, the government—he was even the master of Europe; and before his star those of a Hapsburg and a Napoleon had paled their ineffectual fires! The topic was in truth one that suggested many a striking comparison, many a piquant reminiscence; nor was it one that refused to lend itself to idle comments, to the *plerisque vana miran-*

tibus alluded to by the immortal historian when speaking of striking changes of fortune.

As the great ladies in the Winter Palace looked at the man of the five milliards, they remembered an ambassadress of ten years ago who was heard one day to roundly declare that she really could not afford to pay forty roubles for a dish of early asparagus; and who, on another occasion, very candidly owned that her new diamond earrings were the result of the exchange of a valuable snuff-box, an old gift of the Prince of Darmstadt.* This ambassadress was the wife of M. de Bismarck, then only a baron, now a prince, but still a good fellow, and as affable as ever. He was as easy-tempered, lively, and obliging as when he was envoy. He inquired after his friends, after his acquaintances, after both the great and little people he used to meet; and seemed as though he was taking up the thread of intimacies interrupted but a day ago. The statesman disappeared, and gave place to the courtier and the man of the world. We are told by a sagacious observer that even with Prince Gortchakof he made a point of stepping out of the foreign minister, and appearing in the undress of an old companion, almost a fellow-countryman. M. de Bismarck paid his Russian colleague the affectionate deference of a friend to an elder friend, of a disciple to his master, artlessly enough said his flatterers, forgetting the old saying, *discipulus supra magistrum*; though Alexander Mikhaïlovitch, a good Latin scholar, probably remembered it.

* From the *St. Petersburg Gesellschaft*, vol. ii., p. 89.

The pair often appeared side by side in public at *fêtes* and receptions : the one conspicuous by his great height and remarkable head; the other easily recognisable by his more delicately-cut features, by his keen, witty, and slightly cunning expression. Obeying the ingenious precept of court etiquette first introduced by good old Homer when he made Glaucus and Diomede exchange armour, the Russian minister wore the Order of the Prussian Black Eagle, and the Prussian minister that of St. Andrew of Russia. In truth, this interchange of orders seemed typical of the community of views which had so long united these illustrious diplomatists.

Such a cordial, stable understanding between a couple of statesmen at the helms of two different empires was assuredly an unusual spectacle. It was certainly a striking one, and amidst the solemn pomps of St. Petersburg, it gave reflecting minds much food for thought. The annals of the past were ransacked in vain for such an enduring and brilliant instance of harmonious action. A few celebrated political intimacies, such as those between Choiseul and Kaunitz, Dubois and Stanhope, Mazarin and Cromwell, were only called to mind to be instantly recognised as comparatively misleading and merely apparent analogies.

Nobody miscalculated the considerable and decisive influence which the understanding between the two Chancellors had lately exercised upon the destinies of Europe ; nobody was blind to the prodigious use M. de Bismarck had made of this understanding in his hazardous undertakings. Opinions only began to differ when it became a question of auditing the Russian ledger, of reckoning up the exact profit gained by the Empire of the Czars during this partnership of ten years—the most stormy decade through which the Continent had passed since that which ended on the day of Waterloo.

Some thought that the situation created by Sadowa and Sedan was one of pure gain to Russia. They pointed to the torn fragments of the humiliating treaty of 1856; to Austria, punished for the treachery she had been guilty of at the time of the Crimean war; to France, fallen and diminished; to England, a resigned spectatress of General Kaufman's advance on Bokhara; and, finally, to Russia, rapidly recovering her old prestige, and quietly tasting her revenge—that delicious morsel for the gods, and for such favourites of the gods as Alexander Mikhaïlovitch.

Is there not, they asked, a marvellous good fortune, an impressive singleness of purpose in the career of a minister, who, after the conference at Vienna, solemnly swore to avenge the degradation of his country, and who has so well kept his oath? Does there not seem to be a splendid Nemesis in the punishment, one after the other, of those haughty "allies," who, in 1853, undertook the defence of the Crescent against the Cross of St. Andrew, and who, ten years later, dared to raise the Polish question? To-day, Austria and France outvie each other in obsequious flatteries at the feet of the "northern barbarian" they then professed to despise; while England humbly begs of him a *modus vivendi* in Central Asia. And Russia has attained this enviable and glorious position without a struggle, without a sacrifice; by merely biding her time, while she developed her internal prosperity, and allowed her neighbour—an old and tried friend, whose devotion has never faltered—full liberty of action.

It is but simple justice that Prussia should have reaped the harvest of her bravery and her good faith; and the well-known sentiments entertained by the Emperor William towards the Czar, the family ties which have so long united the two courts, the destinies of the two countries, so distinct, and yet so conformable, are the certain pledges of a permanent and unalterable understanding for the future. How often has not Prussia solemnly sworn that she has no interest in the Eastern question! When the inheritance of the Ottomans comes to be decided, the House of Hohenzollern will show its gratitude to the House of Romanoff. Petty jealousies and petty rivalries have had their day, in common with petty States, and petty artifices to catch influence and to balance power. The future belongs to a rational policy based upon the nature of things, upon geographical facts, and upon homogeneity of race. This policy assigns to Russia and to Germany *rôles* that, while differing, are but the corollaries one of the other.

Taking a broad view, it is, in truth, a matter of congratulation that the sceptre of the West has slipped from the hands of a turbulent, volcanic nation—always engaged in some propaganda, now Jacobin, now Ultramontane, but ever revolutionary—to fall into the grasp of the most orderly, most hierarchical, and best disciplined State in Europe.

And finally, Sadowa and Sedan were Protestant victories over the two chief Catholic powers, and the struggle against Roman Ultramontanism, into which M. de Bismarck has just plunged, is only the logical consequence of these important events in history. Without going so far as to accept certain ideas—ideas, however, very widely spread—as to a possible future fusion of the Protestant and orthodox beliefs, it may certainly be said that it is not for the Church of Photius to lament because the Vatican has been dealt a mortal blow.

To such reasonings, supplemented besides by captious and sarcastic arguments, those who thought differently furnished objections inspired by an equally sincere but a much less sanguine patriotism. They, too, agreed in admiring the ease and the rapidity with which Russia had recovered from the disasters in the Crimea; but they contended that this result had been obtained long before M. de Bismarck had come upon the scene, long before any understanding had been entered into with him; and that, as far back as 1860, when the sovereigns of Austria and Prussia and many minor German princes came to greet the Czar and recognise his moral supremacy at Varsovia, and when Napoleon III. was seeking his friendship and accepting his arbitration, the Russian empire had already reassumed the great position in Europe which of right belonged to it.

The remarkable tact with which Prince Gortchakof had made use of the goodwill of France to promote Russian interests, without yielding a single point of essential importance, without compromising any of the conservative and traditional principles of Russian policy, would always prove his surest claim to his country's gratitude; but it was a matter of regret that he had not shown the same prudent reserve in the close relations with Prussia, which, after the Polish insurrection, took the place of the old understanding with the Tuileries. It was impossible not to perceive that Nesselrode's successor had exaggerated the purpose of the notorious French "remonstrance" about Poland, and the danger likely to accrue from it; as well as the true character of the not really disinterested services at that time rendered to him by his old friend at Berlin. At any rate, the latter constituted no sufficient reason for sulking with the rest of Europe after the matter had been settled to the signal advantage of the Russian Government—for persistently sulking with it year after year, for positively refusing to entertain the idea of any other alliance but that of Prussia, and for obstinately and constantly allowing that power to go where it pleased, do what it pleased, and take what it pleased.

In short, these enlightened patriots were strongly of opinion that, generally speaking, the pith of the mistakes of the last fifteen or twenty years lay in this: that rancour, spite, and ill-nature had been allowed to play too large a part in the settlement of the weightiest affairs. A wretched basis of policy, forsooth! and one which the German Chancellor alone had had the wit to despise.

A rancorous recollection of the behaviour of the St. Petersburg Cabinet in the Italian question had led Austria to extend a helping hand to the Polish insurgents. A feeling of ill-temper against England, for its conduct at the time of the congress, had induced Napoleon III. to throw up the cause of Denmark; while, more than all others, Alexander Mikhaïlovitch had been actuated by these petty motives. He had been the first to yield to them in indulging his "policy of spite" against Austria for the imaginary wrongs she had committed during the Crimean war—he had been, in truth, the most eager to adopt the contemptible "*pourboire* policy," and to promote the selfish "league of neutral powers," that had effectually barred all concerted and generous action.

Many indeed were the splendid opportunities of promoting the welfare of Europe, his country's glory, and the fame of his illustrious master, that had slipped through the Russian Chancellor's hands, as, in infatuated friendship, they obstinately grasped Prussia's calculating fingers. One, for instance, in the spring of 1867, at the time France and Austria offered him such ample concessions in the East; another, in the autumn of 1870, when Austria and England begged him to take the initiative in the work of peace. Much indeed were those mistaken who believed that Prince Gortchakof had sacrificed nothing during his ten years' understanding with his formidable colleague.

Is it nothing, forsooth, that Kiel, the key of the Baltic, has been delivered into the grasp of Germany?—is it nothing that the kingdom of Denmark, the home of the Czarevna, has been rent and dismembered?—nothing that Queen Olga now sits on a vassal's throne?—nothing that a whole phalanx of reigning families, closely akin to the House of Romanoff, have been dethroned and plundered?—nothing that the minor States, from time immemorial the devoted and loyal partisans of Russia, have been robbed of their independence?—In a word, is it nothing that the ancient balance of power—scales, lever, and fulcrum—has been roughly dashed to pieces, and that the Chancellor's whole policy has resulted in the immoderate, gigantic aggrandisement of his country's nearest neighbour?

"The greatness of a State is relative, and a country that suffers no material loss may, in reality, become diminished as new forces accumulate around it."* This saying, addressed to Napoleon III. after Sadowa, might have been well taken to heart by Russia after Sedan, for it is impossible to pretend that the abolition of the second article of the Treaty of Paris was an equivalent for the new resources accumulated by Prussia in the centre of Europe. It may be urged, perhaps, that the recent Russian conquests in Asia constitute the real compensation. But their value is at least doubtful; they have only hitherto succeeded in waking Eng-

* Confidential note of M. Magne, July 20th, 1866.—*Papers and Correspondence of the Imperial Family*, vol. i., p. 241.

land's suspicions, and the time may yet come when they may prove a cause of serious embarrassment to the Empire.

If a huge European conflagration should ever break out, Russia will be obliged either to abandon these distant conquests, impatient of her rule; or else to double and triple her occupying forces there, and so weaken herself in the West, where will lie the real brunt of the struggle. As to her hopes on the Bosphorus, they are mere contingencies, like other expectations of inheritance. The "Sick Man" has over and over again proved the falsity of the prognostications of his doctors; crisis after crisis that was positively to carry him off has passed away. Nor is the postponement of his death-agony, perhaps, altogether a misfortune for Russia; for it is an open question whether the Northern Empire is yet prepared to enter upon such a vast inheritance—whether its outfit of tools and workmen is yet exactly proportioned to such a huge establishment—if, in a word, it is ready with the necessary military and financial resources, with the administrative organisation indispensable for the occupation of such wide territories.

It is impossible to take possession of European provinces in the easy fashion the same extent of soil is annexed on the banks of the Amoor or the Syr-Daria. A second restless Poland may rear its head by the waters of the Danube, at the foot of the Balkans; and the reign of a single system of law, the uniform dominion of the *Svod*, may not prove so easy to establish in lands where the most incongruous institutions, from the rule of the scimitar to that of parliamentary government, have, side by side, confusedly flourished and run riot. Nor is it impossible that the absorption of Turkey may in its turn transform the Muscovite nation, and that history may not have, one day, to inculcate afresh the pathetic lesson of *Græcia capta*.

A Russia, mistress of the Eastern Peninsula, may no longer, perhaps, be Russia; and an empire bathed by the blue waters of the Bosphorus may no longer be able to boast a capital on the ice-bound shores of Finland.

These are weighty and difficult problems—problems that naturally cause hesitation, apprehension, and indecision. On the other hand, one thing is certain, and that is, that when the moment is at hand Prussia will lay down her conditions and stipulate for her compensation. When the hour verily strikes, to pay her old debt of gratitude will be far from her thoughts; she will only think of driving a new bargain. And what will her price be? Holland, or Jutland, or the German territories of Austria?—the frontier of the Vistula, or the provinces of the Baltic?

Perhaps, after all, this long drama of Turkish decadence is destined to wind up with a very unexpected *dénouement*, as illogical as it will be original. Public writers and patriots of Berlin have, before now, been heard to speak of Austria's mission by the Danube and on the Bosphorus—have long ago been heard to say that she was intended by Providence to carry thither Teuton interests—" German civilisation." Since Sedan, particularly, Austria has been eloquently exhorted to "seek her centre of gravity elsewhere than at Vienna," to justify her name of *Ost-reich*, and to become in reality an Empire of the East.

It may well be that a monarchy, constantly threatened with the loss of its German possessions on the banks of the Leitha, may at last be tempted to take this advice and run the risk; especially if it is continually dinned into her ears that the risk is a virtue—nay more, a necessity.

A State that has never undergone any serious process of centralisation, a State that has always oscillated between a dual system of government and a more or less defined federal one, might indeed appear to Europe to possess the very framework with which to enclose and assimilate the medley of races, of creeds, of institutions, which swarm between the Iron Gates and the Golden Horn.

On the Bosphorus, an Empire of the East, subject to German influences and inheriting German traditions; to the south, a kingdom of Greece, enlarged by Thessaly and Epirus; to the north, a united Germany, completed and rounded off by the absorption of the Cis-Leithan Provinces—this is an arrangement that would give satisfaction in many quarters, not excluding England. It is perhaps as good a solution as any other of the tremendous Eastern question; and it is permissible to suggest any hypothesis, any extravagance, when dealing with the world of the fantastic Orient, or with that equally mysterious and portentous world that seethes in the brain of the hermit of Varzin.

The Emperor Alexander, however, is even now face to face with a position that has nothing to do with the world of hypothesis and speculation; a situation that is, unfortunately, but too evident and too palpable. In the place of "a purely and exclusively defensive combination," as Prince Gortchakof once correctly described the ancient Bund—in the place of a league of peacefully inclined States, all the obliged friends of Russia, and forming for her, as it were, a continuous line of rampart, he now sees before him, firmly settled down along the whole line of his frontier, a gigantic power, the strongest of the Continent—ambitious, full of enterprise, and obliged by its very position to henceforward stand up against Russia as the natural champion of what it has been agreed to call "Western interests."

Whenever this power chooses, it can, if it suits it, bring even the Polish question into the arena, and in a somewhat more dangerous manner, forsooth, than that erewhile adopted by the Cabinets of Paris and London. Indeed, a proposal to strike Russia such a mortal blow was warmly discussed in 1871 by a group of Hungarian statesmen, supposed to be to some considerable extent in M. de Bismarck's confidence.

The conduct of the Berlin Government at the time of the last insurrection in Varsovia is no criterion for the future. The passionate speeches uttered by M. de Bismarck in 1849 against the Magyar rising did not prevent him at a later period from encouraging General Klapka. Nor is it possible to be blind to the views held by Prussia in 1863 as to the left bank of the

Vistula, "the natural frontier;" and even now it is sometimes hinted at Berlin that there perhaps lies the most efficacious road to the final annihilation of Polish dreams.

No word, as yet, has been spoken as to the Baltic provinces, as before Sadowa no one had broached the idea of even wishing to cross the Main. But Teuton aspirations are ever on the increase in Courland and Livonia, and the world has by this time learnt to what painful sacrifices the Hohenzollerns are capable of resigning themselves when it is given out that they are summoned by that all-compelling voice—the voice of their German brethren.

In truth, the prince-regent would have shuddered if, in 1848, it had been whispered to him that he would one day find himself arrayed against the Hapsburgs, with Garibaldi as his companion-in-arms; yet, when the time came, he yielded to a supposed necessity, and gave the signal for the fratricidal struggle with grief in his heart and tears in his eyes. It is, moreover, childish to attempt to measure the destinies of nations by the career or the disposition of any single monarch. Germany may one day hail an emperor with neither affection for nor remembrance of Alexander II.—"a Pharaoh who knew not Joseph;" and even if not, there exists a mightier power in the world than that of czar or emperor—the stern force of circumstances, the overmastering necessities of race.

Formidable, indeed, is the race of the victors of Sadowa and Sedan, whose ancient invading and conquering genius has survived a hundred transformations, has accommodated itself to a hundred changes of fortune! Humble and yet daring, temperate but prolific, expansive and yet tenacious, devoutly carrying into practice the spirit of their ancient proverb, *ubi bene, ibi patria*, yet ever preserving a keen affection for their mother country, the Germans insinuate themselves into every country, penetrate into every region, are found in every corner of the habitable globe.

Their connections and their descendants sit on every throne of the world and stand behind its every counter, throng the industrial centres of Europe and people the solitudes of the Far West, throw the casting votes into the Presidential urns of the great Republic and monopolise most of the important posts in the administration of the northern Empire—where people still talk of a statistical return showing that out of every hundred officers of the higher grades in the Russian army, at least eighty per cent. were of German origin.*

Such already were the characteristics of the German before his great strokes of fortune in 1866 and 1870, before the era of "blood and iron," before M. de Bismarck had revealed to him the secret of his might, before he had heard the magic whisper—*tu regere imperio populos!*

---

* This return was published in the *Golos*, some years ago, when it created considerable stir. A story is told to the effect that the sufficiently commonplace name of Kozlof enjoyed a brief popularity in Russia for the following reason:—The Czarovitch was holding a levy of officers, and after an interminable list of purely German cognomens had been called out, the name of Kozlof was suddenly pronounced. "At last! thank God," exclaimed the Czarovitch.—*Russland seit Aufhebung der Leibeigenschaft*. Laibach, 1875.

It is scarcely necessary to recall the hatred which the Germans have always felt towards the Slave, or the extermination to which they have already devoted him by the Elbe and the Oder. The mind recoils horror-struck at the mere idea of a new meeting between the two races—a meeting now more than ever likely to occur. It is the fashion, it is true, to treat such apprehensions as mere pedantic dreams, the empty visions of professors and scribblers; but when has any important problem been less lightly regarded by the conspicuous statesmen, the professional political prophets of our day? Did they not pooh-pooh the Schleswig-Holstein question and the German intentions towards Alsace?—did they not laugh to scorn the unity of Italy and the programmes of the *National-Verein?*

A chapter upon "Diplomatists *versus* Professors" would make an interesting passage of contemporary history, and would show that the most pedantic, the most ideologist of the two classes, are not precisely those generally so considered.

Is it not, for instance, asked the same disapprovers of Prince Gortchakof's policy—more thoughtful for the future and anxious for the present, than blindly fascinated by unseasonable remembrances of the past— is it not simple pedantry to compare the two periods of 1814 and 1840, and to recognise in Moltke the successor of Koutouzof? At the time of the memorable war that followed the heroic burning of Moscow the whole of Europe turned against an insolent master, and brought safety and deliverance to kingdoms bruised and down-trodden by a foot that aspired to universal dominion.

Were the circumstances the same in the last campaign? Should it not rather be said that France, this time, was fighting for the balance of power and the independence of Europe, that she was trying to repair, by a late and badly conceived effort, a whole series of culpable mistakes that had endangered others besides herself?

In truth, the two periods were widely different in their underlying motives, and as broadly contrasted in their external signs and tokens. The Prussian minister at the outset informed M. Benedetti that "he would fight him with revolutions," and he kept his word. He showed attention to, made excuses for, and displayed a sympathy with the Commune he would find it difficult to justify. And later on, he openly protected the Republic against all attempts at monarchical restoration, thus sacrificing the monarchical principle and the weightiest considerations of public order to a selfish and vindictive policy.

This was not the spirit that swayed the allies in 1814. The magnanimous Alexander I. held a very different view of a sovereign's duties, and of the sympathy that should exist between all animated with the spirit of conservatism. And the Emperor Nicholas—can there be any doubt as to the crushing verdict he would have pronounced on the whole gist of the Berlin policy, upon the regeneration of Germany?—a regeneration that, in reality, has ever revealed itself as a species of revolution from above, from its federal execution in Holstein to its arrest of the syndics of the Crown; from its destruction of the Bund to its overthrow of the Guelf dynasty; from its formation of Hungarian legions and its intrigues with Mazzini to its *Kulturkampf* against the Catholic Church.

Let there be no mistake, said the antagonists of the two Chancellors; it is the revolution alone which will profit by the campaign against Catholicism undertaken by Germany. Great and surprising indeed are the illusions of those who flatter themselves that Protestantism and orthodoxy, or tolerant religious feeling in general, will gain anything by the losses the Papacy may suffer. A glance at the swollen battalions of the *Kulturkampf* reveals their god; their banners are plainly embroidered with the symbol in whose name they hope to conquer.

Is it supposed that the sincere Protestants, the Evangelicals to whom the Holy Scriptures are a great truth, are leading the assault, or are even following it with their wishes and their prayers? Assuredly not. All true disciples of the Reformed Church, those who cling not to the empty shadow of the name but to the substance of its doctrine, openly repudiate the struggle, and lament it.

They rightly believe that in our revolutionary epoch—an epoch so undermined by the spirit of negation—there should be such a thing as unity of religious interests as well as political unity of conservative interests. Those eager for the fray, the zealots, " full "—forsooth!—" of the divine Spirit," are, in reality, the very minds who admit the existence of neither deity nor soul, and who have no positive belief but that of positivism. In them a resuscitated Luther would certainly fail to recognise his children.

The great antagonist of Rome in the sixteenth century believed in revelation, in his Bible, in his doctrine of grace—are not all these things ridiculous rubbish in the eyes of the disciples of Strauss and Darwin? The apostle of Wittemberg believed in justification by faith; the apostles of Berlin pin their solitary belief to justification by success.

It is a serious thing, finally observed these alarmed patriots, a very perilous thing, for a great State to abandon, in its relations with the other Powers, certain established maxims, certain rules of conduct assayed by long experience, and become, as it were, *arcana imperii*. Napoleon III. has but just paid a ruinous price for his disobedience to the ancient traditions of French foreign policy.

Russia, on her side, owed Europe a certain obedience to the venerable traditions which had been the foundation of the splendour and the strength of the preceding reigns. In those reigns the liberty of the Baltic was jealously defended, care was taken to maintain a proper balance of power between Austria and Prussia, the friendship and devotion of the minor States of Germany were properly appreciated, and respect for the monarchical principle was everywhere enforced upon the presuming spirit of the revolution. It is devoutly to be wished that Russia may never have cause to regret having turned aside from the track beaten by the triumphant chariot-wheels of Peter the Great, of Catherine II., of Alexander I., and of Nicholas.

Thus thought and spoke on the banks of the Neva many independent minds, while the official world was busy displaying the magnificence of the north in honour of William the Conqueror. Their thoughts and words were, in truth, only the connected expression of a vague presentiment, a deep but veiled doubt that was secretly stirring the heart of Russia.

With that habit of obedience and discipline, which some call a servile instinct, but which in this nation is often the expression of a deep and admirable patriotism, the masses were far from thinking of annoying their Government in the brilliant reception it was giving its Prussian guests; they were content to remain impassive spectators of a display which made no appeal to their hearts.

The press maintained a great sobriety of tone in its descriptions; its remarks were more reserved still. So marked was its reserve, indeed, that with the best will in the world all that could be found to be said at Berlin was that the St. Petersburg press showed a "proper" tone. On the whole, the general feeling in Russian society was a similar one. In the palace itself the true moral was pointed by the surroundings —in the foreground a mass of hot-house flowers, in the distance a perspective of ice. The guests appeared to notice this curious contrast. Mixed with the exquisite perfume of exotic flowers, there occasionally reached them a keen blast of the outer air, the bitter, icy wind of the north.

Even M. de Bismarck himself seemed to feel the effect of this treacherous atmosphere. He displayed more mechanical vivacity than real dash and warmth; his words were far more measured than was usual with him; he seemed to purposely avoid any decided opinion, any too lively discussion.

It is a curious fact that during his fortnight's stay in the Russian capital the once plain-spoken diplomatist gave utterance to none of the sallies, none of the jokes he is generally addicted to; to not one of the bewildering indiscretions which have so often been the delight of society and the dread of men in office.

But one single sensational saying was heard to issue from the lips which had so often pronounced destiny's fiat, the expression that " he could not even admit the thought of ever being hostile to Russia." It seemed an explicit and reassuring declaration enough, offered, perhaps, in reply to concealed apprehensions. But the incredulous and the suspicious felt inclined to remark that, only ten years ago, such an assurance proffered by a Prussian minister to the Russian empire, would have seemed more than superfluous, it would have seemed laughable.

Here ends the task undertaken in writing these two sketches. The meeting of the two Chancellors in the capital of Peter the Great, in the spring of 1873, may be considered the epilogue of the joint action that has lasted ten years, and that has so much contributed to change the face of the world.

Since that period Europe has been free from storms, though angry and threatening clouds have now and again crossed its ever gloomy horizon. Every now and then, indeed, a slight and passing flash has seemed to reveal that the ancient and fatal harmony between the Cabinets of Berlin and St. Petersburg is not more absolute than it was of old, and that it is still interrupted by certain differences of opinion and intention.

The Czar's government, for instance, declined to accompany the German Chancellor on his Spanish campaign, in his feverish adhesion to the presidency of Marshal Serrano; and there seems little doubt that the personal intervention of the Emperor Alexander, strongly backed by England, averted from France last year an iniquitous attack, and prevented a tremendous calamity.

Since then Austria has, to some extent, joined the intimacy of the two northern Empires; and it would be difficult to say whether her arrival has completed or complicated a partnership in which it becomes daily more difficult to discover any common interest, and which up till now has found harmony only in silence. The future alone can unveil the meaning and the value of this triple alliance, so much praised and, perhaps, so little understood. But it is, even now, by no means too soon to be sure that in this interesting trinity it is M. de Bismarck who has really the best of it.

APPENDIX.

The different chapters of this volume appeared in successive numbers of the *Revue des Deux Mondes* for 1875. The second number for the month of September contained the chapter headed, " The Eclipse of Europe ; " and in the number dated October 1st appeared the following :—

"We have received the following letter from M. Benedetti :—

TO THE EDITOR OF THE 'REVUE DES DEUX MONDES.'

PARIS, *September 24th*, 1875.

SIR,—In the last number of the *Revue des Deux Mondes* you published an article by M. Klaczko, which compels me to ask you to insert a short rectification. I should be the last to deny any one the right of placing his own construction upon the events of which M. Klaczko has penned an anecdotic history, or of independently criticising the share in them which fell to me. On the contrary, I am most anxious, both for my own sake and for that of the Government which I had the honour of serving, that they should be discussed and examined. The light that has already been thrown upon them, the reversal of erroneous verdicts that has already taken place, have produced the best results for both of us; but an examination of the past can only prove searching and useful if it is impartially made, and it cannot be impartial if it refuses to notice positive and undeniable facts.

M. Klaczko says:—' Certainly the French Ambassador at the Court of Berlin occupied during 1866 a very onerous and painful, we might almost say, pathetic, position. He had devoted himself to bring about that *connubio* of Italy with Prussia which seemed in his eyes to be of such value to the Imperial policy, to be such a signal victory over the ancient order of things, such a benefit to the "*idées Napoléoniennes*," and to the "new right." In the well-grounded fear of seeing his work collapse and Prussia draw back, if there were any mention made of future compensation or preventative engagements, he was unceasing in his endeavours to dissuade his government from any attempt of the kind . . '.' (page 445). And at page 442, in a note, M. Klaczko remarks:—' M. Drouyn de Lhuys, who had already obtained the cession of Venice from Austria, whatever might be the result of the dispute, insisted at this time on sureties being in a like manner taken from Prussia, the cleverest and most dangerous of the two contending parties. M. Benedetti *did not cease* to oppose such a step, in the fear that, if it were suggested, Prussia would entirely abandon her designs against Austria.'

Now, these assertions either mean nothing at all, or they convey that I was the real originator, perhaps, I should say, the negociator, unknown to my government, of the treaty of alliance concluded in 1866 between Prussia and Italy; and that I had perseveringly prevented M. Drouyn de Lhuys from carrying out his intention of obtaining from the Berlin Cabinet, before the Austrian war, the pledges necessary for the future security of France.

M. Klaczko corroborates these assertions by no quotation of known facts, by no extracts from any official documents. He offers no proof of them in any shape or form.

Yet, he must have been aware, since he continually quotes a work I published in 1871, bearing the title of 'Ma Mission en Prusse,' that I repudiated any participation in the Prusso-Italian treaty; he must have known that I had fully shown this. In such a case, it is scarcely sufficient to offer a simple contradiction; it is necessary, rather, to give proofs to the contrary, to plainly establish that, far from having had nothing to do with the understanding between Prussia and 'Italy, I had been its principal instigator.

I am desirous that the readers of the *Revue des Deux Mondes* should know the truth. They have seen M. Klaczko's article; it is only right to submit to them a few words at least of the despatches I have published.

'The approaching arrival is announced,' I wrote on March 14th, 1866, 'of an Italian officer, General Govone, who is coming to Berlin on an important mission. This news . . . has caused some considerable stir. If it should turn out to be true it will certainly be believed that Prussia and Italy are negotiating a treaty of alliance.'

Two days later I added, 'General Govone reached Berlin the day before yesterday. According to Count Bismarck and the Italian ambassador his mission is simply a military one, and its aim is merely to examine the improvements lately made in weapons of all kinds.'

A couple of days later still I was able to give my government more precise information, and I wrote: 'I informed you, when I reported General Govone's arrival, that, according to M. de Bismarck and the Italian envoy, the general's only object was to study the military organisation of Prussia. Forgetting, no doubt, what he had said to this effect, M. de Bismarck informed me yesterday that General Govone was authorised to ·treat with the Prussian Government. The gist of the communication he has made to the President of the Council is in fact . . .' In concluding this despatch, I added, 'The Italian legation maintains an attitude of complete reserve towards me. Perhaps I ought not to regret it. M. de Bismarck's confidences, which, however, it is impossible for me to decline, already place me in a sufficiently delicate position.'

Finally, on the 27th of March, by which date the plenipotentiaries had already held several conferences, I wrote to

M. Drouyn de Luhys: 'M. de Bismarck has conversed with me about his negotiations with General Govone and the Italian envoy . . . . and I feel all the more able to give you an account of them as M. de Barral, the Italian envoy, *has* AT LAST *decided not to entirely hide from me the proceedings and the intentions of his government.*'

Either M. Klaczko must admit that my official correspondence was sincere, or he must suppose that it was concocted with the object of concealing my real conduct, and the share I was secretly taking in the negotiations. In the first case it is difficult to see on what grounds he affirms that I 'had *arduously* and *passionately* laboured to bring about the understanding between Italy and Prussia.' In the second the circumstances assume a different aspect, and I will wait till M. Klaczko has explained himself before I make any further observations.

For the present I will content myself with producing the only evidence that nobody can possibly suspect—that of the Italian plenipotentiary. Since General Govone's death, and subsequent to the publication of 'Ma Mission en Prusse,' his correspondence has been given to the public by General La Marmora, who has omitted nothing. In this correspondence, where everything is minutely detailed, my name is twice mentioned; the first time in a telegram of the 28th of March, twelve days after the Italian plenipotentiary's arrival at Berlin; and this is what he says about me: 'I ought to tell you that the president (M. de Bismarck) keeps M. Benedetti informed of everything.'

In the letter in which my name appears for a second and last time, a letter dated the 6th of April, two days before the actual signature of the treaty (the dates are most important, and it is necessary to remember them), General Govone gives an account of a visit he paid me, and of what I said to him with reference to the negotiations. I quote word for word:—'Yesterday, after my visit to M. de Bismarck, I had an interview with M. Benedetti; he thought that it would be better for us to sign no treaty, but to have a project proposed, agreed to, and ready to be signed as soon as Prussia had completed her mobilisation.'

APPENDIX.

Do these two extracts, sir, authorise the belief that I was the confidant and the adviser of the Italian envoy? Do they not, on the contrary, entirely confirm the sincerity of my correspondence? Where has M. Klaczko seen or found that I laboured to bring about the understanding between Prussia and Italy? Should he not have told us this before he made such a serious accusation? Can he pretend that it is a matter of reproach to me that I endeavoured to learn what was going on, and kept my government informed of it?

As to M. Klaczko's assertion, twice repeated, that I was continually, before the war, dissuading M. Drouyn de Lhuys from demanding at Berlin conditional compensations and preventative engagements, for fear of arresting Prussia in its coming struggle with Austria, I will answer it by the following extract from a letter which M. Drouyn de Lhuys himself wrote to me on the 31st of March, while negotiations were still pending between Berlin and Florence.

'I have read with a great deal of pleasure,' he wrote, 'the private letters you have sent me in the course of the month. I beg to thank you for them. I did not answer them immediately because I had nothing to add to or alter in the instructions I have at different times given you. Our opinions remain the same. We fully recognise the gravity of the present crisis, but we cannot see that its latest phase contains anything to persuade us to abandon our neutral attitude. We have frankly explained this to the Prussian court. When our intentions were asked by the Cabinet of Vienna we declared our firm intention of remaining neutral, though it was remarked to us that our neutrality would be more favourable for Prussia than for Austria. *We shall await, therefore, the coming war,* if one is to break out, in our present attitude. The king himself has been good enough to acknowledge the justice of your view, that present circumstances afford no foundation for the understanding his majesty desires. The progress of events, the nature and bearing of the interests that may be at stake, the dimensions which the war may assume, as well as the questions to which it may give rise, will *then* furnish a basis for an agreement to be possibly entered into between Prussia and ourselves.'

In this same letter, which is given at full length on the 77th page of 'Ma Mission en Prusse,' M. Drouyn de Lhuys pointed out the reasons which compelled us to maintain a reserved attitude with respect to the efforts made by Prussia and Italy to agree upon concerted action; and he added in conclusion, 'I have now thoroughly laid before you our manner of viewing the question. I quite approve of your attitude and your language, and I shall be obliged to you if you will continue to keep me equally well informed of the minutest details of this crisis.'

Are these the expressions M. Drouyn de Lhuys would have used in acknowledging the receipt of my despatches if their object had been to prevent him from making any conditions for the future with Prussia; if between the minister and his ambassador there had existed differences, the entire responsibility of which M. Klaczko wishes to cast on me? I will not insist any further, but will leave to the penetration of your readers the task of discovering the truth. I may add, however, that if M. Klaczko made himself acquainted with the above letter before writing his article, and I have a right to assume that he did so, it becomes impossible to account for the errors into which he has fallen.

I regret to be obliged to say, moreover, that I should have to refer to every chapter of his work if I wished to point out all its shortcomings; but I will not take undue advantage of my right of reply, and I will go no further. One other mistake, however, on account of its particular importance, you must allow me to correct.

In answer to a telegram from M. Drouyn de Lhuys, I wrote to him on June 8th, 1866, that not a single Prussian, from the king down to his humblest subject, with the exception of M. de Bismarck, would consent to cede us an acre of German territory on the Rhine. After quoting from this despatch, M. Klaczko adds:—'And it is this same diplomatist, who showed such a complete appreciation of the situation before the campaign in Bohemia, it is this same ambassador who afterwards took upon himself to present to M. de Bismarck the demands of the cabinet of the Tuileries; going actually so far as to submit to him, on the 5th of August, an outline of a secret treaty abandoning to France the whole of the left bank of the Rhine, without even excepting the great stronghold of Mayence!'

M. Klaczko is mistaken. This proposal was not made by me; and his assertion, which is corroborated by no proofs, surprises me the more as he might have seen in 'Ma Mission en Prusse,' that the real circumstances were very different; that, on the contrary, I had pointed out the new and serious difficulties to which this proposal would give rise; and that I had asked permission to return to Paris to discuss it before making it to M. de Bismarck, but that I had been instructed to the contrary. Whether I was right or wrong is another matter; but it was all the more incumbent on M. Klaczko to avoid treating this incident in the manner he has done, since, as he takes care to point out, its consequences have been serious and fatal.

If this is the way M. Klaczko interprets the duties of an historian, I can only express my surprised regret. He has doubtless not remembered that party-spirit and personal sympathies suggest statements which a loyal impartiality disavows. I regret this error in judgment in an author who has accustomed the readers of the *Revue des Deux Mondes* to more carefully-prepared and more impartially-written essays. For myself, personally, you will allow, sir, that it was impossible for me to give assent by silence to such utterly unfounded assertions; and that M. Klaczko has driven me to make this protest, in spite of a sincere desire to avoid all controversy, and of a determination, which it is painful to me to forego, to keep aloof from all discussion. This letter has no other object, and in asking you to insert it in the next number of the *Revue*, I beg you to accept the assurance of my distinguished consideration.

BENEDETTI."

"We thought it right to forward M. Benedetti's letter to M. Klaczko, who returned it with the following remarks :—

M. Benedetti confounds the two very different negotiations mentioned in our contributions to the *Revue des Deux Mondes*, as well as the two equally distinct conclusions we drew from them. It was only in the matter that occurred in August, 1866, concerning the treaty in reference to Belgium, that we found fault with M. Benedetti's behaviour to his minister. We did not condemn his attitude in March and April of the same year, with reference to the secret treaty between M. de Bismarck and General Govone; and we certainly did not reproach him with having, *unknown to his Government*, suggested that treaty. We merely attested that his despatches of that date were calculated to prevent the French Government from attempting any preliminary understanding with Prussia, providing against possible results of the war.

M. Benedetti, in fact, continually represented the Berlin cabinet as deaf to any proposal of the kind. On the 8th of June, 1866, just before the war, he wrote : 'The apprehensions with which France fills Germany are still as great as ever, and would be aroused in a violent and unanimous manner at the slightest indication on our part of a wish to extend our possessions towards the east. By no Prussian, from the king to the humblest of his subjects, would the bare supposition of any sacrifice on the Rhine be endured at this moment. The Crown Prince, though convinced of the political dangers by which he is surrounded, declared not long ago, with great energy, to one of my colleagues, that he would prefer war to the cession even of the small county of Glatz.' ('Ma Mission en Prusse,' pp. 171, 172.)

In his other reports and throughout his book, M. Benedetti is always laying stress on the fact that he 'never encouraged any hope' in this direction, and that he 'had plainly pointed out that in no case would Prussia willingly make us any territorial concession on our Eastern frontier. ('Ma Mission en Prusse,' p. 176.)

These, however, were not the opinions of the Italian diplomatists at Berlin. M. de Barral, in a telegram sent on May 6th to General La Marmora, expressed himself thus: 'Considerable stir has been caused here by the busy negotiations which are said to be going on between Austria and France, with the purpose of assuring the neutrality of Italy. Austria is reported to have gone so far as to offer France the frontier of the Rhine. When I remarked to M. de Bismarck on the danger of such an offer by a German power, he shrugged his shoulders, clearly giving me to understand that if he was compelled to face it he would not shrink from such a solution himself.'

And General Govone, in a detailed report of the 7th of May, alludes to the same story in a still more explicit manner. 'M. de Bismarck is anxious to know the intentions and desires of the Emperor (Napoleon III.); he has mentioned his anxiety to M. de Barral, and has asked him to endeavour to ascertain them through M. de Nigra. M. de Bismarck has, in fact, given ground for the belief that he feels disposed to cede Napoleon III. the line of the Rhine, his agents having informed him that the Emperor has been carrying on negotiations with Austria, and that Austria had shown herself willing to give up Venetia, and had even suggested that France might take the left bank of the Rhine. On M. de Barral, to whom the Prussian minister was speaking of these Austrian suggestions, exclaiming, "But Austria would never compromise herself with Germany by ceding territories which belong to the Confederation," M. de Bismarck shrugged his shoulders, as much as to say, "I would cede them too."'

Moreover, in his report of the 3rd of June, five days previous to the date of M. Benedetti's despatch about 'the king and the humblest of his subjects,' General Govone quotes the following reply of the Prussian Minister to his question whether 'some geographical boundary,' might not be found to indemnify France. 'There is the Moselle,' said M. de Bismarck. 'I am,' he added, 'much less of a German than a Prussian, and I should feel no difficulty in agreeing to cede to France the whole territory between the Rhine and the Moselle—the Palatinate, Oldenburg, a small part of Prussia, &c. But the King would be much more scrupulous, and would never be able to arrive at such a decision unless at some supreme crisis, when it came to be a question of losing or gaining everything. Before, however, the King can be brought to agree to any kind of arrangement with France, it is necessary to be acquainted with the minimum (*il limite minimo*) pretensions of that Power.' *

It will be seen, therefore, that the Italian negotiators took a very different view to that of M. Benedetti on this important point. In the confidential, and evidently trustworthy communications they made to their own Government, they treated a preliminary territorial arrangement between France and Prussia as an arrangement difficult to settle, no doubt, but still as a very possible one.

We refrained from discussing in the pages of the *Revue* whether General Govone or M. Benedetti had shown the truest appreciation of the situation; we did not even allude to their difference of opinion; we contented ourselves with asking M. Benedetti, how he could possibly have expected to find Prussia, after Sadowa and Nikolsburg, ready to agree to terms, which she had declined to accept before her stupendous victories, and in the midst of an extremely hazardous crisis; how he came to undertake,† on the 5th of August, to demand for France the whole of the left bank of the Rhine, including the important stronghold of Mayence, when, on the 8th of June, he was convinced that it would be impossible to obtain from Prussia such a pitiful handful of territory even as the small county of Glatz?

---

* La Marmora, "Un po più di luce," pp. 211, 221, 275.

† Our words were: "How came he to take upon himself (*pris sur lui*) to present to M. de Bismarck the *demands of the Cabinet of the Tuileries?*" And M. Benedetti sees in these words, *to take upon himself*, an insinuation that he initiated the proposal. Yet we explicitly said *the demands of the cabinet of the Tuileries*, and we added M. Benedetti's own expressions: "I provoked nothing, neither did I guarantee success; I only allowed myself to hope for it." None of our readers could have misunderstood the meaning of our words, or seen in them the insinuation M. Benedetti gratuitously attributes to them.

We have given the only possible explanation of this contradiction, the only one, it seems to us, that can possibly suggest itself to anyone who has studied these events.

Before the campaign in Bohemia, we said, M. Benedetti did not think himself in a position to obtain territorial concessions from Prussia ; and had the more strenuously insisted upon the difficulties that would attend such a demand, that he feared to see Prussia draw back, and its *connubio* with Italy come to nothing, if too much stress were prematurely laid upon the necessity of compensation. He preferred to rely for the advantages that ought to accrue to his country, upon the upshot of military operations, 'upon the straits to which war might reduce the Prussian Government' ('Ma Mission,' page 172). He expected the thunderbolt of Sadowa as little as any human being.

After Sadowa the success of the Hohenzollerns alarmed him. Patriotic anxiety for his country took the place in his heart of his whilom generous sympathy for Italy; and, as he himself said, 'the important acquisitions of Prussia convinced him that a fresh territorial arrangement was henceforth necessary for France's security' ('Ma Mission,' p. 167). This fresh arrangement he had first hoped to find on the Rhine, 'if only the language of his government were firm, and its attitude a determined one' (p. 178). Afterwards he sought it on the Meuse and the Escaut, and allowed himself to be dragged into the secret negotiations about Belgium, which were destined to prove so fatal to France.

Our having attributed to M. Benedetti a patriotic anxiety on the morrow of Sadowa can scarcely have irritated him. Is he then displeased because we credited him with Italian sympathies ? But a marked partiality for M. de Cavour's cause and country was always a principal and conspicuous feature in the political existence of the former French ambassador at Berlin. By one and all M. Benedetti has ever been considered one of the most distinguished members of a party which wielded a very great influence in the councils of the Second Empire; the party which considered

Italian unity as the most glorious and useful work of the reign, and which looked upon the *connubio* between Italy and Prussia as an immense piece of good fortune for the Imperial policy—a brilliant victory achieved over the traditions of the past in favour of the 'new right' and the '*idées Napoléoniennes*.'

M. Benedetti's diplomatic career in this respect, indeed, is marked by a concentrated singleness of purpose that ought to ensure him the eternal gratitude of all Italian patriots. In 1860 he negotiated, and brought to a successful conclusion, the treaty of Savoy and Nice; in exchange for which the Imperial Government allowed the agreement of Zurich to be torn up, and formally recognised the annexations of Tuscany and Emilia. In 1861 he was appointed Minister Plenipotentiary of France at Turin, to console Italy, as it were, for Cavour's untimely death, and to re-establish beyond the Alps the friendly relations temporarily jeopardised by the invasion of the kingdom of Naples.

In the following summer (August, 1862), fresh troubles arose between France and Italy; brought about by Aspromonte, and by General Durando's circular of the 10th of September, demanding the evacuation of Rome. M. Thouvenel found himself obliged to retire from the hotel on the Quai d'Orsay, in favour of M. Drouyn de Lhuys; and M. Benedetti—as did also his colleague at Rome, M. de Lavalette—hastened to tender his resignation, in order to mark his strong disapproval of a new policy less favourable to Italy's aspirations.

He did not return to his career till two years later, till the 7th of October, 1864; after the convention of the 15th of September had satisfied the wishes of the Turin cabinet with regard to Rome; after, too, M. de Bismarck had paid a visit to Paris, and had there laid the foundations of the combination against Austria. The rank of the French mission at Berlin was then raised to that of an embassy, and M. Benedetti was sent to fill it. His old Roman colleague, M. de Lavalette, was simultaneously summoned to the councils of the Empire; and about the same time General La Marmora, well known for his Prussomania, assumed the lead in the Turin cabinet.

The year 1865 had scarcely dawned before M. de Bismarck inaugurated his first campaign against Austria on the question of the Duchies, and made his first overtures at Florence to compass an understanding with Italy. The *connubio* was not definitively settled till April, 1866, under the eyes of M. Benedetti.

As far as we are aware, no one—ourselves certainly have not—has reproached M. Benedetti with having, *unknown to his Government, favoured this connubio*; though he will scarcely deny that he gave it his best sympathies. We allow that General Govone had no gushing confidences for him at Berlin; it was M. Benedetti, on the contrary, who confided important secrets to the Italian diplomatist; among others, that 'M. de Bismarck was a kind of madman whom he (Benedetti) had known and observed for nearly fifteen years.'* M. Benedetti also advised the General 'to sign no treaty, but to have a plan discussed, agreed upon, and ready to sign as soon as Prussia had completed her mobilisation.' Will M. Benedetti seek to persuade us that in giving this advice he was striving to prevent the *connubio*? Scarcely. In offering it M. Benedetti was simply recommending General Govone to act prudently. He was giving him a piece of good advice; and people are not in the habit of giving good advice about schemes they wish to see break down.

Besides, there was no necessity to waste time in persuading the Italians of the advantages of the *connubio*. They were already more than anxious for it. The real importance lay in winning over the Court of Berlin, in dispelling its scruples, in reassuring it, especially, as to the intentions of France. 'I think it right to inform you,' telegraphed on the 28th of March, the Italian envoy to General La Marmora, 'that the president (M. de Bismarck) keeps M. Benedetti

---

* Del conte Bismarck dice (M. de Benedetti) che è un diplomatico, per così dire *maniaco*; che da quindici anni che lo conosce e lo *segue*.'—General Govone's Report of the 6th April, 1866. 'La Marmora,' p. 139.

informed of everything that is going on.'* M. de Bismarck would scarcely have kept M. Benedetti so well posted in the matter if he had thought him averse or even indifferent to the Italian understanding.

Then as now, in France as abroad, in the opinion of public writers as in that of his own chiefs (we shall prove this presently), the former French ambassador at the Court of Berlin was always considered as the one servant of the Imperial Government who most ardently desired the success of the Prusso-Italian combination. 'Ma Mission en Prusse' has not in the least shaken a conviction which we need not hesitate to call a general one.

We should never have thought of intruding into such an important question our obscure individuality and our humble writings; but as M. Benedetti has been good enough to call some of our former contributions to the *Revue des Deux Mondes*, 'better-prepared and more impartially-written essays,' we feel less hesitation in quoting from them a page, written seven years ago, dealing with this pathetic episode of contemporary history. Speaking, in our 'Préliminaires de Sadowa,' of the treaty negotiated between M. de Bismarck and General Govone, in the spring of 1866, we observed: 'Only such an intellect as that of M. de Bismarck could have come to terms with this messenger of evil, who was backed up by his colleague, Count Barral, while across the background flitted, from time to time, M. Benedetti. Here one involuntarily looks round for one of Machiavelli's volumes; one is seized with a desire to read a chapter of his "Legazioni." How it would have pleased the great Florentine to see his three countrymen matched against a barbarian! . . . . In Paris they could see nothing in this treaty but the unique, prodigious fact of an agreement concluded between a monarch by divine right and a sovereign of the national will. They went into ecstacies about M. Benedetti; only a diplomatist of the new school could have worked such a miracle!'

And in the beginning of the same article, in relating the events which in 1864 recalled to political life the men

* "La Marmora," p. 110.

who had fallen into disgrace in consequence of the Durando incident, we said: 'It was unpleasant, no doubt, to M. Drouyn de Lhuys to have to receive as a colleague M. de Lavalette, who made no secret of his desire to deprive him of his portfolio. It was perhaps still more disagreeable to find himself compelled to accept as his principal agent abroad such a declared adversary as M. Benedetti. Two years later, after Sadowa, the very day he resigned office, the same minister had to sign a decree raising M. Benedetti to the dignity of Grand Cross. Yet, perhaps, in the secret thoughts of M. Drouyn de Lhuys, the second signature somewhat avenged the first. It might almost be said to be a keen stroke of humour, a Parthian shot, thus to highly distinguish a diplomatist for having too well served a policy all responsibility in which for one's-self one firmly repudiated.' *

Did the former chiefs of the ex-ambassador of France entertain a different opinion? M. Benedetti himself furnishes us with some important evidence on this point, evidence we must not forget to mention. In 'Ma Mission' (p. 148), he tells us that in January, 1870, Count Daru, then Minister of Foreign Affairs, had alluded in a letter to the events of 1866 in a manner that keenly affected him. 'The territorial condition of Prussia,' M. Daru wrote, 'is the outcome of a series of events which you, *perhaps*, were unable to prevent.' It seems, therefore, that four long years after Sadowa the French Foreign Office still attributed to M. Benedetti a large share in these fatal events.

The ambassador took an opportunity, in a private letter, dated January 27, 1870, of explaining to his chief 'the part he had played in these matters.' He says: 'I am well aware of everything said on the subject; but a feeling, which I have no doubt you will appreciate, has prevented me from ever publicly repudiating the responsibility thrown upon me, as also from correcting the erroneous statements that have been too easily accepted by a badly-informed public.' He then goes on to show that the information he sent to his Government was 'minute, correct, and far-seeing,' and he refers

---

* See the *Revue des Deux Mondes* for Sept. 15th and Oct. 1st, 1868.

Count Daru to the despatches written by him which were to be found in the archives of the Foreign Office. 'I ought to add,' he says, further, 'that never, *in any of the diplomatic posts which I have held,* have I interchanged any political correspondence except that which you will find in my department, or in the hands of your predecessors; and that *at no period of my career* have I ever accepted any other orders than those they directly gave me.'

But this was not sufficient for M. Benedetti, and in the pages of 'Ma Mission,' he thus triumphantly comments upon his letter: 'The assertion I made in my despatch (to Count Daru), that I had never had the honour *on any occasion* (the italics are M. Benedetti's) of holding a confidential correspondence directly with the Emperor is a perfectly honest and accurate one. His Majesty deigned to repose confidence in me, and to sometimes make me aware of his satisfaction; but he always sent me his orders through his foreign minister, with whom alone I corresponded. Nobody will suppose, I think, that I would have declared this in the positive terms I used in my letter to Count Daru, my immediate superior, if I had not been perfectly free to do so.'

Unfortunately, a few pages further on (p. 194) M. Benedetti is obliged to acknowledge that in the course of his negotiations about the secret Belgian treaty, he had exchanged some despatches which never saw the Quai d'Orsay,* and which the Foreign Minister was quite unaware of. 'I thought it right,' we read, 'to forward to M. Rouher the despatch in which I gave an account of my interview with M. de Bismarck, and which accompanied the outline of the proposed treaty concerning Belgium. As M. Rouher never presided over the Foreign Office, he never placed in its archives the despatches which, for several days, passed between us.' It is true that in palliation of this serious irregularity, M. Benedetti pretends that M. Drouyn du Luhys had offered to resign the seals of the Foreign Office about the middle of August, so that 'there was actually no Foreign Minister at that moment;' but we have

---

* Seat of the French Foreign Office.

shown him that M. Drouyn de Lhuys kept his post till the 1st of September, 1866. Up till that date M. Drouyn de Lhuys had continuously directed his department, and had indulged the hope of remaining there, and preventing the complete abandonment of the traditional French foreign policy.

Indeed, M. Benedetti himself, in his book, quotes several despatches exchanged with M. Drouyn de Lhuys on important matters as late as the 21st and the 25th of August (pp. 204, 223); the negotiations about the treaty relating to Belgium were alone deemed a subject unfit to be unfolded to his immediate chief, and suited only for the information of M. Rouher. These negotiations were not only begun but ended (they were broken off by M. de Bismarck on the 29th of August) *during M. Drouyn de Lhuys' term of office, and entirely without his knowledge.*

Thus, then, there was *one occasion* when M. Benedetti failed to correspond exclusively with the Minister of Foreign Affairs; there was *one period in his career* when he accepted orders that did not reach him from the Quai d'Orsay. Count Daru, therefore, can scarcely be reproached for supposing that what had happened in August, 1866, might very well have also happened in March and April of the same year.

M. Benedetti passes over in complete silence the incident of the treaty relating to Belgium. Yet this is the culminating point, the only really serious one of the argument; and the only matter in which we permitted ourselves to reproach him for having acted *without the knowledge*, not of his Government, but *of his Minister*. Does M. Benedetti, by chance, deem this topic an anecdotic incident, unworthy of the dignity of history? He did, in fact, in a letter published in the *Moniteur* of the 29th July, 1870, attempt to give this most unfortunate circumstance quite a light and anecdotic turn; to assign to this most compromising document a kind of spontaneous generation; he had merely wanted to get a clear perception of M. de Bismarck's ideas, 'had consented to set them down, as it were, from his dictation.'

The ex-ambassador was not long able to persist in this trifling. In his book he found himself compelled to acknowledge that he had been engaged in a serious negotiation; and M. de Bismarck has since given himself the malicious pleasure of throwing a little light upon the different phases of this negotiation by publishing, in the Prussian *Moniteur*, divers extracts from the records of Cerçay, by way of answer to M. Benedetti's book.

'During my long career,' says the ex-ambassador to Berlin, in his preface to 'Ma Mission,' 'I have been entrusted on only three occasions with the task of opening a negotiation that had a fixed object, and that, while allowing me a certain share of independent initiative, left me also a proportional share of responsibility.' He enumerates these three negotiations, and proves that he satisfactorily completed them all; but he is careful not to include his negotiation with respect to Belgium, in which, however, he was assuredly allowed a certain share of independent initiative, and in which we are content to leave him, also, his proportional share of responsibility.

Nor will we attempt to rival his controversial tone; like his diplomacy, it is *sui generis*. We will only say, with M. de Bismarck, '*M. Benedetti est trop fin pour nous.*' "

THE END.

www.ingramcontent.com/pod-product-compliance
Lightning Source LLC
Chambersburg PA
CBHW020229240426
43672CB00006B/464